Multistep Cognitive Behavioral Therapy for Eating Disorders

Multistep Cognitive Behavioral Therapy for Eating Disorders

Theory, Practice, and Clinical Cases

Riccardo Dalle Grave, MD

JASON ARONSON
Lanham • Boulder • New York • Toronto • Plymouth, UK

Published by Jason Aronson
A wholly owned subsidiary of The Rowman & Littlefield Publishing Group, Inc.
4501 Forbes Boulevard, Suite 200, Lanham, Maryland 20706
www.rowman.com

10 Thornbury Road, Plymouth PL6 7PP, United Kingdom

British Library Cataloguing in Publication Information Available

Library of Congress Cataloging-in-Publication Data

Library of Congress Cataloging-in-Publication Data Available
ISBN 978-0-7657-0927-1 (cloth : alk. paper)—ISBN 978-0-7657-0928-8 (electronic)

™ The paper used in this publication meets the minimum requirements of American
National Standard for Information Sciences Permanence of Paper for Printed Library
Materials, ANSI/NISO Z39.48-1992.

For my patients

Contents

Introduction

It is perhaps inevitable that the treatment options offered to patients with eating disorders largely depend on the judgment and training of their assisting clinicians, not to mention local constraints on which treatments can be offered. Unfortunately, in the real world, few of these treatments are based on hard scientific evidence, and even fewer have been evaluated in clinical trials. Although there is a general consensus that the outpatient clinic is the best place for treating the majority of patients, there is a large subgroup who do not respond to outpatient treatment or cannot be managed safely on an outpatient basis, and therefore require a more intensive form of care. In the current state of affairs, the only option in these cases is to hospitalize patients to improve their chances of recovery. However, it is common for patients being transferred from a less intensive (e.g., outpatient) to a more intensive form of care (e.g., inpatient), and vice versa, to receive completely different treatments in terms of both theory and content. This creates discontinuity in the process of care, and inevitably disorients patients regarding the procedures and strategies that must be implemented if they are to overcome their eating problem. It is evident, therefore, that there is an urgent need to improve the process of patient transfer from outpatient to intensive settings, and especially to promote the implementation of evidence-based treatments on a global scale.

In the last ten years a new form of cognitive behavioral therapy (CBT), called CBT-E ("enhanced" CBT) and derived from evidence-based CBT for bulimia nervosa, has been developed by Christopher Fairburn and colleagues in Oxford (UK), with a view to treating the psychopathology behind the eating disorder, rather than the eating disorder itself. CBT-E can truly be described as "enhanced," not only because it uses a variety of new strategies and procedures to improve treatment outcomes in bulimia nervosa, but also because it lends itself to treating all recognized diagnostic categories of eating disorders (i.e., anorexia nervosa, bulimia nervosa, and eating disorder not otherwise specified—NOS) in an outpatient setting. Indeed, the first randomized controlled trial of this innovative approach showed that CBT-E is as effective for not significantly underweight eating disorder NOS patients as it is for patients with bulimia nervosa, with two-thirds of those who completed treatment showing a good outcome. Promising findings have also been reported from a three-site joint UK/Italian study of CBT-E treatment in adult outpatients with anorexia nervosa, by an Italian study in adolescent patients with anorexia nervosa, and by an Australian effectiveness study that successfully used CBT-E to treat a transdiagnostic sample of patients with anorexia nervosa, bulimia nervosa, and eating disorder not otherwise specified.

Having verified the effectiveness of CBT-E for the spectrum of eating disorders in our own clinic, my colleagues and I set out to adapt this original approach for more intensive levels of care. The rationale behind extending CBT-E to inpatient and intensive outpatient settings was based on three main considerations: first, some patients fail to respond to outpatient CBT-E altogether, and some have an eating disorder of such clinical severity that they cannot be managed safely in an outpatient setting; second, data on changing the type of outpatient treatment in patients who are not responding to CBT are inconclusive, but in these cases the alternative to outpatient treatment is generally hospitalization in specialized eating disorder units, which, unfortunately, tend to adopt an eclectic approach not driven by a single theory of empirically supported efficacy; and third, the ineffectiveness of outpatient CBT-E in some patients may depend on insufficiently intensive care rather than the nature of the treatment itself.

It follows then that the availability of a treatment able to address all the diagnostic categories of clinical eating disorders in different care settings (from outpatient to inpatient through intensive outpatient) is sorely needed. In this context, multistep CBT-E offers, for the first time in the field of evidence-based psychotherapy for eating disorders, the concrete possibility of implementing such a treatment within a stepped-care approach in real-world clinical settings. Indeed, the most distinctive and unique characteristic of multistep CBT-E, and perhaps the most significant, is that the same theory and procedures are applied at each level of care. The only difference between the various steps is the intensiveness of treatment, with less-unwell patients being treated using outpatient CBT-E procedures, and the more severely affected sufferers being channeled directly to inpatient CBT-E. Within this three-step approach, non-responders to outpatient treatment, and those who would benefit from more support but whose physical conditions do not warrant hospitalization, can be offered a more intensive form of outpatient treatment within the CBT-E framework. Thus, patients can be moved seamlessly from outpatient to inpatient care, and then on to the final phase of outpatient treatment, with no change in the nature of the treatment itself. It is hoped that this "standardization" of approach will improve the chances for recovery in these patients, as it would avoid subjecting them to confusing and counter-productive changes in therapeutic approach that commonly accompany such transitions. The validity of this hope is supported by a recent Italian study, which tested the effectiveness of CBT-E, previously only trialed in outpatients, in a group of eighty hospitalized patients with severe anorexia nervosa. The results showed that the treatment produced a substantial improvement in weight, eating disorder features, and general psychopathology in these patients, and attenuated the weight loss that typically follows hospitalization for anorexia nervosa.

My confidence in the approach, confirmed by studies such as these, inspired me to actively promote the dissemination of multistep CBT-E in Italy. To this end I set up the First Certificate of Professional Training in Eating Disorders, a one-year course dedicated to preparing clinicians from different clinical backgrounds to use this form of treatment. The success of this initiative led to my being invited to present the multistep CBT-E approach at several national and international workshops, which were gratifyingly well received by colleagues from around the world. Indeed, many of them have begun using multistep CBT-E in their own clinics, and it is thanks to their kind encouragement that I decided to write this book. In essence, I wanted to write a manual illustrating the practical application of CBT-E at different levels of care in real-world clinical settings. To achieve this goal, the book is divided into two parts, part 1 being structured as follows:

- Chapter 1 gives an overview of the various recognized eating disorders, and outlines the arguments supporting the view that it is better to consider them as a single unitary transdiagnostic category, without the subdivisions we are used to today.
- Chapter 2 presents the transdiagnostic cognitive behavioral theory of eating disorders.
- Chapters 3 provides an overview of CBT-E, followed by a description of the distinctive features that set the multistep version apart, and focuses in particular on how to build a multidisciplinary CBT-E team.
- Chapter 4 describes how patients are assessed and prepared for multistep CBT-E.
- Chapters 5–7 set out the general organization, procedures, and strategies involved in the three steps of CBT-E treatment: outpatient, intensive outpatient, and inpatient, respectively.
- Chapter 8 illustrates how CBT-E can be adapted for adolescents (from thirteen to seventeen years of age) and how intensive outpatient and inpatient treatment can best be modified to cater to their needs.

In order to highlight the flexibility of the multistep CBT-E approach, part 2 of the book provides a detailed description of three treated clinical cases. Although details have been largely modified to conceal the identity of the patients, the cases are all authentic and reported with a view to showcasing different aspects of multistep CBT-E. In particular, the first case (chapter 9) illustrates how outpatient CBT-E was adapted to treat a professional sportswoman affected by an eating disorder, the second (chapter 10) describes the procedures and strategies applied in intensive outpatient CBT-E to treat a patient who did not improve with standard outpatient CBT-E, and the third case illustrates the procedures and strategies typically applied in inpatient CBT-E and shows how it can be used to help a patient with a long-standing eating disorder who has failed to respond to several outpatient treatments. Each chapter gives a general description of the case in question and details the main procedures, strategies, and tools used from the assessment stage through to discharge. In addition, abridged transcripts of relevant clinical sessions are included, to give interesting insight into the practical implementation of CBT-E, and the outcomes at the end of the treatment and follow-up are reported. Finally, the book contains, in the appendix, version 2.0 of the Eating Problem Checklist, a self-administered questionnaire designed to help patients monitor the state of their eating problem throughout the course of treatment.

I have endeavored to make this book of interest to all professionals working with eating disorder patients (e.g., psychologists, psychiatrists, physicians, dietitians, nurses, educators, occupational therapists, etc.), as a companion, but not substitute, for the main CBT-E manual (Fairburn, 2008a) and the intensive CBT-E manual (Dalle Grave, 2012), which should be studied by all therapists setting out to practice multistep CBT-E. The book is particularly suitable for professionals working as part of a multidisciplinary team that wishes to adopt a non-eclectic stepped-care approach based on cognitive behavioral theory and treatment.

Before summing up, I would like to take this opportunity to thank the many colleagues who kindly contributed their ideas and suggestions or assisted me in other ways to write this book: Simona Calugi, Arianna Banderali, Marwan El Ghoch, Enrico Patacca, Tiziana Todesco, Maddalena Conti, Igino Marchi, Cristina Scutari, Valeria Monti, Marianna Pisano, Massimiliano Sartirana, Laura De Kolitsher, Annachiara Manganotti, Elettra Pasqualoni, Caterina Cerniglia, Ilaria Gavasso, Maria Zita Sartori, Adalgisa Zanetti, and most especially Christopher Fairburn, who lent his support and helped me to adapt his theory and treatment to an intensive care setting. Particular thanks are also due to Anna Forster for her assistance and competence in editing the English text, and to Amy King for her professional editorial contribution.

It is my fond hope that this book will help promote interest in multistep CBT-E among clinicians, and provide a common theoretical and treatment framework for professionals of different disciplines involved in the management of eating disorders.

Riccardo Dalle Grave, MD

I

Multistep Cognitive Behavioral Therapy for Eating Disorders

Chapter One

Eating Disorders

An Overview

Intense media coverage has left medical professionals and the public alike in no doubt that eating disorders are one of the most common health problems afflicting young females in Western countries today. These disorders are associated with significant impairment of physical health and psychosocial functioning and carry an increased risk of premature death. However, despite the vast body of research conducted to date, their cause is not yet known. Unsurprisingly, therefore, they are very hard to treat, with high relapse rates being reported and some patients resisting all available options. Nevertheless, the work carried out over the last thirty years has led to a progressive improvement in their understanding and management.

CLASSIFICATION

Practitioners will be aware that at present the American Psychiatric Association's Diagnostic and Statistical Manual of Mental Disorders (DSM-IV) recognizes three main eating disorder categories (American Psychiatric Association, 2000): *anorexia nervosa, bulimia nervosa,* and *eating disorder not otherwise specified* (NOS). In addition, a further category, termed *binge eating disorder*, has been recommended for formal inclusion as a separate eating disorder category by the DSM-V proposal (www.dsm5.org). The DSM-V work group also recommends renaming the eating disorders category as *feeding and eating disorders*, so as to include some childhood-onset feeding disorders that will not be described here, being outside the scope of this book.

3

While the DSM is undoubtedly the first point of reference for any physician called upon to treat such patients, there is growing evidence that the traditional eating disorder categories it describes may in fact be misleading. Indeed, the evidence suggests that these disorders may be more closely linked than previously thought, and may in fact be different manifestations of a single eating disorder. Before going on to discuss this idea in detail, however, as the research conducted to date has been centered around the single eating disorder categories, this chapter now presents a brief overview of each, including the relevant facts and figures.

ANOREXIA NERVOSA

Distribution

As specialists will no doubt be aware, anorexia nervosa affects about 0.3 percent of adolescent and young adult women in Western countries (Hoek, 2006); its incidence among males is below one per one hundred thousand persons per year. It has a typical onset in adolescence or early adulthood, although some cases may be seen in older adults or late childhood. The disorder is mainly confined to Western populations, where there is a strong social pressure to be thin, particularly among females. It is uncommon in developing countries, but in the developed world it is distributed fairly evenly across the social classes, although there is anecdotal evidence of a greater frequency in higher social classes. Likewise, in some occupational categories, in particular models, dancers, and athletes, the disorder seems to be very common.

Worryingly, recent epidemiological data appears to suggest that the average age of anorexia nervosa onset has been getting lower over the years, with increasing numbers of patients being affected at ever younger ages. Thankfully, however, its incidence does not appear to be growing—it increased in northern Europe until the 1970s, but since then it has remained stable at around eight cases per one hundred thousand persons per year (Hoek, 2006).

Diagnostic Criteria

According to the proposed DSM-V criteria, a person is diagnosed with anorexia nervosa if he or she displays the following characteristics (see www.dsm5.org for a complete description):

- Active maintenance of significant low weight (defined as a weight that is less than minimally normal, or, for children and adolescents, less than minimally expected).

- Intense fear of gaining weight or becoming fat, or persistent behavior that interferes with weight gain, even though the body weight is significantly low.
- Disturbance in the way in which one's body weight or shape is experienced, undue influence of body weight or shape on self-evaluation, or persistent lack of recognition of the seriousness of the current low body weight.

The presence of amenorrhea, previously required for the DSM-IV diagnosis of anorexia nervosa, is no longer necessary (Attia & Roberto, 2009). The rationale behind this exclusion stems from the observation that amenorrhea is not predicted by psychopathological variables, but only by BMI and excessive and compulsive exercising, and that individuals with all the diagnostic criteria of anorexia nervosa bar amenorrhea respond to the same treatment in a similar fashion (Dalle Grave, Calugi, & Marchesini, 2008a). In addition, this criterion cannot be applied across the board, as it fails to take into account pre-menarchal and post-menopausal females, females taking oral contraceptives, and, of course, males. This does not mean to say, however, that clinicians should ignore the presence of this symptom; indeed, some data have shown that amenorrheic women tend to have poorer bone health than those with regular periods (Miller et al., 2004).

Clinical Features

In typical cases, anorexia nervosa begins in adolescence when the patient embarks upon an extreme and rigid diet. In most cases the food restriction is motivated by extreme concerns about weight, shape, and eating control (often all three), but some cases may be ascribable to other psychological processes (e.g., asceticism, competitiveness, desire for self-punishment, a bid to change the behaviors of significant others). In addition to extreme dieting, some individuals pursue this "irrational" weight loss by exercising excessively, and others use self-induced vomiting or other forms of unhealthy weight control, such as the misuse of laxatives or diuretics. In anorexia nervosa the onset of binge eating (often subjective) is common, and approximately half of these patients migrate to a diagnosis of bulimia nervosa (Bulik, Sullivan, Fear, & Pickering, 1997).

Coexisting Psychological and Psychiatric Disorders

Common psychological symptoms reported by individuals with anorexia nervosa are depression, anxiety, obsessions, irritability, lability of mood, impaired concentration, loss of sexual appetite, and social isolation; these tend to worsen as their body weight decreases, and often disappear altogether once weight is restored. Nevertheless, the most common coexisting psychiatric conditions, namely anxiety disorders, clinical depression, and obsessive-compulsive traits, may predate the onset of anorexia nervosa (Treasure, Claudino, & Zucker, 2010) and may persist after recovery in certain individuals. One subgroup of people with anorexia nervosa are known to engage in psychoactive substances misuse and self-harm practices such as skin-cutting, burning, scratching, banging or hitting body parts, interfering with wound healing, and/or hair-pulling. A further subgroup of anorexia nervosa patients are characterized by the personality traits of perfectionism and low self-esteem—these are generally evident before the onset of the disorder (Fairburn & Harrison, 2003).

Physical Complications

Physical complications are common among patients with anorexia nervosa and are the consequences of three main mechanisms, often operating together: undereating, being underweight, and purging (Mehler & Andersen, 2010). Textbox 1.1 gives an overview of the physical complications to look out for in these patients.

TEXTBOX 1.1. MAIN PHYSICAL FEATURES OF ANOREXIA NERVOSA

Physical Signs

- Stunted growth and failure of breast development (if pre-pubertal onset)
- Bradycardia (heart rate < 60 beats/min); hypotension (< 90 mm Hg systolic)
- Hypothermia; cyanotic and cold hands and feet
- Dry skin; lanugo hair on the back, forearms, and side of the face; orange discoloration of the skin of the palms and soles
- Telogen effluvium
- Purpura
- Erosion of inner surface of front teeth (perimylolysis) in frequent vomit-inducers
- Brittle nails
- Edema (ankle, periorbital)
- Weak proximal muscles (elicited as difficulty rising from a squatting position)

Gastrointestinal Complications

- Gastroesophageal reflux, esophagitis, hematemesis (in those practicing self-induced vomiting)

- Gastroparesis, gastric dilatation and rupture (rare in binge eaters)
- Decreased colon motility
- Abnormal results in liver-function tests
- Elevated serum amylase level (especially in those practicing self-induced vomiting)

Endocrine and Metabolic Complications

- Low serum estradiol (in females), low serum testosterone level (in males); low T3, T4 in low normal range, normal TSH (euthyroid sick syndrome); hypercortisolism, elevated free cortisol level in urine; raised growth hormone concentration; amenorrhea; delay in puberty
- Hypoglycemia, hypercholesterolemia
- Hypokalemia, hypomagnesemia (especially in those with purging); hypophosphatemia (especially during refeeding), hyponatremia (especially in those with high water intake)
- Osteopenia and osteoporosis (with heightened fracture risk)

Hematological Complications

- Anemia, leukopenia, neutropenia, thrombocytopenia

Cardiovascular Complications

- ECG abnormalities (especially in those with electrolyte disturbance): low voltage, prolonged QT interval, prominent U waves

Renal Complications

- Renal calculi

Reproductive Complications

- Infertility
- Insufficient weight gain during pregnancy, and low-birth-weight infants

Neurological Complications

- Enlarged cerebral ventricles and external cerebrospinal fluid spaces (pseudoatrophy)
- Peripheral neuropathy

Course

In some adolescents, anorexia nervosa is of brief duration and remits without treatment or after short-term intervention, but in others it tends to persist, necessitating long and complex specialized treatments. In general, the remission rate is low (around 20 to 30 percent) at short-term follow-up, but this increases to almost 70 to 80 percent after eight years or more (Keel & Brown, 2010). Unfortunately, 10 to 20 percent of individuals do not improve with any of the treatments available to date, and go on to develop a lifelong condition (Steinhausen, 2002). In these cases, the disorder inevitably disrupts education and vocational functioning.

Crude mortality rates of anorexia nervosa have been reported as low as 0 percent and as high as 8 percent, but the most recently reported cumulative mortality rate across studies is 2.8 percent (Keel & Brown, 2010). This figure is lower than those previously reported, presumably due to improved medical stabilization of these patients. Nowadays, deaths are usually the consequence of medical complications or suicide.

The prognosis of the disorder can be influenced by several factors, including young age at onset and short duration of the disorder, which tend to favor remission, while unfavorable prognostic factors include somatic and psychiatric comorbidity (Treasure et al., 2010).

Treatment

In 2004, the UK's National Institute for Clinical Excellence (NICE) published a set of eating disorder guidelines, which significantly improved upon the limitations of traditional narrative reviews or the guidelines issued by professional associations (National Institute for Clinical Excellence, 2004). This is mainly ascribable to the fact that the NICE guidelines are firmly based on evidence and collected expert testimony, the strength of which is used to grade the recommendations from A, denoting strong empirical support from well-conducted randomized trials, to C, expert opinion without strong empirical data. The main recommendations for treating anorexia nervosa proposed by NICE guidelines are the following:

- Family-based treatment (FBT) focused on weight restoration should be provided for adolescents with anorexia nervosa (B).
- There is insufficient evidence to make evidence-based recommendations regarding the treatment of adults with anorexia nervosa. Nevertheless, despite the lack of strong empirical data, the following clinical recommendations can be made (C):
- Most adult patients with anorexia nervosa should be managed as outpatients.
- Dietary counseling should not be provided as the sole treatment for anorexia nervosa.
- Cognitive analytic therapy, cognitive behavioral therapy (CBT), interpersonal psychotherapy (IPT), focal dynamic therapy, or FBT may be considered.
- Inpatient services should combine refeeding and psychosocial interventions.

The absence of grade A recommendations in the NICE guidelines highlights the fact that much still needs to be done in order to provide a comprehensive set of evidence-based recommendations for the treatment of anorexia nervosa. In particular, there is a lack of scientifically proven treatments for adults, and for the more intensive levels of care (e.g., day-hospital or inpatient treatment). Indeed, in the last seven years no evidence-based intervention for adults with anorexia nervosa has been published, although the new *enhanced* treatment (CBT-E) has been shown in two independent studies to produce promising results for adults treated both in outpatient (Fairburn et al., 2012) and inpatient settings (Dalle Grave, 2011b), and therefore provides the basis for the treatment described in this book.

BULIMIA NERVOSA

Distribution

Unlike anorexia nervosa, bulimia nervosa seems more common today than in the past. Nowadays, the disorder affects roughly 1 percent of adolescent girls and young women, and has reached an incidence of about thirteen new cases per one hundred thousand persons per year (Hoek, 2006). Like anorexia nervosa, the onset of the disorder generally occurs in adolescence or in early adulthood. Men are rarely affected and there is no evidence to suggest that the disorder is increasing among males. Bulimia nervosa affects mainly Caucasians, in whom it is evenly distributed across the social classes, while it is uncommon in African Americans and in developing countries.

Diagnostic Criteria

The proposed DSM-V criteria for bulimia nervosa are the following (see www.dsm5.org for a complete description):

- Recurrent episodes of binge eating (i.e., recurrent episodes of uncontrolled overeating).
- Recurrent inappropriate compensatory behavior practiced to prevent weight gain (i.e., self-induced vomiting; misuse of laxatives, diuretics, medications, fasting or excessive exercise).
- The binge eating and inappropriate compensatory behaviors both occur, on average, at least once a week for three months (the DSM-IV required a threshold of twice a week, but this has been revised due to the observation that the clinical characteristics of individuals reporting a frequency of these behaviors once a week are similar to those who report twice-weekly episodes).
- Self-evaluation is unduly influenced by body shape and weight.

- The disturbance does not occur exclusively during episodes of anorexia nervosa.

Comparing these criteria side by side with those pertaining to anorexia nervosa, one is struck by the fact that although the respective manifestations are very different—undereating in anorexia vs. overeating in bulimia, the underlying mechanism seems to be very similar. Indeed, both disorders appear to hinge upon a distorted self of self-worth that rests predominantly upon a person's shape and weight. Moreover, by their very definition, at least according to the DSM, both sets of patients resort to unhealthy means of controlling their weight in order to improve their appearance and therefore boost their self-evaluation.

Clinical Features

Another factor common to both conditions is their mode of onset. Like anorexia nervosa, bulimia nervosa typically begins with an extreme and strict diet motivated by excessive concerns about weight and shape, and about a quarter of cases even involve a period in which the diagnostic criteria for anorexia nervosa are met (Sullivan, Bulik, Carter, Gendall, & Joyce, 1996). However, in bulimia, dieting is periodically interrupted by episodes of binge eating. The combination of dietary restraint, binge eating, and purging rarely produces a persistent calorie deficit, which explains why individuals with bulimia nervosa, although rarely obese, are usually overweight, normal weight, or slightly underweight.

The difference in presentation of the two disorders explains why bulimia nervosa patients tend to seek treatment more frequently than those with anorexia nervosa. Indeed, most individuals with bulimia nervosa are worried by their binges, rather than their unhealthy attempts to control their weight. However, since they are often ashamed of their behavior, they usually seek help many years after the onset of their disorder.

Coexisting Psychological and Psychiatric Disorders

As in anorexia nervosa, anxiety and depression are common symptoms associated with bulimia nervosa, and, likewise, a subgroup of affected individuals is known to engage in alcohol or psychoactive substance misuse and self-harm (Treasure et al., 2010). Common coexisting personality traits and psychiatric disorder diagnoses are low self-esteem, perfectionism, mood intolerance, and affective disorders (Fairburn, Cooper, & Shafran, 2003; McElroy, Kotwal, & Keck, 2006); once again, the similarities between anorexia and bulimia are striking.

Physical Complications

One area in which the two disorders differ is the physical impact of their condition. Although disturbed eating behavior can be extremely dangerous for the patient, physical complications are minor in most cases of bulimia nervosa. Nonetheless, in patients who manifest a high frequency of self-induced vomiting, it is common to find electrolyte disturbances, esophagitis, swelling of the parotid and submandibular glands, dental damage, and Russell's sign (a thickening or scarring on the dorsal surface of the hand caused by pressing the hands against the teeth while inducing vomiting) (Dalle Grave, 2011a).

Course

As with anorexia nervosa, the remission rate for bulimia nervosa is low at short-term follow-up (27 to 28 percent at one-year follow-up) and improves as duration of follow-up increases (up to 70 percent or more by ten-year follow-up) (Keel & Brown, 2010), but with nearly 23 percent on average going on to develop a long-standing course (Steinhausen & Weber, 2009).

Crude mortality rates of bulimia nervosa reported across studies range from 0 percent to 2 percent, and the cumulative mortality rate is 0.4 percent, which is almost five times lower than that observed in anorexia nervosa (Keel & Brown, 2010). Like anorexia, however, in bulimia nervosa vocational and educational functioning is below expectations.

Childhood obesity, low self-esteem, and personality disorder seem to be associated with poor prognosis (Fairburn & Harrison, 2003). Although, as previously mentioned, a significant number of bulimia nervosa cases may qualify for a diagnosis of anorexia nervosa at some time during their course, definitive crossover to anorexia nervosa is rare. In contrast, migration to binge eating disorder, also characterized by repeated overeating, or eating disorder NOS has been described in almost 20 percent of cases (Steinhausen & Weber, 2009).

Treatment

The NICE guidelines are more emphatic about recommending CBT as a treatment for adults with bulimia nervosa (CBT-BN), giving it a grade (A) (National Institute for Clinical Excellence, 2004), a conclusion also confirmed by two systematic reviews (Shapiro et al., 2007; Wilson, Grilo, & Vitousek, 2007). This recommendation is based on empirical support for this therapy, which has been extensively tested in more than twenty randomized control efficacy trials, in which it showed its superiority to other psychological and pharmaceutical interventions. Indeed, CBT-BN results in a demonstrable substantial and persistent improvement, with (on intent-to-treat analyses) a third to a half of the patients making a complete and lasting recovery (Wilson & Fairburn, 2002).

NICE guidelines also recommend, albeit with a precautionary grade (B), self-help with CBT manuals (preferably guided) and/or antidepressant medication at full doses (e.g., fluoxetine 60 mg daily) as an initial step in treatment. However, patients should be informed that although antidepressant drugs could reduce the frequency of binge eating, and any beneficial effects will be rapidly apparent (B), their long-term effects are unknown. Finally, IPT may be an alternative to CBT-BN, but patients need to be informed that it takes eight to twelve months longer for IPT to produce effects equivalent to CBT-BN (B).

Although CBT-BN received a grade (A) recommendation for adults with bulimia nervosa, it is by no means a cure-all solution. Although a 30 to 50 percent remission rate is far higher than any other treatment strategy can boast, efficacy is still arguably limited, and an extensive research can development campaign is therefore essential. Furthermore, the effectiveness of CBT-BN, or in fact any other treatment, has yet to be confirmed in the real world, and even fledgling treatments for adolescents are notable by their absence.

BINGE EATING DISORDER

Like bulimia nervosa, binge eating disorder is characterized by recurrent episodes of overeating. In stark contrast to bulimia nervosa, and indeed anorexia nervosa, however, extreme weight-control behavior (e.g., purging or extreme, strict dietary restraint) is absent. The lifetime prevalence of binge eating disorder in the community is around 3 percent (Hudson, Hiripi, Pope, & Kessler, 2007), and as many as a quarter of those afflicted are males. It has a later age of onset than both anorexia nervosa and bulimia nervosa, and individuals typically seek treatment in their forties (Barry, Grilo, & Masheb, 2002).

Diagnostic Criteria

Binge eating disorder, previously included in the DSM-IV appendix as a disorder requiring further study, has been recommended for formal inclusion in its own category in the forthcoming DSM-V, following a comprehensive review of the literature (Wonderlich, Gordon, Mitchell, Crosby, & Engel, 2009). The main proposed DSM-V criteria for binge eating disorder are the following (see www.dsm5.org for a complete criteria description):

- Recurrent episodes of binge eating (i.e., recurrent episodes of uncontrolled overeating).
- Binge eating episodes occurring, on average, at least once a week for three months (the DSM-IV appendix suggested assessing frequency of binge days, rather than the number of episodes, and required a minimum average frequency of twice a week over six months—the rationale behind this change derives from the observation that criteria identical to those for bulimia nervosa do not significantly alter caseness).
- The binge eating is not associated with the recurrent use of inappropriate compensatory behavior (for example, purging).

Clinical Features

Individuals with binge eating disorder have recurrent bulimic episodes not followed by the use of regular compensatory behaviors (e.g., self-induced vomiting and laxative or diuretic misuse). The bulimic episodes occur against the background of a general tendency to overeat rather than dietary restraint, as typically occurs in bulimia nervosa. This explains the strong association of the disorder with obesity.

In spite of the fact that, on paper, this disorder may appear to diverge significantly from the two categories discussed so far, in particular by the absence of attempts to mitigate weight gain, on closer inspection there seems to be a common underlying theme, namely the concerns about weight and shape. These are also reported to varying degrees in individuals with binge eating disorder, although these are generally less extreme than those observed in anorexia nervosa and bulimia nervosa.

When binge eating disorder is severe and characterized by daily bulimic episodes it impairs the quality of life, and individuals may miss work, school, or other social activities. In most cases, sufferers try to control their eating by themselves, but only succeed for a short period of time. Hence, many patients request treatment for their excess weight and not the eating disorder itself. It is estimated that about 7 to 12 percent of patients seeking treatment for obesity suffer from binge eating disorder (Dalle Grave, 2011a).

Coexisting Psychological and Psychiatric Disorders

Parallels between the three DSM categories are also evident in terms of the psychological health of their respective patients. Indeed, low self-esteem, depressive features, and mood intolerance are also common in binge eating disorder. The most frequently seen personality traits and coexisting psychiatric disorders diagnosed in individuals with binge eating disorder include impulsive traits, affective disorders, and alcohol or psychoactive substance misuse (Treasure et al., 2010).

Physical Complications

Individuals with binge eating disorder often have an unhealthy lifestyle characterized by daily smoking, low exercise frequency, poor nutrition—as bulimic episodes usually involve foods that are high in fat, sugar, and/or salt but low in vitamins and minerals—and alcohol abuse. This explains why they present both the typical complications associated with obesity (e.g., metabolic syndrome, type 2 diabetes, gallbladder disease, heart disease, and certain types of cancer), and also some independent of the excess weight but related to their unhealthy lifestyle, such as irritable bowel syndrome, alcohol and smoking complications, neck and shoulder pain, lower back pain, and chronic muscle pain (Bulik & Reichborn-Kjennerud, 2003).

Course

Little data is available on the course of binge eating disorder. Patients typically report long histories of binge eating, with an increase in frequency at times of stress, but many also report long periods free from this behavior. Indeed, findings from short-term natural history studies and drug trials indicate that binge eating disorder is characterized by high spontaneous remission rates (Dingemans, Bruna, & van Furth, 2002; Fairburn, Cooper, Doll, Norman, & O'Connor, 2000). Four-year remission rates have been reported in 82 percent of binge eating disorder cases, as compared to 47 percent in bulimia nervosa and 57 percent in anorexia nervosa (Agras, Crow, Mitchell, Halmi, & Bryson, 2009). In non-remitting patients, the migration from binge eating disorder to anorexia nervosa or bulimia nervosa is rare.

Treatment

NICE recommends that adults with binge eating disorder should be offered a specifically adapted form of CBT derived from the CBT-BN (A) successfully used to treat bulimics (National Institute for Clinical Excellence, 2004), a recommendation also confirmed by a systematic review (Brownley, Berkman, Sedway, Lohr, & Bulik, 2007). Possible initial steps in treatment are self-help CBT (preferably guided) and/or antidepressant medication (B). IPT and Dialectic Behavior Therapy-based treatments are potential alternatives to CBT (B).

Patients should, however, be informed that psychological treatments have a limited effect on body weight (A), an outcome confirmed by a study showing that IPT and guided self-help CBT were significantly more effective than behavioral weight loss in eliminating binge eating after two years, but that none of the three treatments managed to obtain significant long-term weight loss (Wilson, Wilfley, Agras, & Bryson, 2010).

EATING DISORDER NOS

The diagnosis of eating disorder NOS was introduced by DSM-IV in 2004 for individuals who have an eating disorder of clinical severity not meeting the diagnostic criteria of anorexia nervosa or bulimia nervosa. The diagnosis of eating disorder NOS was initially defined with the intent of creating a residual diagnostic category of eating disorders, although recent studies have found that around half of patients seeking treatment receive this diagnosis in both outpatient and inpatient settings (Dalle Grave & Calugi, 2007; Ricca et al., 2001). It has even been reported that the proportion of patients seeking treatment for an eating disorder later diagnosed as suffering from eating disorder NOS may even be as high as 70 percent (Fairburn & Bohn, 2005). In spite of the prevalence of eating disorder NOS, very few data are available about its distribution in the community, although clinical reports suggest that this disorder mainly affects adolescents and young adult women.

Diagnostic Criteria

The DSM-V Work Group has recommended that the category eating disorder NOS should be replaced by a section termed *feeding and eating conditions not elsewhere classified*. These conditions should only be diagnosed if the individual has an eating problem judged to be of clinical significance that does not meet the criteria for any of the eating disorders described above (see www.dsm5.org for a complete criteria description). Both this description and, indeed, the prevalence of this rather eclectic and poorly defined category, lend weight to the theory that the distinctions between separate eating disorders are more ephemeral than they may at first seem.

Clinical Features

Indeed, although the eating disorders NOS can be arbitrarily divided into two main subgroups, there is no clear line of demarcation between them. The first subgroup includes individuals who have a disorder similar to anorexia nervosa and bulimia nervosa but do not completely meet their diagnostic criteria. For example, they may have a weight slightly above the threshold necessary for the diagnosis of anorexia nervosa or a frequency of binge eating slightly below the minimum threshold required for the diagnosis of bulimia nervosa. These cases may be described as *subthreshold disorders* of anorexia nervosa and bulimia nervosa (Fairburn & Bohn, 2005).

The second and larger subgroup of eating disorder NOS patients is composed of people in whom the clinical features of anorexia nervosa and bulimia nervosa are combined in a different way to those described for the two disorders. These cases may be described as *mixed eating disorder* (Fairburn

& Bohn, 2005). Here are two examples: (i) an individual with BMI>17.5, self-induced vomiting four times a week but no objective bulimic episodes, and overvaluation of body shape and weight—this disorder is also called *purging disorder* (Keel, 2007); and (ii) an individual with a BMI > 17.5, extreme dietary rules, excessive and compulsive exercising, and overvaluation of body shape and weight—this disorder is also known as *restrained eating disorder*.

Here the similarities between anorexia nervosa, bulimia nervosa, binge-eating disorder, and the eating disorder NOS umbrella, which encompasses at least 40 percent of eating disorder patients (Fairburn & Bohn, 2005), are self-evident, and once again it strikes even the untrained eye that in the latter too the affected individuals are unduly preoccupied with their figure and attempts to control it. Are we really to believe that these disorders are separate entities fuelled by distinct psychopathological mechanisms? Or would it be more plausible to suggest that they all stem from a common pathology that merely manifests itself in different ways, according to the individual psychological makeup of a patient?

Although not yet recognized by the medical profession as a distinct disorder, *night eating syndrome* is another disorder that might be incorporated within the diagnosis of eating disorder NOS, and therefore within the postulated universal eating disorder category. Though its definition is still a matter of debate among researchers, in 2010 the International NES Working Group proposed provisional diagnostic criteria for night eating syndrome research (Allison et al., 2010); the proposed core criterion of this disorder is an abnormally increased food intake in the evening and during the night, manifested by (i) consumption of at least 25 percent of daily calorie intake after the evening meal, and/or (ii) nocturnal awakenings accompanied by food ingestion at least twice weekly. The overall prevalence of night eating syndrome has been estimated at 1.5 percent (Rand, Macgregor, & Stunkard, 1997), and, although it does occur among non-obese persons, it appears to be more common among the obese, and its prevalence increases with increasing adiposity (Aronoff, Geliebter, & Zammit, 2001). The disorder seems to have a chronic course and to be exacerbated by stressful life situations.

Course

Little is known about the course of eating disorder NOS as a whole, although what is known generally appears to support the theory of a single eating disorder category; while some studies suggest that eating disorder NOS patients recover more quickly than those with anorexia nervosa or bulimia nervosa (Agras et al., 2009; Ben-Tovim et al., 2001), another found no differences in terms of remission between eating disorder NOS and bulimia nervosa. At five- and twenty-year follow-ups, no significant differences were found in remission rates between eating disorder NOS characterized by bulimic symptoms and "pure" bulimia nervosa, with a remission rate of around 70 to 75 percent being reported for both (Keel & Brown, 2010). Moreover, an observational study found that the cross-diagnostic flux of eating disorder NOS to anorexia nervosa and bulimia nervosa is common, and that eating disorder NOS is a less stable diagnosis than bulimia nervosa and anorexia nervosa (Milos, Spindler, Schnyder, & Fairburn, 2005). Although eating disorder NOS is sometimes viewed as a less severe form of eating disorder, a recent study observed a crude mortality rate of 5.2 percent, similar to that found in anorexia nervosa (Crow et al., 2009).

Treatment

NICE guidelines stated that it is not possible to make evidence-based recommendations regarding the treatment of eating disorder NOS because there has been no research carried out to date (National Institute for Clinical Excellence, 2004). The advice is therefore that disorders resembling bulimia nervosa should be treated as if they were, and an equivalent extrapolation should be made for disorders resembling anorexia nervosa (C). This recommendation, is supported by data from two independent studies showing that the enhanced form of CBT (CBT-E) is suitable both for bulimia nervosa for eating disorder NOS patients who are not significantly underweight (Byrne, Fursland, Allen, & Watson, 2011; Fairburn et al., 2009), once again lending weight to the idea that these disorders could be more closely related than previously thought.

THE CLINICAL REALITY: DOES THE DSM CLASSIFICATION REFLECT THE TRUE PICTURE?

Thus three fundamental flaws in the DSM classification (Fairburn et al., 2003) start to become evident. First, the supposedly residual diagnostic category, eating disorder NOS, is in fact the most common eating disorder diagnosis in both outpatient and inpatient settings, and it has thus far been almost completely ignored by researchers. Second, the DSM classification is of limited diagnostic validity, as it is common to observe a migration between eating disorder diagnostic categories (e.g., from anorexia nervosa into bulimia nervosa or eating disorder NOS, and from bulimia nervosa into eating disorder NOS) (Milos et al., 2005). This diagnostic migration does not reflect recovery from one disorder and the onset of another, as the DSM classification would suggest, but rather the evolution of a single eating disorder. Third, the DSM classification is of scarce clinical utility, since the eating disorder diagnostic categories have poor prognostic and therapeutic implications.

These considerations led Fairburn and Bohn (2005) to propose a *transdiagnostic* solution, designed to overcome the limitations of DSM classification. They recommend the creation of a single unitary diagnostic eating disorder category without any subdivisions. Although this may seem a controversial idea, it is supported by several observations, which are outlined in the following paragraphs.

Eating Disorders Share the Same Clinical Features

The thing that most strikes a clinician when meeting patients with anorexia nervosa, bulimia nervosa, and eating disorder NOS is the similarity between them. Indeed, all three diagnostic categories share the majority of their clinical features (Fairburn & Bohn, 2005); in particular, the *overvaluation of shape and weight* (i.e., judging self-worth largely, or exclusively, in terms of shape and weight) is a characteristic common to almost all eating disorder patients. It is observed only in eating disorders, it explains the main clinical features observed in anorexia nervosa, bulimia nervosa, and eating disorder NOS, and for this reason has been called their *core psychopathology* (Fairburn et al., 2003).

The most characteristic expressions of the overvaluation of shape and weight are the *extreme concerns about weight and shape* and the associated *weight and shape checking* or *avoidance* behaviors. Other expressions of the core psychopathology are *feeling fat*, *pursuit of thinness*, and *fear of gaining weight*, which are not mitigated by the loss of weight. The core psychopathology also explains the extreme weight control behaviors adopted by people with eating disorders, such as the *extreme and rigid dietary rules*, the *excessive and compulsive exercising*, the *self-induced vomiting*, and the *misuse of laxatives and diuretics*. The only feature that is not a direct expression of the overvaluation of shape and weight is the *bulimic episode*. However, this behavior is in most cases a consequence of the extreme dietary rules adopted by individuals with eating disorders, regardless of whether these rules produce a real energy deficit or not (Fairburn et al., 2003).

In one subgroup of individuals with eating disorders, the core psychopathology is the *overvaluation of eating control* (Dalle Grave, Calugi, & Marchesini, 2008c). Sometimes this psychopathology coexists with the overvaluation of shape and weight, but this is not always the case. Indeed, certain individuals do not report the fear of gaining weight, extreme concerns about shape and weight, body checking and avoidance, or feeling fat. Instead, in these cases there is an extreme concern about eating control, associated with the adoption of extreme and strict dietary rules and frequent and unusual *food checking* (e.g., repeatedly weighing and/or checking the calorie content of the food they eat).

In all eating disorder categories, psychological problems, such as general symptoms of *depression* and *anxiety* (see above), often coexist and typically meet the diagnostic criteria for mood or anxiety disorders. In general, depression is observed more frequently in individuals with bulimic episodes, while anxiety is more common in those with high levels of dietary restraint. *Obsessive symptoms* are frequently reported by calorie restricting and underweight patients, and in many cases are the consequence of the state of malnutrition, as will be discussed later (Dalle Grave, Pasqualoni, & Marchesini, 2011). Another subgroup of patients, particularly those who binge eat, are known to *self-harm*, and a comparable group reported a *misuse of psychoactive substances*. Common in all eating disorder categories are several personality traits, such as *perfectionism*, *low self-esteem*, and *mood intolerance*, which in some patients precede the onset of the eating disorder itself (Fairburn et al., 2003).

Eating Disorders Migrate between Diagnostic Categories

Longitudinal studies that follow patients over time have frequently observed a migration of eating disorders from one diagnostic category to another (Fairburn & Harrison, 2003; Milos et al., 2005). Research has also found that eating disorders rarely migrate to other mental disorders (Fairburn & Harrison, 2003). These observations indicate that eating disorders represent a distinct diagnostic category (they do not migrate to other psychiatric disorders), and that the division into three diagnostic categories is probably an artifact of the classification, rather than a reflection of the clinical reality.

To illustrate the point, let us examine the case of Chiara, a patient who, in the space of ten years, was diagnosed as having three separate eating disorders. DSM diagnosis:

At the age of fourteen, Chiara was given a diagnosis of anorexia nervosa by her family physician. This diagnosis was motivated by her weight of 34 kg, and reported extreme undereating, excessive and compulsive exercising, fear of weight gain, overvaluation of shape and weight, and amenorrhea. Four years later, at the age of eighteen, after a trip to England, she began to binge eat and self-induce vomiting almost every day. Her weight rose to 52 kg, and her overvaluation of shape and weight became extreme. Accordingly, a psychiatrist gave her a diagnosis of bulimia nervosa. At age twenty-four, however, she stopped vomiting after bulimic episodes, and her weight went up to 60 kg; nevertheless, she continued to report an extreme overvaluation of shape and weight. She was started on CBT, and her therapist gave her the diagnosis of binge eating disorder.

Thus, adhering to the DSM-IV classification, Chiara received three different psychiatric diagnoses during her illness. This begs the question of whether this is a true representation of her condition, or whether it is more likely that she suffered from one eating disorder whose clinical features changed over time.

Eating Disorders Respond Well to a Single Same Treatment

Implementation of the new CBT-E for eating disorders in Italy, in England, and in Australia has shown that anorexia nervosa, bulimia nervosa, and eating disorder NOS all respond well to the same single transdiagnostic treatment (see chapter 5 for details) with little difference between their short- or longer-term outcomes, another finding that raises questions about the clinical utility of distinction between DSM eating disorder categories (Byrne et al., 2011; Fairburn, 2008c; Fairburn et al., 2009; Fairburn et al., 2012).

THE TRANSDIAGNOSTIC SOLUTION

In response to this question, the transdiagnostic solution, which considers eating disorders as a single diagnostic category rather than three separate disorders (Fairburn, et al., 2003), has been proposed. From this perspective, a person might be diagnosed with an eating disorder of clinical severity if he or she satisfies the following four criteria:

- Overvaluation of shape, weight, and eating control.
- Persistent disturbance of eating habits or weight-control behaviors.
- Impairment of physical health or psychosocial functioning.
- The behavioral disturbance is not secondary to any medical or psychiatric disorder.

This means of classifying eating disorders transdiagnostically has been used as a starting point for the cognitive behavioral theory outlined in chapter 2, and the CBT-E multistep described later in this book.

Chapter Two

The Cognitive Behavioral Theory of Eating Disorders

Several psychological theories have been proposed to explain the development and maintenance of eating disorders, but cognitive behavioral theory has been the most influential in producing evidence-based treatments. The theory, in its last incarnation (Fairburn et al., 2003), has been extended to cover all forms of eating disorders (anorexia nervosa, bulimia nervosa, and eating disorder NOS), thereby making it *transdiagnostic* in scope (see the main arguments for the transdiagnostic solution in chapter 1). The theory is principally focused on the processes maintaining the eating disorder, rather than on the DSM diagnosis, which is more relevant to the manifestation of the disorder.

According to the transdiagnostic theory, the overvaluation of shape, weight, and eating control is central in the maintenance of all manifestations of a single eating disorder. Other clinical features stem directly (e.g., strict dieting, excessive and compulsive exercising, compensatory vomiting/laxative misuse, the underweight state and starvation syndrome, body checking and avoidance, and feeling fat) or indirectly (e.g., binge eating) from this core psychopathology, and, in turn, act to reinforce it.

The theory also proposes that in certain patients, one or more of three adjunctive maintenance mechanisms interact with the eating disorder psychopathology, creating an additional obstacle to change. The three proposed adjunctive maintenance mechanisms are (Fairburn, Cooper, Shafran, Bohn, & Hawker, 2008): (i) clinical perfectionism, (ii) core low self-esteem, and (iii) interpersonal difficulties. Indeed, data from randomized controlled trials support the view that correction of these processes is necessary for recovery.

This chapter describes the principal, the core and the adjunctive maintenance mechanisms of the eating disorder psychopathology, interpreted according to cognitive behavioral theory. Knowledge of these mechanisms is
essential to understand and apply multistep CBT-E, and readers interested in
learning more about the development of theory and the evidence supporting
it should therefore refer to Fairburn, Cooper, and Shafran (2003).

THE CORE MAINTENANCE MECHANISMS OF EATING DISORDER PSYCHOPATHOLOGY

Overvaluation of Shape and Weight: The Core Psychopathology

According to cognitive behavioral theory, *overvaluation of shape and weight*
is central to the maintenance of eating disorders because the main clinical
features of these disorders derive either directly or indirectly from it. Overvaluation of shape and weight must be differentiated from body dissatisfaction, a term used when people do not like their appearance. Indeed, body
dissatisfaction is a common feature among Westerners and does not necessarily represent a clinical problem (Fairburn, 2008b). In contrast, individual
who overvalue their shape and weight tend to judge themselves predominantly, and in some cases exclusively, in terms of their shape, weight, and their
control thereof. This system of self-evaluation adopted by individuals with
eating disorders is dysfunctional for three main reasons (Fairburn et al.,
2008, pp. 99–100):

- Individuals who judge themselves predominantly on a single domain (e.g.,
  the control of shape and weight) risk the collapse of their entire system of
  self-evaluation should failure in this domain be perceived.
- In some domains, such as the control of shape and weight, it is almost
  impossible to achieve success, because a person with an eating disorder
  can never be thin enough or achieve the perfect figure.
- The overriding commitment to controlling shape and weight inevitably
  marginalizes other important areas of life (e.g., school, relationships,
  work) that usually contribute to the development of a functional, stable,
  and well-balanced system of self-evaluation.

Overvaluation of Eating Control

As previously mentioned, the core psychopathology in a subgroup of individuals with eating disorders is the *overvaluation of eating control* (Fairburn,
2008b, p. 12). Although this feature often coexists with the overvaluation of
shape and weight, this is not always the case. Indeed, some individuals tend
to report an excessive preoccupation with eating control associated with the

adoption of strict dieting and food checking behaviors of (see below), rather than the fear of gaining weight or concern about weight and body shape. The most common reasons for the overvaluation of eating control reported by patients are concerns over digestion, fears about food and eating, asceticism, intolerance of postprandial fullness, dyspeptic symptoms (e.g., abdominal pain or bloating, constipation or diarrhea), lack of hunger, and a fear of being greedy (Dalle Grave et al., 2008c).

Preoccupation about Shape, Weight, and Eating Control

The inevitable consequence of people judging themselves predominantly or exclusively in terms of shape, weight, and eating control is the development of recurrent *preoccupations about shape* (e.g., "My thighs are enormous and covered with cellulite," "My belly sticks out too much—it's awful!"); *weight* (e.g., "My weight gain is out of control—I must weigh myself after every meal," "I weigh too much—I have to lose weight"); and *eating* (e.g., "I have to count all the calories I eat if I want to control my weight," "Carbohydrates make me fat—I must cut them out of my diet").

When these preoccupations are of short duration and focused on appropriate, real, objective issues, they are healthy cognitive strategies aimed at solving problems and associated negative emotions (Davey, 1994). However, if the problem is impossible to solve (e.g., curbing the natural drive to eat and to have a body weight above the underweight range), the individual remains helplessly locked in a specific *mindset* (Harvey, Watkins, Mansell, & Shafran, 2004), which has the following effects in eating disorder patients (Fairburn et al., 2008, p. 119):

- It filters internal and external stimuli in a particular way (e.g., preferentially noticing people who have a flat stomach or minimal body defects).
- It pressures the individual to follow specific unhealthy behaviors such as extreme and strict dieting, excessive and compulsive exercising, self-induced vomiting, misuse of laxatives, and body checking and avoidance behaviors.
- It causes them to mislabel some physical and emotional experiences from, for example, "I feel sad" to "I feel fat."

In addition, this mindset is associated with negative emotions such as anxiety and apprehension about the capacity to control eating, fear of weight gain, guilt, and mood swings related to minimal changes in the control exercised on eating, weight, and shape.

Strict Dieting

As people with eating disorders judge themselves predominantly or exclusively in terms of shape, weight, and eating control, it is easy to understand why they usually adopt a strict diet characterized by *extreme and rigid dietary rules*. These rules dictate *when* to eat (e.g., never before dinner), *what* to eat (e.g., only fruit and vegetables) and *how much* to eat (e.g., very small portions) (Fairburn, 2008b, p. 13). Other typical rules include not eating with others, eating less than the others present, not eating food of uncertain calorie content or that prepared by others, not eating in the absence of hunger or despite a calorie deficit, eating as late as possible, and not eating in restaurants, fast-food outlets, or other people's homes, etc.

A behavior typical of individuals following a strict diet is *food checking*, both *during meals* (e.g., counting calories while eating; counting the number of pieces of pasta on the plate; checking what others eat), and *outside meals* (e.g., counting the calories before and after meals; checking the food labels; weighing food several times). Although food checking helps individuals to adhere to extreme, rigid dietary rules, it reinforces their condition by increasing their preoccupation with food and preventing social eating.

The persistent attempt to limit food intake (*dietary restraint*) may or may not produce a persistent calorie intake lower than the energy expended and consequently lead to weight loss. In the first case, the condition is defined as *dietary restriction* (Fairburn, 2008b, p. 13), whereas in the second case, typical of many individuals with bulimia nervosa or not-underweight eating disorder NOS patients, the attempt to reduce calorie intake does not produce an energy deficit and weight loss because it is interrupted by recurrent bulimic episodes.

In both cases, however, the strict diet contributes to maintaining the eating disorder through several mechanisms:

- Increasing preoccupation with eating control.
- Provoking anxiety and distress, as eating becomes an unpleasant experience.
- Impairing social life, as it makes eating with others difficult.
- Promoting bulimic episodes (see below).
- Intensifying the core psychopathology, both through a positive cognitive reinforcement associated with the feeling of controlling shape, weight, and eating and, if it produces a persistent calorie deficit, through a need to increase control over eating in consequence of the effects of being underweight and starvation syndrome (see below).

The Underweight State and Starvation Syndrome

Successful adherence to extreme and rigid dietary rules produces a condition of *dietary restriction* and *being underweight*, which is in turn associated with severe physical and psychosocial consequences, some of which encourage further undereating. The key reference on the effect of dietary restriction and weight loss in normal weight individuals is considered to be a study carried out at the University of Minnesota between November 19, 1944, and December 20, 1945 (Keys, Brozek, Henschel, Mickelsen, & Taylor, 1950). The study was designed to evaluate the physiological and psychological effects of severe and prolonged dietary restriction, and the effectiveness of nutritional rehabilitation strategies. The principal aim of the research was to gather data from a laboratory simulation of starvation with a view to guiding assistance to famine victims in Europe and Asia during and after World War II.

More than one hundred male volunteers came forward to participate in the study in lieu of military service. Of this initial sample, thirty-six men in the best physical health, with good psychological functioning and high motivation to participate were selected. The participants were all Caucasian males in the age range from twenty-two to thirty-three years. Of the thirty-six volunteers, twenty-five were members of the historic peace churches (Mennonites, Church of the Brethren, and Quakers).

The study was divided into three phases: a control period of twelve weeks, twenty-four weeks of semistarvation, and twelve weeks of rehabilitation. During the control period the mean daily intake of the participants was 3,492 calories, which was reduced to a mean of 1,570 during the period of semistarvation, then returned to the former levels during the period of rehabilitation. In the semistarvation period, participants were fed foods most likely to be consumed in European famine areas, and on average lost approximately 25 percent of their body weight. Four participants withdrew during or at the end of the semistarvation phase, meaning that complete data are only available for thirty-two participants. Nevertheless, despite the heterogeneity of the individual reactions to semistarvation and weight loss, most participants experienced dramatic effects traditionally called *starvation symptoms* (see textbox 2.1).

TEXTBOX 2.1. EFFECTS OF STARVATION REPORTED BY THE MINNESOTA STUDY VOLUNTEERS

Behavioral Effects
- Eating rituals (eating very slowly, cutting the food into small pieces, mixing the food in a bizarre way, ingesting very hot food)
- Reading cookbooks and collecting recipes

- Increasing coffee and tea consumption
- Increasing the use of salt, spices, gums, hot soup, and water
- Nail-biting
- Increased smoking
- Bulimic episodes
- Increased exercise to compensate for the increase in the calorie content of the diet
- Self-mutilation

Psychological Effects
- Impaired concentration
- Poor insight and critical judgment
- Preoccupation with food and eating
- Depression
- Mood swings
- Irritation
- Hunger
- Anxiety
- Apathy
- Psychotic episodes
- Personality changes

Social Effects
- Social withdrawal
- Loss of sexual appetite

Physical Effects
- Abdominal pain
- Gastrointestinal discomfort
- Sleep disturbances, vertigo
- Headache
- Reduction in strength
- Hypersensitivity to light and noise
- Edema
- Cold intolerance
- Paresthesia
- Reduction of basal metabolism
- Decreased heart and respiratory frequency

Source: Keys et al. (1950)

Many of these symptoms are similar to those found in patients with ano-rexia nervosa, an observation that significantly improved the understanding and the treatment of eating disorders. Indeed, today, it is widely accepted that many symptoms, once attributed to the psychopathology of anorexia nervosa, are instead the consequences of severe weight loss and calorie restriction. These symptoms are not only those related to food and eating, but embrace all the areas of the individuals' psychosocial functioning (Garner, 1997).

However, the *effects* of starvation symptoms differ between individuals with eating disorders and those without. In absence of eating disorder psychopathology, starvation symptoms have a positive function, both to reduce energy expenditure and to focus the attention of individuals on the search for food, and, when food becomes available, allowing them to eat without being concerned about losing control of their shape and weight. In contrast, in eating disorder sufferers, starvation symptoms interact with the underlying psychopathology, reinforcing the overvaluation of eating control. In particular, it has been suggested that some symptoms of starvation (e.g., hunger, heightened satiety, reduction in rate of weight loss, poor concentration, and dizziness) actually stimulate further dietary restriction by undermining one's sense of being in control of his or her eating, shape, weight, or self in general. Likewise, other symptoms appear to exacerbate the tendency to use control over eating as an indicator of self-control (Dalle Grave, Di Pauli, Sartirana, Calugi, & Shafran, 2007; Shafran, Fairburn, Nelson, & Robinson, 2003). It has also been proposed that some people with eating disorders interpret the symptoms of starvation as a positive sign of being in control, and as evidence that they are working hard to achieve their goal of controlling their eating, shape, and weight (Shafran et al., 2003).

Thus, a knowledge of starvation symptoms and how they interact with the eating disorder psychopathology will have important implications on both the understanding and treatment of eating disorders. Clinicians should therefore be aware that many psychosocial symptoms reported by underweight eating disorder patients are the consequences of dietary restriction and being underweight, and not the expression of their eating disorder psychopathology. Since many of the symptoms reported by eating disorder patients, often suggested to be the cause of their disorder, are instead the consequences of being underweight and dietary restriction, it follows that the weight must be completely restored before a final assessment of the psychological functions and personality of patients can carried out with any hope of accuracy (Garner, 1997).

To sum up, the underweight state and starvation symptoms play a powerful role in the maintenance of the eating disorder through several mechanisms:

- Deteriorating physical health and psychosocial functioning.
- Increasing the need to control eating.
- Increasing the preoccupation with eating.
- Promoting bulimic episodes (see below).

Bulimic Episodes

Binge eating and bulimic episode are terms used to describe a behavior characterized by the loss of control over eating associated with the consumption of what would generally be regarded as a large amount of food. This type of binge eating is also termed an *objective bulimic episode*, to distinguish it from a *subjective bulimic episode*, in which the loss of control over eating is not associated with the consumption of what would generally be regarded as a large intake (Fairburn & Wilson, 1993).

According to cognitive behavioral theory, several processes interact in the development and maintenance of bulimic episodes (Fairburn et al., 2003, pp. 511–12). The first occurs in individuals who adopt extreme and rigid dietary rules and tend to interpret any infraction of their dietary rules as evidence of their lack of self-control. As a consequence, they usually abandon their previous intense efforts to restrict their eating. However, the resultant bulimic episode further intensifies concerns about their ability to control eating, shape, and weight, and encourages further dietary restraint, which, in turn, increases the risk of further bingeing.

A second process that contributes to the maintenance of bulimic episodes occurs in individuals who misuse compensatory vomiting/laxatives or diuretics after binges, in the belief that in so doing they will eliminate all of the calories ingested while bingeing. Not only is this assumption mistaken, since vomiting only eliminates part of what has been ingested (Kaye, Weltzin, Hsu, McConaha, & Bolton, 1993), and laxatives and diuretics have little or no effect on energy absorption, this behavior encourages them to relax their control over eating and thereby increases the risk of further bingeing and purging.

The third process reinforcing bulimic episodes is related to external events and the mood changes they provoke. In this case, binge eating can be used as a distraction from concerns associated with the negative events and/or to mitigate intense and intolerable emotional states (Fairburn, 2008b, p. 19). Finally, in some individuals, binge eating may be also precipitated by alcohol intake, which promotes a lack of inhibition and relaxed control over eating restraint (Gadalla & Piran, 2007).

Whatever their trigger, bulimic episodes contribute to maintaining the eating disorder through several mechanisms:

- Increasing preoccupation with shape, weight, and eating control.
- Promoting the perception of poor self-worth, as patients tend to blame their lack of willpower, rather than their unrealistically harsh dietary standards, for their loss of control over eating (Fairburn, Marcus, & Wilson, 1993), leading them to strive even harder to pursue success in controlling their eating, shape, and weight.

- Encouraging the use of compensatory behaviors (e.g., self-induced vomiting, misuse of laxatives or diuretics, excessive and compulsive exercising, fasting).
- Modulating mood in a dysfunctional way.

Excessive and Compulsive Exercising

Excessive and compulsive exercising is a common feature of patients with eating disorders, particularly those who are underweight (Dalle Grave, Calugi, & Marchesini, 2008b). Exercising is defined as *excessive* when it significantly interferes with important activities, occurs at inappropriate times or in inappropriate settings, or continues despite injury or other medical complications. Exercising is defined as *compulsive* when it is associated with a subjective sense of being driven or compelled to exercise; it takes priority over other activities (e.g., school or work) and is associated with feelings of guilt and anxiety when postponed. For most eating disorder patients, exercise is both excessive and compulsive, and disentangling the two components is difficult to say the least (Dalle Grave, 2009).

Three primary forms of excessive and compulsive exercising have been described (Fairburn et al., 2008, p. 86):

- Excessive and compulsive exercising in routine daily activities (e.g., walking most of the day, standing rather than sitting while studying or watching television).
- "Overdoing it" in sports activities (e.g., training above and beyond a planned schedule or going to the gym several times a day), a form of exercising that can be exhibited by those who practice sports either competitively or recreationally.
- Practicing abnormal activities in an excessive and compulsive fashion (e.g., doing extreme numbers of push-ups or sit-ups at home or in unusual places such as public restrooms).

Excessive and compulsive exercising can be classified into two main categories according to its function (Fairburn et al., 2008, p. 86):

- *Excessive and compulsive exercising to control body shape and weight.* This is the most common function observed in eating disorder patients, and can be divided in two subcategories:

1. *Compensatory exercising*—practiced to compensate for an excessive calorie intake (actual or perceived). Individuals who exercise to burn calories before eating, to create a kind of "calorie bank," and those who eat only if they have already practiced some form of exercise are included in this category.
2. *Non-compensatory exercising*—used routinely to control shape and weight, independent of the quantity of food ingested. This form of exercising has a similar function to other weight control strategies (e.g., dieting or taking diet pills) practiced without any link to eating.

• *Compulsive exercising to modulate mood*, used by a subgroup of individuals with mood intolerance (see below).

According to the cognitive behavioral theory of eating disorders, excessive and compulsive exercising plays a central role in the maintenance of eating disorder psychopathology through several possible reinforcement mechanisms (Dalle Grave, 2009):

• Deteriorating physical health.
• Promoting social isolation—individuals with eating disorders typically exercise alone and inevitably reduce the time spent with others, and the resulting marginalization of social life acts to increase the overvaluation of shape and weight.
• Determining (in association with dietary restriction) weight loss and the maintenance of the underweight status.
• Favoring bulimic episodes—some patients who view exercise as an effective means of weight control tend to relax and ultimately lose control over food intake, increasing their propensity to binge, a mechanism that may occur in both compensatory and non-compensatory exercising.
• Intensifying preoccupation with shape and weight.
• Modulating mood in a dysfunctional way.

Purging

Purging is a common and potentially very dangerous behavior adopted by several individuals with eating disorders (Dalle Grave, Calugi, & Marchesini, 2009). The most common forms of purging are self-induced vomiting, laxative misuse, diuretic misuse, and spitting with or without rumination (rare). Whichever form it takes, purging has two main functions (Fairburn et al., 2008, pp. 82–83):

• *Compensatory purging*—used to compensate for objective or subjective bulimic episodes.

- *Non-compensatory purging*—the routine ingestion of large doses of laxatives or diuretics practiced irrespective of food intake—this needs to be directly addressed by treatment.

Other less common functions of purging are the following (Fairburn et al., 2008, p. 83):

- To manage the experience of feeling full—some patients vomit or take large doses of laxatives in order to avoid this sensation.
- To manage the experience of feeling bloated—some patients take diuretics in order to avoid feeling bloated. However, the state of dehydration induced by diuretics may in fact accentuate the bloated feeling when their effects wear off.
- To obtain a flat or concave stomach—some patients vomit or take large doses of laxatives in order to get a flat or concave stomach (when lying down). However, it is well known in the medical community that vomiting does not completely empty the stomach and that laxatives empty the colon by producing diarrhea, neither of which eliminates ingested fat from the stomach.
- To modulate mood—self-induced vomiting may be used, like excessive and compulsive exercising, to cope with changes in mood.

Purging maintains the eating disorder psychopathology through several mechanisms:

- Negatively affecting physical health and psychosocial functioning.
- Causing weight loss and the underweight state—this is particularly true of self-induced vomiting after subjective bulimic episodes.
- Encouraging bulimic episodes, especially in patients who believe that purging will rid them of the calories they introduce with food intake; instead, it is more likely to cause them to relax their rigid control and, subsequently, binge eat.
- Modulating mood in a dysfunctional way.

Body Checking

Body checking is common among healthy individuals, but in those with eating disorder psychopathology it manifests far more frequently and in very unusual ways, for example, standing naked in front of the mirror for long periods of time and looking at the body from different angles (Rosen, 1997; Shafran, Fairburn, Robinson, & Lask, 2004). Typical body checking behaviors include:

- Frequent weight checking.
- Using the mirror to check specific parts of the body.
- Measuring body dimensions with a tape measure.
- Pinching parts of the body to assess how fat they are.
- Repeatedly touching the abdomen, thighs, and arms.
- Feeling bones.
- Checking that there is a gap between the thighs when standing with the knees together.
- Placing a ruler across the iliac crest when lying down, to check that the surface of the abdomen does not touch it.
- Looking down when sitting (especially during assisted eating) to assess the extent to which the abdomen protrudes or the degree to which the thighs spread out.
- Making comparisons with the body, or specific parts of the body, of other individuals.

The most common functions of body checking reported by patients are to help them understand what their figure looks like, and to check whether their shape is changing or whether they are putting on weight (Fairburn et al., 2008, p. 106). Most patients report that they feel bad after checking, although some underweight patients may say that they feel reassured about being thin, but this in no way arrests their preoccupation with their shape.

Body checking maintains the eating disorder through several mechanisms:

- Increasing body dissatisfaction through the repeated scrutiny of "unsatisfactory" parts of the body.
- Increasing the likelihood of detecting perceived defects—seek and you shall find.
- Magnifying apparent defects as a consequence of scrutinizing specific parts of the body in isolation rather than the body as a whole.
- Reinforcing the apparent need for a strict diet and other extreme weight control measures by increasing body dissatisfaction.

Body Avoidance

While some patients cannot refrain from checking their weight and shape, others abstain from these behaviors with as much fervor. Indeed, body avoidance is another typical expression of the overvaluation of shape and weight (Shafran et al., 2004), and is common in individuals when they put on weight and feel powerless to change their weight and the body shape. However, it can be also observed in underweight individuals with extreme body dissatisfaction. Typical body avoidance behaviors include:

- Avoiding checking the weight and eschewing the bathroom scales.
- Staying away from mirrors and avoiding looking at the body.
- Refusal to expose the body to others.
- Wearing baggy clothes that hide the body shape.
- Steering clear of certain places (e.g., swimming pool, beach, gym, etc.) where there is a risk of body exposure.
- Shrinking from physical contact with other people.

Shape avoidance acts to maintain body dissatisfaction and therefore the eating disorder itself, because concerns and fears about shape and appearance tend to persist in the absence of a real idea of what one actually looks like. In addition, it hinders socializing, intimacy with a partner, and activities such as going to the swimming pool and buying new clothes (Fairburn et al., 2008, p. 112).

Feeling Fat

Feeling fat is a common experience in individuals with eating disorders; it fluctuates in intensity from day to day, and even over the course of a single day. According to cognitive behavioral theory, it is the result of mislabeling certain negative emotions (e.g., anxiety, depression, anger), physical sensations (e.g., feeling full or bloated) or behaviors (e.g., body checking) (Fairburn et al., 2008, p. 115). Individuals with eating disorders commonly equate the sensation of feeling fat to being fat, and this tends to maintain the eating disorder by encouraging dieting and the use of extreme weight control behaviors (Fairburn et al., 2008, p. 114).

THE COMPOSITE TRANSDIAGNOSTIC FORMULATION OF EATING DISORDERS

The transdiagnostic formulation is a device central to the implementation of CBT-E. Figure 2.1 illustrates the interactions between the main eating disorder maintenance mechanisms and can therefore be used to inform the patient about his or her particular issues and as a framework for the treatment itself. The formulation can be adapted to all the diagnostic categories of eating disorders, or rather the individual manifestation of a patient's eating disorder, with minimal modification, and provides a guide to those processes that need to be addressed in treatment. For example, the formulation of an individual with bulimia nervosa does not contain the "underweight and starvation syndrome" box, but can feature all the other mechanisms and symptoms described in the composite formulation shown in the figure. In contrast, the formulation pertaining to an individual diagnosed with anorexia nervosa–type eating disorder will always feature the "underweight and starvation syndrome" box, along with a combination of several of the other features included in the composite formulation. Cases of anorexia nervosa featuring binge eating and purging will require the inclusion of a greater number of maintenance mechanisms, while the formulations of patients with binge eating disorder will contain fewer (Fairburn, 2008b, p. 20).

ADJUNCTIVE MAINTENANCE MECHANISMS

In its latest incarnation, the transdiagnostic cognitive behavioral theory proposes that in *certain* individuals with an eating disorder, one or more of three external, or adjunctive, maintenance mechanisms interact with the eating disorder psychopathology, thereby creating an additional obstacle to change. The three external maintenance mechanisms proposed are (Fairburn, Cooper,

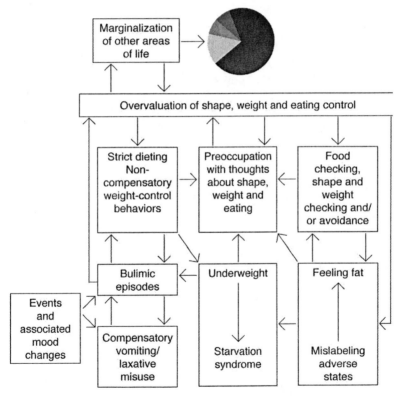

Figure 2.1.   A Composite Transdiagnostic Formulation Showing the Main Maintenance Mechanisms of Eating Disorders. Originally published as a combination of figure 2.5 and figure 8.2 in *Cognitive Behavior Therapy and Eating Disorders* **by Christopher G. Fairburn, 2008. Copyright Guilford Press. Reprinted with permission of The Guilford Press.**

Shafran, Bohn, & Hawker, 2008, pp. 197–220) (see figure 2.2): (i) *clinical perfectionism,* (ii) *core low self-esteem,* and (iii) *interpersonal problems.* In the original version of the transdiagnostic cognitive behavioral theory, the fourth external mechanism *mood intolerance* was included (Fairburn, et al., 2003, pp. 517–18), but this has been subsequently integrated into the standard, focused form of the treatment designed to address external events and moods.

Clinical Perfectionism

Clinical perfectionism may precede the eating disorder and even increase the risk of developing it. The core psychopathology of clinical perfectionism has been defined as a dysfunctional self-evaluation system through which the individual judges him or herself exclusively or predominantly on his or her struggle for, and achievement of, personally demanding standards, despite the adverse consequences that ensue (Shafran, Cooper, & Fairburn, 2002). It is evident that the core psychopathology of clinical perfectionism is similar in nature to that underlying eating disorder, as both are based on a dysfunctional system of self-evaluation.

In fact, it has been hypothesized that when clinical perfectionism coexists with the eating disorder, an interaction between the two psychopathologies occurs, because the perfectionist becomes focused on achieving "perfect" shape, weight, and eating control, in addition to "perfecting" other aspects of his or her life (e.g., performance at work or sports). Cognitive behavioral

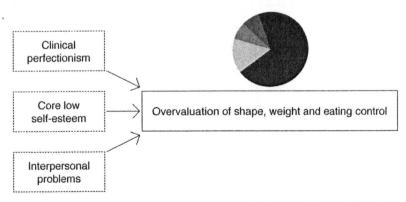

Figure 2.2.   Three Adjunctive Maintenance Mechanisms of Eating Disorders Proposed by the Transdiagnostic Cognitive Behavioral Theory. Derived from chapter 13 of *Cognitive Behavior Therapy and Eating Disorders* by Christopher G. Fairburn, 2008. Copyright Guilford Press. Reprinted with permission of the Guilford Press.

theorists therefore believe that the presence of clinical perfectionism intensifies certain aspects of eating disorders, making them more difficult to treat
(Shafran et al., 2002).

Core Low Self-Esteem

One subgroup of individuals with eating disorders suffers from a pervasive
perceived lack of self-worth influenced neither by events or circumstances,
nor by any change in the state of the eating disorder (Fairburn, et al., 2003).
This form of negative self-evaluation, whose importance has been stressed
by CBT theorists of anorexia nervosa (Garner, Vitousek, & Pike, 1997), has
been called *core low self-esteem*, and must be differentiated from the more
common self-critical attitude of individuals with eating disorders that results
from their failure to achieve their goals of controlling their shape, weight,
and eating (Fairburn et al., 2003).

Core low self-esteem acts to maintain the eating disorder through two
main mechanisms (Fairburn, Cooper, Shafran, Bohn, & Hawker, 2008): (i) it
creates a sense of helplessness and lack of confidence in an individual's
ability to change, adversely affecting his or her adherence to treatment; (ii) it
prompts the individual to pursue success in the domains he or she considers
important in the evaluation of self (e.g., the control of shape, weight, and
eating) with particular determination, making changes in these areas even
more difficult.

Interpersonal Problems

The important role of interpersonal processes in the maintenance of eating
disorders has been emphasized by FBT (Lock, Le Grange, Agras, & Dare,
2001) and IPT (Fairburn, 1997; McIntosh, Bulik, McKenzie, Luty, & Jordan,
2000) theorists, and is supported by findings showing the efficacy of IPT in
the treatment of bulimia nervosa (Agras, Walsh, Fairburn, Wilson, & Kraemer, 2000; Fairburn, Jones, Peveler, Hope, & O'Connor, 1993). According to
IPT proponents, interpersonal problems may influence the maintenance of
the eating disorder through all four general areas in which a person may
experience relationship difficulties (Klerman, Weissman, Rounsaville, &
Chevron, 1984). Here are some examples:

- *Grief* (i.e., delayed or distorted): after the death of her mother, a young
  woman develops persistent low self-esteem, feelings of emptiness, and
  loss of control, which she attempts to counter by controlling her shape,
  weight, and eating.

- *Role dispute* (i.e., experiencing nonreciprocal expectations of a relationship with another person): constantly treated like a child by her mother, a girl of eighteen years attempts to wrest control by imposing strict dietary restrictions, which have the self-defeating effect of causing her mother to treat her even more like a child.
- *Role transition* (i.e., when an individual is "forced" to give up an old role and take on a new, unfamiliar one): a young woman begins to binge and self-induce vomiting to modulate negative emotions after being left by her boyfriend.
- *Interpersonal deficits* (i.e., difficulties in forming or maintaining interpersonal relationships): a friendless sixteen-year-old girl begins to diet with the aim of becoming thin, attracting others, and developing more intimate and satisfying friendships, but the consequences of weight loss only serve to increase her isolation.

CLINICAL REASONS FOR ADOPTING THE TRANSDIAGNOSTIC COGNITIVE BEHAVIORAL THEORY

There are several good reasons why this transdiagnostic cognitive behavioral theory of eating disorder should be adopted. First and foremost, the theory is backed up by evidence (for a detailed discussion see Fairburn, et al., 2003). Second, the theory is very clear about the postulated mechanisms maintaining the eating disorder psychopathology, which provides a focus for both clinicians and patients. Third, the transdiagnostic nature of the theory, and its focus on the psychopathology at work in the patients, helps to go beyond the narrow criteria of the DSM diagnosis. Fourth, the formulation derived from the theory, a diagram that can be constructed together with the patient to illustrate the maintenance mechanisms to be addressed during the treatment, is a key tool for integrating the work of a multidisciplinary team, commonly called upon to treat eating disorder patients in intensive settings of care. Fifth, the treatment rooted in the theory is time limited, and requires shorter training periods in comparison with other forms of eating disorder psychotherapy (a fact that may facilitate the dissemination of the approach). Finally, but no less importantly, the treatment stemming from the theory (CBT-E), targeting the maintenance mechanisms it proposes, is demonstrably effective in the outpatient management of patients with bulimia nervosa and eating disorder NOS with a BMI > 17.5, and promising in those with anorexia nervosa.

Chapter Three

Multistep CBT-E for Eating Disorders

This chapter begins with a brief overview of the *enhanced* CBT (CBT-E) for outpatients with eating disorders. This treatment is based on the theory described in chapter 2, and in turn provides the foundations for multistep CBT-E. The overview is followed by a description of the distinctive features that set the multistep version apart.

AN OVERVIEW OF CBT-E

CBT-E, developed by Fairburn, Cooper, and Shafran (2003), is based on the transdiagnostic interpretation of eating disorders. It was derived from CBT specific for bulimia nervosa (CBT-BN) (Fairburn et al., 1993), the leading treatment for this condition in adults (National Institute for Clinical Excellence, 2004). It is described as enhanced for three main reasons. First, it introduced new, potentiated procedures and strategies, inspired by the most recent development in the field of CBT (Beck, 1995; Greenberger & Padesky, 1995; Segal, Williams, & Teasdale, 2002). These enhancements were introduced in particular to address the overvaluation of shape and weight, along with its various manifestations (the Achilles heel of CBT-BN). Second, it is designed to be suitable not only for treating bulimia nervosa, but for all forms of clinical eating disorders. Its content can therefore be tailored to suit a particular individual, whose treatment is dictated by the psychopathological features of the individual's particular eating disorder and the processes that appear to be maintaining it (transdiagnostic approach), rather than by his or her diagnosis according to the DSM. Third, it includes modules to address certain obstacles to change (i.e., clinical perfectionism, core low self-esteem, and interpersonal problems) that are considered *external* to the eating disorder psychopathology.

39

CBT-E was originally designed for treating individual adult patients with any eating disorder of clinical severity deemed to be manageable in an outpatient setting (Fairburn et al., 2003), but was later adapted by the Oxford group for treatment of adolescents (Cooper & Stewart, 2008). The treatment may be administered in one of two forms, a *focused* form, which exclusively addresses the processes maintaining the eating disorder psychopathology, or a *broad* form, which also addresses one or more of the three external maintenance mechanisms proposed by the transdiagnostic cognitive behavioral theory (i.e., clinical perfectionism, core low self-esteem, and/or interpersonal problems).

To further refine the treatment, its intensiveness can also be selected according to the patient in question. In this system, a *twenty-session treatment plan* would be scheduled for patients with a BMI >17.5, and a *forty-session treatment* would be reserved for those with a BMI ≤ 17.5 (Fairburn et al., 2003). The initial step in both programs is an *evaluation interview* to assess the nature and extent of the patient's psychiatric problems and to engage patients in the subsequent treatment, which develops over the course of *four distinct stages* (see chapter 5).

Effectiveness of CBT-E

The effectiveness of focused and broad forms of CBT-E have been compared in an English two-site randomized controlled trial, which recruited 154 outpatients with bulimia and eating disorder NOS and a BMI of over 17.5 (Fairburn et al., 2009). 22.1 percent did not complete treatment or were withdrawn due to lack of response, but, at the end of treatment, 52.7 percent and 53.3 percent of the remainder, with bulimia nervosa and eating disorder NOS, respectively, had a level of eating disorder features less than one standard deviation above the community mean, while at sixty-week follow-up the figures were 61 percent and 46 percent. In the full sample, the subgroup with marked additional psychopathology, which received the broad form of CBT-E, did better than an analogous group that received the focused version. These data suggest that CBT-E might be more effective than CBT-BN, which has been linked to a cessation of bulimic episodes and purging in only 30 percent to 50 percent of patients, and that the broad form of the enhanced version is able to improve the outcome of patients with marked additional psychopathology.

An Australian open trial also evaluated the effectiveness of CBT-E in 125 patients (thirty-four with anorexia nervosa, forty with bulimia nervosa, and fifty-one with eating disorder NOS). In this case 47 percent of patients did not stay the course (Byrne et al., 2011), but by the end of treatment two thirds of completers had achieved either full remission (cessation of all key eating disorder behaviors, BMI ≥ 18.5, failure to meet DSM-IV criteria for an eating disorder) or partial remission (meeting at least two of these criteria). The results, with the exception of the higher dropout rate, which was associated with a longer waiting list, compared favorably to those reported in the English trial.

Promising data are also emerging from the application of CBT-E in outpatients with anorexia nervosa; indeed, a Phase II trial with sixty-week posttreatment follow-up recently conducted in 99 patients treated in two community-based clinics in the UK and Italy revealed that the two-thirds of the subjects who completed treatment displayed a substantial and sustained improvement in weight, eating disorder features, and general psychopathology. Half of these patients met the strict criteria for a full response (i.e., BMI ≥ 18.5 and Eating Disorder Examination Questionnaire score below 1 SD above the community) (Fairburn et al., 2012). Finally, the data emerging from the CBT-E adaptation for adolescents (thirteen- to seventeen-year-olds) with anorexia nervosa are also encouraging (Dalle Grave, Calugi, Doll, & Fairburn, 2012).

Main Procedures of CBT-E

The procedures involved in CBT-E have been detailed in full in the main treatment guide (Fairburn, Cooper, & Shafran, 2008, pp. 26–28), but a brief summary is provided here. In short, CBT-E is a treatment that aims to address the eating disorder psychopathology, rather than the disorder itself as diagnosed according to the DSM. The treatment is therefore primarily concerned with the processes that act to *maintain* the patients' eating disorder psychopathology, with cognitive processes being viewed as of central importance.

The key strategy is to create a *formulation* of the main maintenance mechanisms at work, a type of "to do" list of things to be targeted by the treatment. Patients are actively involved in constructing their own personal formulation, which can be revised to deal with any mechanisms emerging during the course of the treatment. The aim of this concerted effort is to create a bespoke treatment suited to address the patient's individual psychopathology. This *collaborative approach* continues throughout the CBT-E course, which sees therapist and patient work together as a team in order to overcome the eating problem (collaborative empiricism).

CBT-E theorists have compared the eating disorder psychopathology to a house of cards, and suggest that the key strategy in its treatment is to identify and remove the cards that hold up the eating disorder, thereby bringing down the entire house (Fairburn et al., 2008, p. 47). Hence the eating disorder psychopathology is addressed by means of a flexible series of sequential cognitive behavioral procedures and strategies, integrated with progressive patient education. Simpler procedures are preferred over complex ones, and the *principle of parsimony* (it is better to do a few things well than many things badly) governs the approach (Fairburn, Cooper, & Shafran, 2008, p. 27). To modify thinking, the treatment privileges the use of strategic changes in behavior, rather than direct cognitive restructuring. Ongoing self-monitoring and the accomplishment of strategically planned homework are of fundamental importance in achieving the change.

In this way, patients are gradually helped to decenter from their eating problem. In the first phase of treatment they are encouraged to observe themselves enacting their formulation (in real time), and to engage in an attempt to change their behavior by considering its effects. In the later phase of the treatment, when the main maintenance processes have been disrupted, patients are shown how to shift their dysfunctional mindset when it is triggered.

DISTINCTIVE FEATURES OF MULTISTEP CBT-E

The main idea behind multistep CBT-E is to expand the range of clinical applicability of standard outpatient CBT-E. In order to accomplish this, the treatment introduces a CBT stepped-care approach (multistep treatment) and an appropriately trained multidisciplinary CBT-E team, all working off the same page. In addition, it introduces further procedures, described in chapters 6 and 7, such as assisted eating and group sessions, to potentiate the treatment in the more intensive settings of care (Dalle Grave, 2011b).

Multistep Treatment

In the real world, the treatment options offered to patients with eating disorders largely depend on the judgment and the training of the examining clinicians and the local availability of treatments. There is a general consensus that outpatient treatment is the best option for the majority of patients, because it is less disruptive than inpatient or day-patient treatment and more likely to be effective in the longterm, since patients make the changes required while living in their usual environment. However, there is a subgroup of patients that does not respond to outpatient treatment or cannot be managed safely on an outpatient basis. In these cases, a more intensive form of care is required. Unfortunately, in the real world, it is common for outpatients to receive completely different treatments, in terms of both theory and content, when they go from a less intensive form of care (e.g., outpatient) to a more intensive treatment (e.g., inpatient) and vice versa. This creates discontinuity in the process of care, and understandably disorients patients about the procedures and strategies that need to be adopted to overcome their eating problem.

In answer to these problems, a stepped-care approach for eating disorders was proposed (Dalle Grave, Ricca, & Todesco, 2001; Wilson, Vitousek, & Loeb, 2000), comprising treatments arranged in empirical and logical steps based on cost, intrusiveness, and good outcome prospects. The first treatment step should be the least intrusive, dangerous, and expensive, though not necessarily the most successful. Hence, if it is seen to be failing, the patient is channeled onto the second step, which entails stepping up the intensiveness of treatment (along with the cost), and so on, until a positive outcome is obtained. Within this framework, multistep CBT-E introduces an original approach, whereby the same theory and procedures are applied at different levels of care. The only difference between the CBT-E dispensed in these settings is its intensiveness, which is stepped down for outpatients and stepped up for inpatients.

Although the effectiveness of the stepped-care approach has not yet been evaluated by rigorous research, the rationale behind extending CBT-E to intensive levels of care is based on three robust considerations. First, some patients fail to respond to outpatient CBT-E (Fairburn et al., 2009), and some have an eating disorder of such clinical severity that they cannot be managed in an outpatient setting. Second, data on changing the *type* of outpatient treatment (e.g., interpersonal psychotherapy or fluoxetine) in patients who are not responding to CBT are inconclusive (Mitchell et al., 2002). In those who do not respond to outpatient treatment, the alternative is currently almost always hospitalization in specialized eating disorder units. Unfortunately however, as previously mentioned, most intensive units adopt an eclectic approach not driven by a single theory, and their effectiveness is not empirically supported. Third, the ineffectiveness of outpatient CBT-E in some patients may depend on insufficiently intensive care rather than the nature of the treatment itself. To overcome these problems, multistep CBT-E was designed to include three steps of care: (i) outpatient, (ii) intensive outpatient, and (iii) inpatient.

Most patients are initially treated as outpatients, with the exception of those deemed unsuitable to be managed in such a setting—these will be immediately referred for inpatient care. As treatment unfolds, a patient's progress is continually monitored, and should there be no measurable improvement after a reasonable period of time, the patient is encouraged to step up to intensive outpatient CBT-E. For instance, if there is no appreciable weight gain in underweight patients after twelve weeks of outpatient treatment, or if not-underweight patients fail to improve their eating habits after eight weeks, a more intensive treatment may be indicated. Likewise, if at any time the medical conditions of a patient becomes unstable or starts to deteriorate, his or her treatment intensiveness is stepped up. If intensive outpatient CBT-E is not an option in a particular local context, this can be replaced by day-hospital treatment, as proposed in the original description of this multistep approach (Dalle Grave, 2005), although this may be a more costly alternative. Nevertheless, it still represents a considerable saving as compared to hospital admission, the last resort should a patient fail to improve in response to intensive outpatient/day-hospital treatment.

As the treatment intensiveness is stepped up in patients requiring specialist care, so it is stepped down when they show concrete signs of improvement. Thus, outpatient CBT-E is offered to all patients successfully completing inpatient CBT-E. Then, should a patient relapse in post-inpatient outpatient CBT-E, a short period of intensive outpatient treatment is proposed and, should this prove insufficiently intensive, the patient is readmitted. In this way, CBT-E implemented according to the stepped-care philosophy aims to provide the maximum benefit to patients while minimizing the financial burden of their treatment, and without changing the theory and the content of the treatment along the way.

Multidisciplinary CBT-E Team

In order to implement such an all-encompassing treatment strategy, it is inevitable that a multidisciplinary team will be called into action. However, it should be mentioned that outpatient CBT-E has been designed for delivery by a single therapist for good reason. Indeed, CBT-E theorists emphasize that, as well as aiding research, this practice avoids the common problems observed in multidisciplinary treatment, in which patients partition their problems and discuss specific issues with specific therapists. In this scenario, there is a high risk that no one is in a position to appraise the full clinical picture, and patients may therefore receive conflicting and confusing advice about how to address the same problem (Fairburn, Cooper, & Shafran, 2008, p. 30). Another potential advantage of treatment delivered by a single therapist is that it is more practical and therefore easier to disseminate than those involving multiple therapists.

Nevertheless, it should be stated that many clinicians who work in the real world advocate a comprehensive treatment team consisting of psychiatrists, psychologists, dietitians, primary care physicians, and social workers (Halmi, 2009). Clinicians challenge researchers, saying that they fail to include patients with high clinical severity (Seligman, 1995), who require multiple and complex professional skills and inevitably a multidisciplinary approach, in their investigations. This perceived failing is perhaps one of the main reasons that have limited the dissemination of evidence-based treatment, such as CBT-E, in standard clinical practice.

However, the criticisms of clinicians are refuted by researchers, who affirm that patients with severe eating disorders and several coexisting medical and psychiatric problems have been included in their trials (Wilson, 1998). Indeed, it its rare even in controlled trials that only a single therapist sees a patient. The general praxis is that the evaluation interview is administered by a senior clinical researcher, often a physician, who assesses and engages the patient, while the treatment itself is conducted by a highly trained psychologist, under the constant supervision of senior researchers. In addition, underweight patients have a named physician who will take responsibility for their physical health, and all the patients see a psychiatrist if there is a need for pharmaceutical treatment of comorbid psychiatric problems (e.g., clinical depression). Likewise, patients who are underweight or overweight or adhering to vegetarian or vegan diets may also be offered counseling by a specialist dietitian (Fairburn, Cooper, & Shafran, 2008, p. 30). Unfortunately, these optimal conditions are difficult to replicate in standard, non-research clinical settings.

This problem does not arise in intensive settings of care (e.g., day-hospital or inpatient), because the involvement of several health professionals is inevitable. Traditionally, intensive treatments are provided by a multidisciplinary team, which includes psychiatrists, physicians, psychologists, dietitians, and nurses (Vandereycken, 2003). This choice depends mainly on the need to address the multiple medical and psychiatric problems common in eating disorder patients admitted to intensive units, which a single therapist is rarely able to manage alone. Unfortunately, however, it appears that most multidisciplinary teams adopt an *eclectic* approach, which can involve a wide variety of procedures, including medical, psychological, nursing, and social intervention, stemming from different and even conflicting theories (Dalle Grave, 2005). For example, the psychologist will swear by psychoanalytical theory, the dietitian may adopt some basic cognitive behavioral procedures and strategies, and physicians are likely to follow a biomedical prescriptive model. In other words, each member follows the theory and practice of his or her field, pursuing therapeutic goals related to his or her professional role rather than those of the team as a whole.

While each of these approaches undoubtedly has it merits, and will benefit the patient to a certain degree, their coadministration inevitably entails some significant drawbacks:

- Patients receive conflicting information about their eating disorder and the strategies required to address it. This mishmash of information will inevitably create confusion and a sense of losing control in already unstable patients, and perhaps even compromise the effectiveness of the individual treatments themselves.
- Therapeutic boundaries are unclear. Therapists may, unwittingly or otherwise, cross over into the territory of another team member, generating further confusion in the patient. For example, a dietitian, frustrated by the

eating difficulties exhibited by some patients, may give patients a naïve psychological interpretation of their resistance, thereby effectively taking on the role of psychologist.

- Conflict among team members becomes more likely in this scenario, and also is particularly likely to arise between those who have different beliefs about the way eating disorders should be treated and the problems that need addressing with patients. As well as potentially compromising therapeutic outcomes, friction between therapists is often exploited by patients in their resistance to treatment.
- Dissemination and replication of treatment strategies is limited. Without effective communication between units, it is impossible to evaluate the effectiveness of a particular approach to the standards required by evidence-based medicine.
- Treatment development is hampered. Without a unifying theory, it is almost impossible to understand which are the active and inactive elements of a treatment method, and substantial evolution in treatment approaches is therefore unlikely to occur.

As the involvement of more than one therapist will be inevitable in intensive outpatient and inpatient settings, multistep CBT-E has been designed to ensure a *unified*, rather than eclectic, multidisciplinary approach. To guarantee that all members of the team are cognizant of the full clinical picture, and to prevent conflicting advice being given to patients, four main strategies are adopted. First, when the treatment is delivered by multiple professionals, as in intensive levels of care, all therapists involved in treating eating disorder patients (i.e., physicians, psychiatrists, psychologists, dietitians, and nurses) receive extensive training in CBT-E before joining the team. This ensures that while the therapists maintain their specific professional roles, they all share the same philosophy (cognitive behavioral theory and treatment) and therefore use a similar language with patients. Thus, after assessment by an expert clinician from the team, CBT-E can be implemented either by a single therapist (outpatients) or by the multidisciplinary team (intensive outpatients and inpatients). Although most outpatient cases only require the intervention of a single team member, generally the CBT psychologist, under this system, periodic examination by a team physician can be integrated without interrupting the general flow, as can other disciplines should they be necessary to treat patients with coexisting psychiatric disorders (e.g., clinical depression), medical conditions (e.g., obesity, type 2 diabetes), or complications associated with their low weight and/or purging. In addition, regular counseling by a CBT dietitian may be considered in severely underweight (i.e., BMI < 16) or obese (i.e., BMI $\geq$ 30) outpatients, or those who want to stick to a vegetarian or vegan diet.

Second, in order for the flexibility of this unified multidisciplinary approach to be fully exploited, it is vital that therapeutic roles are well defined and coordinated within the team. Thus, in intensive outpatient and inpatient CBT-E, the dietitian is primarily concerned with addressing modification of eating habits and weight, while the psychologist addresses the overvaluation of shape and weight, the physician oversees the physical health of the patients and the prescription of any medication (Dalle Grave, Bohn, Hawker, & Fairburn, 2008), and, in the inpatient setting, the CBT nurse supervises the administration of medication and assists patients in weighing and managing everyday difficulties. Other professionals, such as educators to help the young patients with school homework and physiotherapists who run the physical exercise sessions, can also be trained in CBT and integrated into the unit.

Third, a weekly review meeting (round table) between the patient and all of his or her therapists is organized in intensive outpatient and inpatient CBT-E. In this meeting, the patient's progress is reviewed and the various elements of the treatment and their relationship to one another are discussed. This allows all team members to form a complete picture of the patient's eating problem, and gives the patient a sense of empowerment, at the same time obviating the risk of mixed messages arising (see chapters 6 and 7).

Fourth, the personal formulation, a visual representation of the processes that appear to be maintaining the patient's eating disorder, built collaboratively with the patient, integrates each staff member's contribution to treatment. This will ensure that no therapist oversteps the boundaries of his or her professional role, and that the patient receives comprehensive and coherent individualized treatment.

Thus, the many potential advantages of the unified multidisciplinary approach to multistep CBT-E start to become apparent. Rather than relying on a single therapist for outpatients and resorting to hospitalization in order to provide more severe, complicated cases with the multidisciplinary treatment they need, a team of professionals can be mobilized to treat more severe cases in an outpatient setting. This can be achieved by stepping up the intensiveness of their care, implementing measures such as meal supervision, should they fail to respond to standard outpatient CBT-E (see chapter 6).

This considered, concerted approach can therefore render the more costly inpatient treatment unnecessary in most cases, with only the most severely disabled non-responders being admitted. Furthermore, unlike the eclectic multidisciplinary approach, unified CBT-E gives the patient the opportunity to benefit from a theory-based treatment, even at intensive levels of care, and the treatment itself can be continually refined and adjusted to suit. Moreover, it facilitates the construction of a collaborative therapeutic relationship with the patient, who is reassured by the support from different professionals on several fronts, and benefits from being treated as a whole person with a coherent non-contradictory approach. Last but not least, uniting the team behind a common line of attack facilitates evaluation of the strengths and limitations of the treatment itself, something that is invaluable from a research perspective and can ultimately only lead to improvement in therapeutic strategies.

Textbox 3.1 gives some suggestions of how to build a multidisciplinary CBT-E team.

TEXTBOX 3.1. PRACTICAL ADVICE ON BUILDING A MULTIDISCIPLINARY CBT-E TEAM

1. Select, if possible, open-minded young therapists who are not committed to other theories and therapeutic practices. Strong alternative influences may be dangerous because they may cause a therapist to deviate too far from the treatment guidelines.
2. Train all therapists (psychologists, dietitians, physicians, and nurses) in multistep CBT-E and in the team approach before they start to see patients. Neither universities nor psychotherapy schools (even CBT-based) tend to prepare therapists in both CBT-E and teamwork.[a]
3. Monitor therapist adhesion and consistency by adopting the following procedures:

   a. Planning a weekly peer-supervised meeting between therapists to discuss clinical work freely and at length
   b. Asking the therapists to record individual sessions and encouraging them to listen to selected recordings of each other's treatment sessions
   c. Asking the therapist to give evidence of the topics covered in each session, as part of the medical records
   d. Providing the therapists with a written treatment protocol to implement
   e. Introducing new procedures and strategies only when mutually agreed upon

4. Provide procedures to improve the team approach:

   a. Maintaining the highest standard of professional skill in the team with regular group updates on eating disorder literature

b. Pooling knowledge to be gained in the field with ALL team members
c. Helping other team members to solve the problems of implementing multistep CBT-E
d. NEVER criticizing other team members (in the presence of the patient or the other team members)
e. Organizing a weekly team meeting to set out the professional tasks of each member in detail, to address any difficulties raised by the implementation of the treatment, and to integrate new strategies and procedures.

[a] The First Certificate of Professional Training in Eating Disorders and Obesity is an annual training course for medical doctors, psychologists, and dietitians, designed to train specialists from different disciplines on the theory and cognitive behavioral therapy of eating disorders and obesity, and how to work as a unified multidisciplinary team. Thus far, more than five hundred clinicians have taken this course in Italy, and twenty non-eclectic multidisciplinary teams have been trained to follow the procedures described in this manual.

Chapter Four

Assessing and Preparing Patients for Multistep CBT-E

Assessment and preparation of patients is a crucial stage in multistep CBT-E, and has several aims: first, to establish the nature and the severity of the eating problem; second, to evaluate whether CBT-E is the appropriate form of treatment; third, if CBT-E seems appropriate, to decide the intensiveness of care required and to inform the patient regarding the main aspects of the indicated treatment; fourth, to encourage patients to make the most of the opportunity to overcome their eating problem; and fifth, to assess the presence of barriers that could hinder treatment. Preparation for multistep CBT-E usually takes a minimum of two sessions, but further sessions are often required to engage very reluctant patients.

GENERAL PRINCIPLES FOR ENHANCING MOTIVATION TO TREATMENT

Most eating disorder patients referred for the evaluation interview are ambivalent toward treatment for various reasons. Some, in particular many underweight patients, do not consider their eating disorder a problem, and instead see the control of shape, weight, and eating as an *achievement* or a means to becoming special or increasing their personal value. Other patients may have an extreme fear of becoming fat if they abandon their rigid and extreme control over eating. Still others have a fear of change, and may have concerns about setting themselves up for failure. In contrast, some seem very motivated to change, most likely not-underweight patients with recurrent binge eating, but rather than tackling their eating problem, their main goal is to address the obstacles to losing weight (i.e., binge eating episodes). Finally, other patients have had adverse experiences of treatment in the past and are therefore understandably reluctant to repeat the experience. It is therefore vital that these issues are addressed in ambivalent patients, as motivation is a key factor in ensuring the success of treatment.

Conceptualization of Motivation

Motivation is a dynamic entity, waxing and waning as a function of shifting personal, cognitive, behavioral, and environmental factors (Miller & Rollnick, 2002). In eating disorder patients in particular, even minor changes in weight or eating may trigger a collapse of the motivation to change and lead to their abandoning the treatment. Thus, a patient's motivational state may require continuous attention, not only during the initial engagement process, but also throughout the course of treatment.

Adopting an Engaging Therapeutic Style

In order to motivate patients, it is vital that therapists adopt an *engaging* style from the very first session. The approach to engaging patients will vary according to their individual motivation to change, but in all cases it essentially involves transmitting empathy, understanding, and expertise, instilling hope and giving a clear picture of what the treatment will entail (Dalle Grave, 2012). Although there are no simple formulas for becoming a good engaging clinician of eating disorder patients, here is a list of general guidelines, which, in association with good training and periodic supervision by a senior therapist, may help to get patients to invest in their multistep CBT-E treatment.

- *Show empathy.* Patients, particularly those with eating disorders, who tend to place a high value on the judgment of others, will appreciate a kind, friendly therapist who shows interest in them as a person (Dalle Grave, 2012).
- *Be aware of the egosyntonic nature of the drive for thinness and self-control.* As emphasized by Vitousek, Watson, and Wilson (1998, p. 398), the control of weight and shape is not a means to an end, but an end in itself, and the failure to appreciate this is the most basic error made by clinicians working with eating disorder patients.
- *Show sensitivity to ambivalence.* Ambivalence toward treatment is the norm in eating disorder patients (Vitousek et al., 1998), and the assessing clinician should always be attuned to this, making sure to inquire as to their concerns at the assessment interview and throughout treatment.

- *Don't stigmatize.* By appearing to stigmatize patients, a clinician is likely to thwart the engagement process. Hence, clinicians should always keep in mind that an eating disorder is a psychological problem and not due to lack of willpower. Patients should therefore be treated accordingly and provided with the respect and support they need (Gowers & Shore, 1999).
- *Be honest.* The need to feel in control is central to the psychopathology of individuals with eating disorders (Fairburn, Shafran, & Cooper, 1999), and giving them realistic expectations about the nature and duration of treatment, the level of commitment required, and the achievable results can not only reduce treatment anxiety, but may also facilitate the decision to start treatment by giving patients a sense of control.
- *Exploit self-evaluation.* Informing patients that although treatment will be hard, it should become a priority in their lives because it will be well worth the effort will appeal particularly to clinical perfectionists, who are attracted by difficult challenges. Not only will this approach help to engage patients, it will also foster the idea that their energies might be better invested in "excelling" at overcoming the eating problem rather than attempting to control their shape, weight, and eating.
- *Support self-efficacy.* This is an important strategy in eating disorder treatments (Steele, Bergin, & Wade, 2011), and clinicians should therefore promote self-efficacy even in the initial assessment, raising the hope that there are good possibilities of recovery. This encouragement is particularly important in patients with core low self-esteem, and those who have failed to benefit from previous treatment. During the treatment itself, self-efficacy should be nurtured by designing individualized tasks and aims that patients are confident they will be able to achieve and stick to.
- *Avoid commenting on patients' assumptions.* Commenting on patients' assumptions about shape, weight, and eating control during assessment may hinder the development of a trusting and empathetic therapeutic relationship.
- *Inform.* At this early stage, it is useful to ask patients whether they are interested in improving their knowledge about their eating problem. Informing them about the main mechanisms maintaining the patients' eating disorder—the targets of the multistep CBT-E—through the construction of a provisional personal formulation (see below), promotes engagement, allows patients to recognize themselves in the processes described, and helps them understand the aims of treatment (Dalle Grave, 2012).
- *Empower.* Clinicians should empower patients by eliciting, rather than providing, a functional analysis of the pros and cons of starting the treatment. As change is facilitated by a sense of personal investment (Miller & Rollnick, 2002), patients should be encouraged to think for themselves on this issue, as they will undoubtedly, with proper guidance, arrive at the conclusion that their excessive control of shape, weight, and eating is a

problem worth tackling. Similarly, any sign of ambivalence should be approached with a functional analysis of the variables maintaining it. In reluctant patients, it may also be helpful to propose treatment as a sort of experiment, leaving the door to old habits open should patients fail to perceive a benefit after an agreed period of time (Garner et al., 1997).

- *Create a dialogue.* Asking patients during the evaluation interview, and throughout treatment, whether they have any concerns or questions facilitates engagement and the development of an open and empathetic relationship (Fairburn et al., 2008, p. 49).

In some cases, especially in patients with a condition of severe medical instability, engagement may be better facilitated by adopting a persuasive and directive style. This, however, should never become argumentative. At no time during the treatment should the relationship degenerate into a debate or squabble, as this will increase resistance and weaken the engagement process (Garner et al., 1997).

PRACTICAL SUGGESTIONS FOR CONDUCTING THE EVALUATION INTERVIEW

In my experience, the following simple yet practical suggestions are useful to bear in mind when conducting the evaluation interview.

Assess the Patient's Attitude toward the Interview

A constructive start to the initial assessment is to ask patients whether they came to the consultation freely, or whether they felt pressured by others to attend. This key question, almost always appreciated by patients, helps to create an atmosphere of empathy and favor the patients' willingness to disclose information about their eating problem (Dalle Grave, 2012). In fact, a large proportion of patients with eating disorders, in particular adolescents and those of low body weight, are likely to say they were coerced into attending the consultation by significant others. They themselves may be uninterested in addressing their eating problem, and in these cases, the main focus of the evaluation interview should be to engage the patients in their treatment. Conversely, in patients autonomously seeking help, usually not-underweight adults or binge eaters, after assessment, the focus of the interview can be quickly switched to the explanation of treatment options.

However, it is also necessary in these cases, for the assessing clinician to carefully investigate whether patients genuinely wish to overcome their eating problem or, as described above, only to address some egodystonic aspects of their problem (e.g., binge eating or perceived excess of weight). In the latter case, it is crucial that the assessing clinician gently explain that the treatment will not only address binge eating, but also the overvaluation of shape, weight, and eating control, since this is the psychological core from which the binge eating indirectly originates (see chapter 2).

Settle the Purpose of the Interview

Another key initial question is asking patients whether they agree that the purpose of the interview is to exchange information about their potential eating problem and the treatment options available. In general, even very reluctant patients accept this as the purpose of the interview, because they are reassured by the fact that they will not immediately be obliged to begin treatment and change their eating habits (Dalle Grave, 2012).

Assess the Nature and Severity of the Eating Problem

After a patient has agreed upon the purpose of the interview, the assessing clinician should ask the patient about the evolution and the current status of his or her eating problem. As the main aim of the assessment is to evaluate the nature and severity of the eating psychopathology and discern the principal mechanisms operating to maintain it, key points to assess are the following:

1. *Onset of eating problem*

- Age of onset and nature of the eating disorder behavioral precursor (e.g., dieting, excessive and compulsive exercising, self-induced vomiting, binge eating for at least three months).
- Reasons for dieting or adopting other extreme weight control behaviors (e.g., to lose weight, changing shape, to address symptoms of dyspepsia, loss of appetite, other).
- Weight at the onset of the eating problem.

2. *The twelve months preceding the onset*

- Events (precipitant factors) that may have triggered the control of eating, shape, and weight.

3. *The six to twelve months following the onset*

- How did they feel? Most patients report they felt well and in control during this period, which some describe as the best time in their life (*the honeymoon phase of the eating disorder*).

4. *Since then*

- Any changes in eating habits (e.g., the onset of binge eating) and weight control behaviors (e.g., the adoption of self-induced vomiting or of other extreme weight control behaviors) in this period. These often occur as the main maintenance mechanisms described in chapter 2 are fully operational, and the eating disorder tends to become self-perpetuating and more or less autonomous (Fairburn et al., 2008).

5. *Current state of the eating problem* (the last four weeks and last three months for DSM diagnosis).

- Current weight and height.
- Frequency of menstruation.
- Weight changes.
- Dietary rules (e.g., skipping meals, reducing portions, avoiding specific foods, calorie counting, calorie limitation, avoiding social eating) and reaction if any of these rules are broken.
- Extreme weight control behaviors (e.g., self-induced vomiting, laxative misuse, diuretic misuse, excessive and compulsive exercising): frequency and triggers.
- Bulimic episodes (objective and subjective) and other eating habits (e.g., chewing and spitting, rumination, eating rituals, picking at food): frequency and triggers.
- Drinking (e.g., water, alcohol, other), smoking and substance misuse, and their connection to the eating problem.
- Weight and shape checking and avoidance: frequency and triggers.
- Degree of fear of weight gain.
- Degree of preoccupation with shape, weight, and eating control.
- Degree of feeling fat, feeling full, feeling bloated.
- Effect of the eating problem on physical health, psychological state, social functioning (with partner, parents, and friends), and study or work.

6. *Personal and family medical history*

- Current and past medical and psychiatric comorbidity.
- Current medications.
- Family medical and psychiatric history.

7. *Domestic situation*

- Living arrangements, occupation, and marital status.

The assessment can be improved by asking patients to complete, prior to interview, the Eating Disorder Questionnaire (EDE-Q 6.0; Fairburn & Beglin, 2008) and the Clinical Impairment Assessment (CIA 3.0; Bohn & Fairburn, 2008). The EDE-Q provides a measure of the eating disorder features, and the CIA assesses the influence of the eating disorder psychopathology on psychosocial functioning, both focusing on the twenty-eight days prior to completion. For a thorough assessment of the clinical features of the eating disorder, and for research purposes, the Eating Disorder Examination interview (EDE 16.0D; Fairburn, Cooper, & O'Connor, 2008) can be employed at the beginning of the treatment, since it is too detailed and time consuming to use during the initial evaluation interview(s).

Explore the Nature and Outcome of Previous Treatments

The next step is to assess the patient's previous treatment for his or her eating problem, if any, and the assessing clinician should therefore ask about the type and the duration of any treatment, the improvement achieved, and the reasons for failure. It is important to investigate whether the patient has previously had any CBT-based outpatient treatment or experience of a conceptually different approach (e.g., psychoanalysis), as this will affect the treatment suggested. If patients report that they engaged well with CBT, but failed to improve, the assessing clinician should consider suggesting an intensive form of multistep CBT-E (i.e., intensive outpatient CBT-E or inpatient CBT-E). If, on the other hand, patients state that they did not engage with CBT at the time, but their conditions have changed and they are now willing to make treatment a priority, outpatient CBT-E can be suggested. If patients have not previously been exposed to CBT, outpatient CBT-E can be proposed to the majority of patients as their first treatment step.

Assess the Patients' Physical Health

Assessment of patients' physical health needs to be undertaken by a physician, preferably one trained in multistep CBT-E, as many patients with eating disorders may be in a condition of severe medical instability. In particular, some symptoms and signs (e.g., fainting, dizziness, arrhythmic pulse, marked bradycardia and hypotension, edema, and weakness of proximal muscles) are the expression of severe malnutrition and could indicate the need for urgent hospitalization.

Thus, if the assessing clinician is not a physician, the patients should be referred to one, expert in the assessment and management of eating disorder medical complications, for a thorough physical examination. This should include measurement of height and weight, assessment of vital signs (e.g., temperature, blood pressure, pulse, and respiratory rate) and characteristic eating disorder physical signs and symptoms (see textbox 1.1). If patients are reluctant to be weighed, the assessing clinician should explain that this measurement is necessary for the assessment, and that body weight (the number) will not be disclosed against their wishes.

The physician should also ensure that patients undergo several laboratory and instrumental tests to assess the presence of complications associated with low body weight and the use of extreme weight control behaviors. Here is the routine list used in assessing underweight patients prior to multistep CBT-E:

- Complete blood count (to detect any anemia, leucopenia, or thrombocytopenia).
- Aspartate and alanine aminotransferase, alkaline phosphatase (to assess hepatic function).
- Blood urea nitrogen and serum creatinine (to assess kidney function).
- Serum potassium, sodium, calcium, magnesium, phosphorus (to determine electrolyte status).
- Erythrocyte sedimentation rate, serum ferritin, and albumin (to determine nutritional status).
- Thyroid-stimulating hormone test (to assess thyroid function).
- Estradiol in women or testosterone in men (to assess reproductive function).
- Urinalysis (to determine hydration status).
- Electrocardiogram (to detect any heart rhythm alterations).
- Blood pressure (to detect any hypotension).
- Dual energy X-ray absorptiometry (DEXA) in patients amenorrheic for > 6 months and/or with a BMI < 15.0 (Mehler & Andersen, 2010) (to detect osteopenia or osteoporosis).

Explore What the Patient Thinks about His or Her Eating Problem

The next step is to explore what thoughts the patient has about his or her eating problem. This can be achieved by asking a closed-response question (of which two responses are possible) such as: "Do you think the control of shape, weight, and eating is a *healthy choice* or a *problem*?"

Some patients, in particular underweight adolescents, will state that *it is a healthy choice*. In this case, the assessing clinician should ask them why they feel this way. If patients, as is usual, affirm that it is a healthy choice because they feel well, the assessing clinician may ask something like this: "If you were a doctor, would you prescribe the diet you are following to your patients?" or "Would you recommend your weight loss methods to your sister or your best friend?" Most patients will admit that they would not, and in this case the assessing clinician can then go on to investigate the reasons for their reluctance to change.

In very egosyntonic patients, it may be useful to explore what meaning they attribute to making a choice. By placing a series of open questions, the assessing clinician should help patients to reach the conclusion that two requisites are necessary for making a choice: first, the presence of two or more options; second, the freedom to choose between the options. Then the assessing clinician may ask: "Do you feel free to eat, or are there some psychological forces influencing your eating?" In most cases, patients report that they do not feel free to eat because they are extremely concerned about shape, weight, and eating, and they have a morbid fear of gaining weight.

Other patients will respond that their shape, weight, and eating control *is a problem*. In this case, the assessing clinician may ask something like this: "What makes you think that the control of shape, weight, and eating is a problem?" The typical reasons reported by patients include incessant worrying about shape, weight, and eating control; the adoption of unhealthy weight control behaviors; the concerns expressed by significant others; and the negative effect of the disorder on their physical health, mood, relationships with others; and their capacity to study or work.

Whatever the patient's response to the above question, the aim of this intervention is not for patients to fully internalize the fact that they have a problem, rather to instill in them a state of cognitive dissonance between the belief that control over shape, weight, and eating is a personal choice and the belief that it might be a problem.

Educate Patients about Their Eating Problem

Education, predominantly through the provisional formulation, has several aims: first, to interest and engage patients with their eating problem, second, to help patients to understand the principal mechanisms operating in maintaining their eating problem, and third, to facilitate the description of multistep CBT-E targets. At this point in the interview the assessing clinician should therefore ask patients if they would be interested in hearing some information about eating problems. If they agree to learning more, as is usually the case, a useful way of raising their awareness of their condition is the collaborative creation of a *provisional personal formulation* of the eating problem, based on the information collected during the assessment. Explanation should focus on describing that the core problem of the eating problem is a dysfunctional scheme of self-evaluation, based predominantly or exclusively on the control of shape, weight, and eating, and that most clinical features of the eating problem derive directly or indirectly from this psychopathological core. Underweight patients should be also educated in detail about starvation symptoms and the mechanisms (see chapter 2) that are acting to maintain their eating problem. Likewise, those with bulimic episodes should be educated that these are the consequences of extreme and rigid dietary rules and/or a response to external events and changes in mood.

Explain the Nature of Multistep CBT-E

The next step is to fully inform the patient about multistep CBT-E. In case of doubts about the intensity level to recommend, the assessing clinician should give only a general description of the principles of multistep CBT-E and about the three intensiveness steps of the treatment. However, if a specific form of multistep CBT-E seems indicated (i.e., outpatient, intensive outpatient, inpatient), the assessing clinician should give a detailed description of this type of treatment. It is also useful to provide patients with a previously prepared information sheet summarizing the main features of the treatment.

Set Homework for the Second Evaluation Session

The last task of the first evaluation session is to ask patients if they would agree to do the following homework assignments for the next evaluation session:

- Considering the pros and cons of starting the treatment.
- Reading the information sheet on the treatment.
- Creating a list of questions about the treatment to discuss with the assessing clinician.

As regards the first item of homework, patients should be encouraged to evaluate the short- and long-term effects of the eating problem on their health, psychological functioning, relationships, school or work performance, and whether the control of eating, shape, and weight provides them with a benefit that they would be afraid or unwilling to lose.

Involve Significant Others

Informants of adult patients (the procedure for adolescent patients is described in chapter 8) are not required to attend. Indeed, some patients prefer to keep their eating problem hidden from others and would refuse to attend or cooperate if disclosure were required from the outset. However, many adult patients do arrive accompanied by their significant others (i.e., partner, parents, siblings). In this case, during the one-to-one assessment, the clinician should ask patients whether they would be willing to get significant others involved. If so, these will then be invited to meet with the patient and the clinician, who will provide them with basic information on eating disorders, the mechanisms involved in their maintenance according to cognitive behavior theory, and the nature of multistep CBT-E, once the patient has been fully apprised. If significant others ask about the *cause* of the eating problem, the assessing clinician should maintain a neutral stance. It is also a good idea to ask to significant others if they would agree to participate in some sessions during the course of treatment, and whether they have any questions about the treatment itself. At the end of this meeting, the assessing clinician should emphasize that the decision to start the treatment belongs exclusively to the patient, because it is destined to fail if this decision is made under the pressure of others.

Procedures in the Second Evaluation Session

In the second evaluation session, generally held one week after the first, the assessing clinician should review the pros and cons of starting the treatment with the patient, reinforcing interest in change and addressing any questions the patient may have. During this discussion, patients should be helped to analyze their life aspirations (long-term goals) and not focus solely on the present. Every reason for change should be reinforced. The cons of starting a treatment must also be analyzed, the main aim being to help patients reach the conclusion that the positive aspects of eating problems are transitory and are always associated with a severe impairment to the quality of their life, and that addressing their eating problem will be a positive opportunity for a new life, no longer conditioned by the unhealthy need to control shape, weight, and eating.

A sign that patients see their present situation as problematic is when they make statements such as "If I didn't have an eating problem I would . . ." (Fairburn et al., 2008, pp. 167–68). In these cases, the assessing clinician should make a confirmatory statement such as, "I understand that you have decided to try to address your eating problem. That's a great choice." This type of reinforcement is important with eating disorder patients because they tend to be indecisive and often need help making the decision to change.

In ambivalent patients, the assessing clinician may suggest they *take the plunge* (Fairburn et al., 2008, p. 168) and *make an experiment* (Garner et al., 1997) to see if the treatment enables them to attain a better quality of life and a more functional way of achieving good self-evaluation. Patients should be informed that, in the first weeks of the treatment in particular, when they will address changes in their eating habits, levels of anxiety and concerns about change may well increase, but are sure to taper off, and this will be associated with gaining the benefits of leading a healthy lifestyle.

Patients who manifest strong ambivalence or reluctance to change, particularly if they do not see their low weight as problematic or they have a morbid fear of losing control over weight, will need additional sessions. As in all CBT-E sessions, all patients' questions and concerns must be elicited, reviewed, and addressed.

Deciding the Treatment Intensiveness

At the end of the second evaluation session, the type of treatment to be undertaken is generally decided jointly with patients. In the following paragraphs, the possible options are described.

Outpatient CBT-E

This option is recommended for most patients with an eating disorder manageable in an outpatient setting. In general there is no BMI threshold under which patients cannot be treated by outpatient CBT-E, because the team includes a physician expert in the assessment and management of medical complications associated with eating disorders. However, if a very low BMI (e.g., <15.0) is associated with *high or moderate physical risk*, the patient should be referred for admission to a department of internal medicine until his or her medical conditions are stabilized, after which he or she may start outpatient CBT-E. Some examples of high or moderate physical risk conditions are the following:

- Rapid weight loss (< 1 kg per week) for several weeks.
- Episodes of feeling faint or collapsing.
- Episodes of disorientation.
- Confusion or memory loss.
- Awareness of the heart beating unusually or chest pains.
- Unusual muscle twitches or spasms.
- Shortness of breath.
- Swelling of the ankles, arms, or face.
- Extreme weakness and exhaustion.
- Difficulty climbing stairs or getting up from a chair without using the arms.
- Blood-stained vomit.

The presence of a *high suicide risk* is another contraindication to outpatient CBT-E. In most cases this is confined to patients with coexisting clinical depression, and those who feel hopeless about the possibility of recovery. In this case, psychiatric evaluation and management are essential, and admission to an acute psychiatric unit may be indicated. Once the acute crisis has been resolved, the patient may begin outpatient CBT-E. This approach is also adopted with patients showing signs of *acute psychosis*.

Evident signs of *clinical depression* (e.g., tearfulness, neglect of personal appearance and hygiene, extreme and pervasive negative thinking, and hopelessness about the chances of changing as a result of the program), although not an absolute contraindication to outpatient CBT-E, may interfere in three main ways (Fairburn, Cooper, & Waller, 2008, p. 246). First, depressive thinking is associated with hopelessness about the potential to change, a formidable obstacle to active engagement in the treatment. Second, it impairs concentration and affects retention of information. Third, it reduces determination and the ambition to achieve change. Hence, it is more constructive for clinical depression to be addressed before outpatient CBT-E is begun. Fortunately, however, a large number of eating disorder patients with coexisting clinical depression can be treated successfully with psychiatric drugs (e.g., full dose fluoxetine or sertraline) (Fairburn, Cooper, & Waller, 2008, p. 248), without the need to complicate the psychological groundwork undertaken in the individual CBT-E sessions. After the resolution of the depressive episode, outpatient CBT-E may be initiated.

Another important contraindication to outpatient CBT-E is the presence of *daily substance misuse*. While intermittent misuse in not a contraindication (Fairburn, Cooper, & Waller, 2008, p. 252), patients who misuse substances daily must be informed that intoxication during treatment sessions will render the sessions useless, and persistent intoxication outside sessions undermines their ability to benefit from CBT-E. Although some patients give up or reduce their intake of the substance in question (usually alcohol) without any professional help, others are unable or unwilling to do this. In this case, they should be referred for specialist help before outpatient CBT-E can be initiated.

Finally, if patients have some *impediment to attending treatment sessions* with continuity (e.g., a pre-booked vacation) it would be better to postpone the start of the treatment to avoid a false start.

Intensive Outpatient CBT-E

Intensive outpatient CBT-E has been developed as a less costly alternative to day-hospital for patients not responding to conventional outpatient treatment (Dalle Grave, 2011b; Dalle Grave et al., 2008; Dalle Grave, Pasqualoni, & Calugi, 2008). This option is recommended for patients having difficulties modifying their eating habits in response to conventional outpatient-based CBT-E. Examples include underweight patients not succeeding in eating more and regaining weight after twelve weeks, and patients who, despite not being underweight, have severely dysfunctional eating habits (e.g., frequent binge eating and vomiting) and are unable to modify their behavior by week 8 (of their twenty-week treatment).

In rare cases, patients need to be channeled directly to intensive outpatient CBT-E as the first treatment step. Examples are: patients with long-standing eating disorders who have not responded to several outpatient treatments; very underweight adolescent patients who receive no parental support during meals; patients with core low self-esteem who openly state during the evaluation session that they will not be able to address the meals without assistance.

Intensive outpatient CBT-E has the same contraindications as outpatient CBT-E (see above).

Inpatient CBT-E

Inpatient CBT-E was developed to give a possibility of care and recovery to patients who have not responded, or are unlikely to respond, to outpatient treatments, and has been in use since 2004 at the Department of Eating and Weight Disorder of Villa Garda Hospital near Verona, Italy, with promising results (Dalle Grave, 2011b, 2012; Dalle Grave et al., 2008). Derived from outpatient CBT-E, inpatient CBT-E is indicated for patients whose eating disorder has not improved with well-delivered outpatient treatments, and those with high or moderate physical risk (see above). Other indications include severely high frequency and intensity of binge eating and vomiting, excessive and compulsive exercising, severe interpersonal problems, and/or an abusive family.

Like all the CBT-E treatments, this therapeutic approach is contraindicated in patients with daily substance misuse (intermittent substance misuse is not a contraindication), acute psychosis, high suicide risk, and medical conditions requiring acute and urgent treatment. Nevertheless, after the resolution of these acute states, all these patients can be admitted to inpatient CBT-E.

Recommending Referral Elsewhere

Patients are referred elsewhere when the problem is not an eating disorder (e.g., anxiety disorder), or there are conditions that contraindicate the adoption of multistep CBT-E (see above).

Observation Period

Observation without treatment is indicated in two situations: first, when the nature of the eating disorder is not yet clear (e.g., the disorder is remitting or there are some clinical features but no clinical impairment, as may occur in adolescents), and second, when patients would benefit from CBT-E but refuse it point-blank. In these cases the assessing clinician should ask patients to undergo periodic assessment to keep an eye on the evolution of their eating problem (in the first case), or to try to engage them in active treatment for their eating problem (in the second).

Recommending Compulsory Treatment

Compulsory care should be considered only in rare cases that force the difficult decision on the clinician. Balancing the respect for a patient's wishes with the patient's right to receive a treatment that may save his or her life is a difficult task, and the possibility of compulsory treatment should only be entertained, after consultation with colleagues, in patients at high risk of death who are not prepared to undertake any kind of treatment.

A NOTE ON NON-ATTENDANTS

Some patients assessed as suitable for multistep CBT-E fail to attend the second or subsequent evaluation sessions. In the past, the percentage of non-attendants was roughly 30 percent, but in multistep CBT-E the percentage is now around 10 to 15 percent. This reduction is presumably due to the implementation not only of better engagement strategies, but also of a protocol for dealing with non-attendance. This involves encouraging patients to attend subsequent evaluation sessions, even if they are not interested in pursuing an opportunity to evaluate the pros and cons of change in depth. The assessing clinician should also take on the responsibility of calling patients who do not present to the appointment, expressing concern about their absence and attempting to schedule a new session. Many patients are pleased with this concern for their well-being and agree to reschedule the appointment.

Chapter Five

Step 1: Outpatient CBT-E

Outpatient CBT-E is the form of treatment indicated for the majority of patients with an eating disorder of clinical severity. CBT-E, originally developed in Oxford (UK) for outpatient treatment of all eating disorder categories (bulimia nervosa, anorexia nervosa, and eating disorder NOS) in adults (Fairburn et al., 2003), has since been adapted by the same Oxford group (Cooper & Stewart, 2008) so that it is also suitable for treating adolescents. A comprehensive account of the approach and its implementation can be found in the original CBT-E treatment guide (Fairburn, 2008a); this chapter merely aims to provide an outline of its main strategies and procedures, which will help readers to follow the description of Case Study A (chapter 9) in the second part of the book. After a description of the core procedures of outpatient CBT-E for normal-weight eating disorder patients, this chapter then goes on to discuss their specific adaptations for underweight and obese patients, the latter recently developed in Italy.

CORE TREATMENT PROCEDURES

The treatment for patients who are not underweight is generally scheduled to last twenty weeks. The treatment has been designed for delivery by a single clinician in individual sessions and unfolds over four well-defined stages, each with specific goals and procedures.

Stage One

This is the most intensive stage of treatment, and appointments should therefore be fixed twice weekly. Several reports indicate that the magnitude of change in the first four weeks is the most powerful predictor of treatment outcome (Fairburn, Agras, Walsh, Wilson, & Stice, 2004), which explains why CBT-E theorists stress the importance of helping patients to *get off to a good start* via effective engagement (Fairburn et al., 2008, pp. 47–72).

Engaging Patients with the Treatment and Change

It is crucial that the therapist seek to engage patients in treatment and prepare them for change right from the assessment stage. This is particularly important since most patients with eating disorders are ambivalent or even unwilling to commit. Nevertheless, engagement can be greatly facilitated by a *collaborative* approach, which enables and encourages patients to take an active role in their own treatment (see chapter 3).

Creating the Formulation in Collaboration with the Patient

In particular, patient collaboration is actively sought in the creation of a patient's *formulation*. The formulation is a personalized visual representation, essentially a flow chart, of the processes that appear to maintain the patient's eating disorder, and therefore the targets of treatment (see chapter 2). To avoid complicating matters and confusing the patient, the formulation should only include the most powerful of these maintenance mechanisms. Despite its fundamental importance, the formulation should be considered provisional rather than set in stone. Indeed, a core process of the therapy itself is its regular updating during the course of treatment as more information about the key maintenance mechanisms comes to light.

Creation of a formulation has four main aims (Fairburn et al., 2008, p. 44). First and foremost, it helps to *engage* patients in the treatment, by actively seeking their collaboration and giving them the opportunity to invest in the therapeutic approach. Second, it helps patients to adopt a *decentered stance* toward their eating problem, allowing them to analyze their issues objectively (a key strategy in helping patients embrace change). Third, it illustrates that the eating problem is maintained by a variety of interacting, self-perpetuating mechanisms, enabling patients to visualize and *understand* the nature and function of their psychopathology. Finally, it provides the backbone of treatment, a readily consultable guide to the issues that need to be addressed.

Thus the first CBT-E session after assessment is dedicated to the creation of a provisional formulation, with the therapist taking the lead. At the end of this session, and indeed every session thereafter in this stage, patients should be given a copy of their latest formulation. After briefly reviewing it together with the patient, the therapist should make it clear that in order for treatment to progress, the patient needs to reflect upon the formulation at home (homework), and to write down any modifications he or she would like to make to bring the next session (Fairburn et al., 2008, pp. 53–54). Since this continuous process means that the patient's formulation evolves as the treatment progresses, the patient should be reminded to bring his or her copy, and any thoughts he or she may have had on the subject, to all sessions; particularly since it provides a guiding focus to the treatment and needs to be in evidence throughout.

Setting Up Real-Time Self-Monitoring

Patients are trained to monitor their eating, along with other relevant behaviors, thoughts, and feelings, by writing them down in real time on an apposite monitoring record (see chapter 9). Real-time self-monitoring is introduced in the initial session (session 0) and is the main procedure used throughout the course of the entire treatment. In order to maximize patient adherence and understanding, the therapist should explain to the patient the four main aims of real-time self-monitoring. The first of these aims is to help both patient and therapist improve awareness of the mechanisms maintaining the eating problem of the former. The second is that it helps to identify progress, providing a concrete record of changes made. Third, it facilitates change itself, because awareness and ownership of maintenance mechanisms as they occur enables patients to gain the upper hand and exert their will on behaviors that previously seemed automatic or impossible to control. The fourth aim of real-time self-monitoring is that it helps dictate the agenda of the session. Indeed, to improve the patient's adherence to self-monitoring it is essential that these records are reviewed together with the therapist in detail each session, extending objective analysis not only to any progress made, but also to the process of recording itself, and any difficulties or obstacles the patient experiences.

Establishing Collaborative Weekly Weighing

Patients are firmly encouraged to refrain from weighing themselves during the course of the week; instead, under the new regime, a weekly weighing session is planned, with patients checking their weight in session with the assistance of the therapist. Their weight is then plotted on the weight graph, and patients are helped to interpret any variation over the last four weeks.

The benefits of weekly in-session weighing are threefold. In particular, it is an ideal opportunity for the therapist to educate patients about body weight and its regulation, and to train patients to interpret their weight changes objectively. It also gives patients accurate data and clear evidence of the effect changing their eating habits has on their weight. Perhaps most importantly, however, it directly addresses excessive weight checking or its avoidance, two behaviors that fuel unhealthy concerns about weight.

Providing Education

From the initial session onward, patients are educated about the physical and psychosocial effects of their eating problems and weight regulation (e.g., body mass index [BMI] and its interpretation, natural weight fluctuation, effect of treatment on weight), the ineffectiveness of purging (vomiting, laxatives, and diuretics) as a means of weight control, and the adverse effects of dieting (e.g., the types of dieting that promote binge eating; self-imposed dietary rules versus general dietary guidelines). The rationale behind providing education is that patients are likely to labor under several misconceptions about these issues that are instrumental in maintaining their eating problem.

Establishing Regular Eating Patterns

Patients are encouraged to take up healthy eating patterns, i.e., three planned meals each day plus two or three planned snacks. This ensures that there is rarely an interval greater than four hours between eating. Two principal strategies can be taught by the therapist and employed by the patient to help the patient resist eating between meals. These comprise two lists of tasks, which can be drawn up beforehand and referred to by the patient when he or she feels temptation knocking. These tasks, or distractive behaviors, should be loosely grouped under the headings: *Things to Do* and *Things to Say* (to oneself). For example, the former should include activities that are incompatible with eating and therefore distract from the urge to binge (e.g., taking a bath, doing a crossword) or those that reduce the risk of eating (e.g., going to a place where food is not accessible). The latter group, *Things to Say*, comprises external vocalizations of statements reiterating, for example, that the urge to eat is a temporary phenomenon that can be tolerated and overcome.

During meals, on the other hand, patients are free to eat whatever they wish, with the sole condition that the meals and snacks not be followed by purging. The pattern of regular eating should be the priority of the day, and must therefore take precedence over other activities. That being said, mealtimes may be adjusted each day to suit the patient's commitments.

The therapist should explain to patients that there are three main reasons why establishing a pattern of regular eating is fundamental to the success of treatment. First, it addresses one of the most important types of unhealthy dieting (skipping meals and delaying eating) that fuel bulimic episodes. Second, it gives structure to the patient's day, which is often chaotic. Third, it introduces meals and snacks that can be gradually increased in size and variety, thereby helping patients to tackle their aversion to certain food groups (i.e., it is the foundation on which the other forms of dieting are addressed).

Involving Significant Others

The involvement of adult significant others (e.g., parents or partner), if a patient agrees, is only considered if they are in a position to assist patients in making changes (e.g., helping them manage regular eating) and/or if they represent an obstacle to change (e.g., habitually making negative comments on a patient's eating or appearance).

Stage Two

This is a brief transitional stage with the aim of assessing progress to date and setting up the subsequent stage. The appointments are weekly from this point on. While continuing the procedures of Stage One, the therapist and patients review the treatment so far; the therapist should praise patients that are making any progress (however minimal), and help those who are not progressing to identify their obstacles to change. At this stage there is also a review of the personalized formulation and a formal assessment if clinical perfectionism, core low self-esteem, and interpersonal problems (see chapter 2) present obstacles to change and need to be addressed in Stage Three.

Stage Three

This is the main body of treatment. The mechanisms to address, and the order in which they are tackled, should be decided on the basis of their relative importance in maintaining the patient's psychopathology.

Addressing Overvaluation of Shape and Weight

Whatever the patient's particular psychopathology, this is doubtless the main issue to be addressed. This process can be articulated as follows:

1. Identification of the overvaluation and its consequences. For unhealthy preoccupation with weight and shape to be overcome, the patient must first be able to recognize it as such. Thus the therapist needs to educate patients on the concept of self-evaluation and help them identify how they judge themselves. For educational purposes, the relative importance of the various relevant self-evaluation domains are represented as a pie chart. In patients with eating disorders this will in most cases be dominated by a large slice representing shape, weight, and eating control, along with a few other small slices (e.g., good performance at school, work, etc.). Using this visual representation as a starting point, the therapist then begins to elicit from the patient the advantages and disadvantages of using a system of self-evaluation based predominantly on shape and weight.

This analysis usually leads to the conclusion that although having a predominant domain of self-evaluation may give some short-term advantages, i.e., the simplicity of judging oneself based on a single, controllable, and measurable domain (e.g., shape, weight, and eating control), with respect to multiple domains that are not fully controllable (e.g., school marks, relationships, sports performance, personal qualities, etc.), in the long term, this is a dysfunctional means of assigning self-worth, for several reasons (Fairburn et al., 2008, pp. 99–100). First, it marginalizes other important aspects of life (e.g., relationships, school, work, hobbies, etc.); second, it is directly responsible for behaviors that characterize and maintain eating problems (e.g., strict dieting, binge eating, etc.), producing severe physical and psychosocial complications; and third, it may function when things go well, but if something goes wrong (e.g., an increase in weight or a bulimic episode) it inevitably leads to a collapse of self-esteem.

Having obtained agreement that a stable, balanced self-evaluation system is preferable, the therapist then helps patients create an "extended" personal formulation to include the main expressions of the overvaluation of shape and weight that maintain their preoccupation (e.g., body checking and body avoidance, feeling fat, and marginalization of other areas of life), and therefore need to be addressed in treatment.

2. Enhancing the importance of other domains for self-evaluation. This involves helping patients to identify any activities or areas of life that they would like to work on (e.g., taking up a new hobby, changing the way they react to certain events, etc.). In other words, the aim is to increase the number and significance of other domains to draw on for self-evaluation, and indirectly to reduce the patient's overvaluation of shape and weight.

3. Targeting the main expressions of overvaluation of shape and weight. The main expressions to tackle are the following:

Body checking. This behavior is strongly implicated in the maintenance of the overvaluation of shape and weight as it fuels body dissatisfaction (see chapter 2); since patients are often not aware of this, they need to be educated about the adverse effects of this habit. Patients can also often be unaware of the frequency of their anomalous body checking, and should therefore be asked to monitor any episode occurring over a two-day period. Typical body checking behaviors to address are dysfunctional mirror use and excessive scrutiny of certain body parts (which magnify apparent defects), and comparison with thin, attractive people (a behavior that can only lead to the conclusion that one is fat and unattractive). Where celebrities shown in magazines are the object of this unhealthy comparison, it is worth pointing out to patients that the vast majority, if not all, of these images have been doctored and are therefore not representative of realistic body models (the Internet is full of videos, for example, illustrating the "The Photoshop Effect," one of which the therapist may judge to be helpful in a particular case).

Body avoidance. This behavior, as described in chapter 2, maintains body dissatisfaction through several mechanisms. First and foremost, it makes it impossible to challenge the dysfunctional beliefs and fears about one's body. Indeed, it prevents realistic information about one's body being assimilated, exacerbating the aforementioned fears and beliefs and creating situations of stress and anxiety when exposure of the body is required. Thus, it is likely to prevent socializing, intimacy between partners and the practice of any activities (e.g., swimming, going to the beach, trying on clothes) where the body, or an offending part thereof, will be revealed. As this type of behavior leads inevitably to isolation, effectively confining a patient to a world ruled by their psychopathology, patients who practice body avoidance are likely to need considerable help. They should be assisted to progressively become accustomed to the sight and feel of their body, and eventually to become comfortable exposing it in the presence of others.

Feeling fat. This experience, reported by many women, is extremely intense and frequent among people with eating disorders. It seems to be the consequence of mislabeling certain emotions (e.g., anxiety, depression), sensations (e.g., feeling full, bloated, or hot, being sweaty, wearing tight clothes, etc.) or behaviors (e.g., body checking). As *feeling* fat is often equated by eating disorder patients with *being* fat (even if they are in reality of normal or low weight) it is an issue that needs urgent attention. Hence patients, when they feel fat, are encouraged to ask themselves what *else* they are feeling at the time, and then to address that emotion or circumstance directly.

Addressing Dietary Rules

Patients should be educated that extreme and rigid dietary rules impair their quality of life and are potent mechanisms that maintain their eating problem. They should then be helped to identify their many extreme, rigid dietary rules and associated beliefs, and to gradually and systematically break them. For instance, patients who binge eat are encouraged to gradually introduce food they would prefer to avoid into their diet, as food avoidance is a major contributor to binge eating.

Addressing Events and Moods Changes

It is common for patients with an eating disorder to change their eating behavior in response to external events and associated changes in mood. In certain circumstances therefore, they may restrict their diet or binge. If these changes are frequent, patients should be helped to cope with adverse events using proactive problem-solving methods, coupled with functional means of modulating mood.

Addressing Clinical Perfectionism, Low Self-Esteem,
and Interpersonal Problems

The broad version of CBT-E includes strategies and procedures aimed at addressing one or more external, or additional, processes that may be maintaining the eating disorder. These processes are addressed in specific modules as follows if their contribution to the patient's psychopathology emerged during the review in Stage Two (Fairburn et al., 2008, pp. 197–220).

Clinical perfectionism. CBT-E tackles clinical perfectionism using strategies mirroring those used for the overvaluation of shape and weight, and for this reason the two tendencies are addressed almost in parallel. The clinician should add clinical perfectionism to the patient's personal formulation, and assess the patient's consequences on his or her self-evaluation pie chart. Patients should then be helped to enhance the importance of other self-evaluation domains not related to performance. They should also be encouraged to consider their rigid and extreme goals in a particular domain of life that they value (e.g., school or sports), and assess whether these goals are counterproductive and actually impair their performance. Finally, they should be helped to address dysfunctional performance checking (including selective attention to failure), avoidance and procrastination.

Core low self-esteem. If present, this is addressed slightly later than the overvaluation of shape and weight. Patients are educated about the role of core low self-esteem in maintaining their eating problem, and helped to identify and modify its main cognitive maintenance processes (e.g., discounting positive qualities, selective attention to information consistent with their negative view of themselves, double standards, overgeneralization, dichotomous appraisal of self-worth and dysfunctional beliefs). When possible, it is better to address core low self-esteem indirectly by enhancing the patient's interpersonal functioning and setting the patient up for success during other aspects of treatment, because this approach is easier to manage and more readily accepted by patients with this particular problem.

Interpersonal problems. This module is reserved for patients in whom interpersonal problems have a significant effect on the maintenance of their eating problem. CBT-E theorists suggest the integration of IPT, an evidence-based treatment that helps patients identify and address current interpersonal problems, during the CBT sessions. However, since only few therapists are trained in this form of psychotherapy, CBT procedures and strategies can be used to achieve the same ends.

Learning to Control the Eating Disorder Mindset

Toward the end of the treatment, many patients begin to experience prolonged periods in which they are not preoccupied with shape and weight. This phenomenon becomes particularly evident in patients whose main eating problem maintenance mechanisms have been eroded. When this situation arises, patients are made aware of the eating disorder mindset (or frame of mind) and taught how to control it. The procedures by which this is achieved, part of the CBT-E core protocol (Fairburn et al., 2008, pp. 119–23), are derived from the work of Teasdale et al. (2002), and entail the following steps: (i) educating patients about the concept of the eating disorder mindset; (ii) helping patients to identify stimuli that reinstate the eating disorder mindset; and (iii) teaching them how to decenter from the eating disorder mindset. This latter phase involves training patients to spot the early signs of the eating disorder mindset re-exerting itself (Fairburn et al., 2008, pp. 121–22), and to counter its onset by *doing the right thing* (e.g., doing the opposite of the behavior driven by the eating disorder mindset) and engaging in distracting interpersonal activities (e.g., meeting a friend, going out to a party, etc.).

Exploring the Origins of Overvaluation

An additional strategy that may help patients to distance themselves from their eating problem is to explore the origins of the patients' sensitivity to shape and weight. This may help patients to become consciously aware of how their eating problem arose, and highlight how its early positive function (e.g., the feeling of being in control) may no longer be applicable.

Stage Four

This is the final stage of the treatment and the primary focus is on the future. The appointments are scheduled at fortnightly intervals and their aims are to ensure that changes will be maintained over the subsequent twenty weeks until a review appointment is held, and to reduce the risk of relapse in the long term.

During this stage patient discontinues self-monitoring and begins weekly weighing at home. Then, the therapist and patient build together a personalized plan to address both the residual eating disorder problems (e.g., dietary restraint, body checking), to develop new interests and activities, and to identify and to address as early as possible setbacks (see chapter 8 for details).

OUTPATIENT CBT FOR UNDERWEIGHT PATIENTS

The treatment of underweight patients (i.e., BMI < 18.5) mirrors those used to treat patients of normal weight, but includes some distinctive procedures and strategies designed to address the specific needs of this group of patients (underweight module). Specifically, this type of treatment has three main phases, and its duration is more flexible, tending to be longer than that aimed at normal-weight patients. Nevertheless, in typical cases the treatment can be concluded successfully within forty sessions held over the course of forty weeks.

The emphasis of the first phase of treatment is on helping patients think afresh about their current state and the processes maintaining it. This is followed by a detailed collaborative analysis of the pros and cons of addressing their eating disorder and regaining weight, a phase that may last from one to eight weeks. Following the analytical phase, patients, if willing, are helped to regain weight while tackling their eating disorder psychopathology. This phase may vary in length from two to three months in fully engaged patients to several months in the very ambivalent. The objectives behind the third and final phase are to help patients accept and maintain their new body shape, to address residual dietary restraint, and to develop personalized strategies for the rapid correction of setbacks. This phase typically lasts about eight weeks. Timewise, the sessions are initially scheduled twice a week until patients start a regular process of weight regain, and then once a week, with the last three sessions fixed at two-week intervals.

Addressing Poor Motivation to Change

This is a crucial step in the treatment, as underweight patients tend not to regard being underweight as a problem. They should therefore be encouraged to independently arrive at the conclusion that weight regain should be their treatment goal. This may be achieved through several strategies. In particular, the inclusion in the formulation of the psychosocial effects of being underweight may help patients to understand that several problems they are experiencing (e.g., social isolation, irritability, mood alterations, compulsive behavior, lack of sexual desire) are the consequences of malnutrition and not characteristics of their true personality, as proven by the Minnesota Starvation Study. Moreover, developing a good therapeutic alliance, showing interest in patients as people, and collaboratively weighing up the pros and cons of change may help ambivalent patients make the decision to begin the process of weight regain. Finally, encouraging patients to take the plunge and to directly test their theories as regards the benefits and drawbacks of gaining weight may prompt them to stop procrastinating and instead embrace change.

Addressing a Patient's Undereating and Being Underweight

Patients are educated about the effects of being underweight and dietary restriction, and they are helped to create a personalized formulation in which the contribution of being underweight is given particular prominence. They are also actively involved in planning their energy intake and interpreting changes in their weight. In particular, they are educated about the surplus of energy required to gain 0.5 kg per week (i.e., 500 kcal per day), and helped to draw up a daily eating plan that should enable them to accomplish this goal (*meal planning*). Aside from weight regain, the secondary objective is to help patients to achieve predictability and control during this process.

In my clinical experience, a useful strategy when discussing meal planning is to suggest that patients consider food as they would a medication, and to eat mechanically, without being influenced by any external (e.g., offers of food) or internal (e.g., anxiety and thoughts) cues (Garner et al., 1997). This new form of eating must be continued until patient's eating habits are no longer influenced by anxiety and preoccupation regarding shape, weight, and eating control. Significant others, especially if patients are adolescents, may need to be involved in the weight regain process to facilitate the dietary changes.

Addressing Feeling Full and Feeling Bloated

Feeling full and feeling bloated are problems frequently experienced by underweight patients, and are intensified during refeeding and weight regain. These sensations commonly arise due to the mislabeling of other, often coexisting, experiences (e.g., being physically full or bloated, considering food eaten as excessive, perceiving the abdomen as excessively sticking out, wearing clothes that are tight over the stomach, feeling fat), and are often interpreted as evidence of having have eaten too much. This often prompts patients to ask for a diet with fewer calories, or to refuse to eat planned foods. Alternatively, they may attempt to compensate for the perceived overeating with exercising or vomiting (even one hour after eating) or give up on the treatment altogether. If feeling full or feeling bloated are proving to be a barrier to weight regain, these issues need to be addressed with specific cognitive behavioral strategies (see chapter 11).

Addressing Dietary Restraint

Once patients have normalized their weight, the treatment is focused on addressing dietary restraint and any residual dietary rules. This is approached in much the same way as in normal-weight patients. The aim is that patients learn to achieve and maintain a healthy body by adopting a flexible nutritious diet based on national nutritional guidelines.

Addressing External Events and Mood Changes

External events and associated alterations in mood may hinder the process of weight regain. For this reason, during the weight restoration phase patients are trained to deal with events likely to trigger mood alterations and changes in eating using functional means of modulating mood and proactive problem solving.

Addressing Overvaluation of Shape and Weight

To overcome the patients' tendency to overvalue their shape and weight, they are helped, as in normal-weight patients, to address shape checking, body avoidance, and feeling fat. They are also encouraged to develop additional domains of self-evaluation (see above). However, as frequent body checking increases body dissatisfaction and is therefore likely to hamper the process of weight restoration, it is advisable to give this feature priority in the early phase of treatment in these patients.

Addressing Overvaluation of Eating Control

About 20 percent of underweight patients with eating disorders do not report the overvaluation of shape and weight, but only the overvaluation of eating control (see chapter 2) (Dalle Grave et al., 2008c). In this case, patients are encouraged to increase their spectrum of self-evaluation domains, but also to reduce food checking and any form of selective attention to eating and/or digestive function.

OUTPATIENT CBT-E FOR PATIENTS WITH OBESITY

Most patients with obesity and eating problems have a DSM-IV diagnosis of binge eating disorder; however, a subgroup may be diagnosed as having bulimia nervosa or eating disorder NOS. In any case, CBT-E management of patients with an eating disorder and coexisting obesity, briefly described by Fairburn, Cooper, and Waller (2008), is identical to that of normal-weight patients, but should include some distinctive procedures and strategies designed to target the specific needs of this particular subset.

Whether to Address the Eating Disorder, the Excess Weight, or Both

The fundamental question for the clinician is to decide whether it will be possible for these patients to confront their eating problem while trying to lose a healthy amount of weight, or whether these two goals will be too much for a patient to handle simultaneously. Though research findings on this issue are controversial and inconclusive, patients with binge eating disorder, contrasting with bulimia nervosa sufferers, tend to report a low level of dietary restraint, in many cases considerably lower than people without eating disorders (Ardovini, Caputo, Todisco, & Dalle Grave, 1999). In other words, while in bulimia nervosa there is an alternation of dietary restraint and bulimic episodes, in binge eating disorder bulimic episodes occur in a context of excessive eating. In addition, recent studies have shown that a moderate and flexible calorie restriction does not increase the frequency of bulimic episodes, but, on the contrary, tends to diminish them (Dalle Grave, Calugi, Corica, Di Domizio, & Marchesini, 2009; Dalle Grave, Calugi, Petroni, Di Domizio, & Marchesini, 2010; Stice, Presnell, Groesz, & Shaw, 2005). Hence, increasing the levels of dietary restraint appears to have a positive effect on the management of binge eating disorder.

However, if patients have previous history of bulimia nervosa or anorexia nervosa, being encouraged to increase the levels of dietary restraint may reactivate the perceived need to adopt extreme and rigid dietary rules and/or increase the frequency of bulimic episodes. Hence, the practical approach adopted by CBT-E is the following (Fairburn, 1995): (i) to promote a healthy, moderate weight loss if the association between attempts to diet and bulimic episodes seems to be absent; but (ii) to discourage any attempt to lose weight if patients report a worsening of the frequency of bulimic episodes associated with dietary restraint.

Addressing Clinical Depression

There is a subgroup of patients with binge eating disorder who report several coexisting symptoms of clinical depression rather than the overvaluation of shape and weight. This may partly explain the low levels of dietary restraint seen in this subset of patients, who should be prescribed full-dose antidepressant medication (e.g., fluoxetine 60–80 mg day) before they undergo outpatient CBT-E, as clinical depression interacts negatively with eating disorders (i.e., promoting bulimic episodes), as well as the patient's capacity to benefit from CBT itself.

Assessing and Managing Coexisting Medical Complications

Overweight and obese patients, particularly those with body fat prevalently distributed in the visceral region, the so-called "apple shaped," appear to have a higher risk of several dangerous medical complications (e.g., metabolic syndrome, type 2 diabetes, cardiovascular diseases, obstructive sleep apnea, nonalcoholic fatty liver disease, and certain types of cancer). It is evident that these will need to be addressed or ruled out before outpatient CBT-E is begun. Indeed, while many cases of these medical complications may be treated successfully with a weight loss of as little as 5 to 10 percent (National

Institutes of Health, 1998), in some cases it will be necessary to accompany lifestyle modification with specific drugs for optimal management of conditions such as hypertension, hypercholesterolemia, and type 2 diabetes.

The Concept of Healthy Weight

As mentioned in the preceding paragraph, to treat most medical complications associated with obesity successfully, it is sufficient for the patient to lose a modest amount of weight. This has been shown in several studies in which, for example, it has been observed that a 5 to 10 percent weight loss significantly reduces the risk of developing type 2 diabetes in susceptible people (Diabetes Prevention Program Research Group, 2002), and eliminates most of the other risks associated with obesity (National Institutes of Health, 1998). Moreover, this modest amount of weight loss also often goes hand in hand with an improvement in psychological functioning, leading to a significant improvement in mood, body image, interpersonal relationships, and self-esteem. Rather than relying strictly on generic height/weight charts therefore, this research tends to suggest a new definition of the concept of *healthy weight*, i.e., the weight associated with a low level of health risk that can be achieved by adopting a flexible, healthy diet and active lifestyle. In most cases this will correspond to a weight loss of between 5 percent and 10 percent.

Addressing Bulimic Episodes

The procedures and strategies for addressing bulimic episodes in overweight and obese eating disorder patients are similar to those adopted in normal-weight patients (see above), and include: (i) establishing regular eating patterns; (ii) addressing extreme and rigid dietary rules (if present); (iii) addressing external events and mood changes; (iv) collaboratively making a binge analysis after every bulimic episode to understand and plan how to address the mechanisms that triggered the loss of control over eating.

Adopting an Active Lifestyle: The 10,000-Steps-a-Day Goal

Several studies have shown that adopting an active lifestyle is the key strategy to controlling weight in the long term, as well as being associated with several health benefits. Patients should be made aware that an active lifestyle does not necessarily involve grueling sessions at the gym, but can be attained merely by including some form of movement, such as walking, in the daily routine. The goal is to help patients to build up to at least 10,000 steps a day. To assess the number of steps they take, patients are encouraged to use a pedometer and to report their daily total in the appropriate column of their monitoring record (Dalle Grave, Calugi, Centis, El Ghoch, & Marchesini, 2011).

Adopting a Healthy Diet

In the Italian version of CBT-E for eating disorders coexisting with obesity, patients are encouraged to adopt the so-called Mediterranean diet and, assisted by the CBT dietitian, to follow a healthy but flexible eating plan based on national nutritional guidelines. It is vital that the diet includes a reasonable combination of foods, i.e., representatives from all the food groups, and should never completely eliminate the food that the patient likes. The main suggestions to give patients are: (i) to reduce the amount of fat (in particular those of animal origin); (ii) to increase the intake of complex carbohydrates (preferably unrefined), and to decrease the amount of simple carbohydrates (sugars); and, last but certainly not least, (iii) to increase the amount of fruits and vegetables they eat.

If the goal is to achieve a modest amount of weight loss with the treatment, the CBT dietitian may help patients to follow a diet that does not increase concern about eating and therefore the risk of binge eating. In most cases this goal can be achieved with a daily calorie content not lower than 1,500 kcal.

Addressing Weight and Shape Avoidance

A large number of patients with obesity and eating disorders avoid checking their weight. The main reasons reported are so as not to dwell on their body dissatisfaction and to avoid feeling guilty while continuing to adopt a lifestyle not oriented to weight control. Unfortunately, however, as well as allowing weight to get out of control, weight avoidance also *maintains concerns* about weight. Furthermore, available data shown that regular weighing needs to be employed for weight to be maintained long-term (Wing & Phelan, 2005). Thus, overweight patients, as for those of normal weight, should be encouraged to check their weight once a week during a CBT-E session, with the reading being plotted on their weight graph and the number in the scale interpreted (see above).

Likewise, shape avoidance may help to reduce anxiety and body dissatisfaction short-term, but in the long term it fuels body image dissatisfaction and increases stress levels, particularly in situations requiring body exposure. In addition, the negative consequences of body exposure so feared by these patients (e.g., staring, unkind comments) are perhaps less likely to occur than predicted, while concerns about body shape do tend to grow, reinforcing the belief of having an unacceptable body that must be hidden. Finally, if body exposure is not risked, it will be impossible for afflicted patients to put into practice strategies they have learned to cope with the feared consequences, should they occur, thereby depriving them of the opportunity to "do well" and gain confidence.

Shape avoidance is addressed using the same procedures and strategies adopted with normal-weight patients, but since overweight patients may in fact receive negative feedback from prejudiced or tactless people, they should be trained to deal with such situations, and clinicians should help them prepare a repertoire of assertive ripostes, just in case.

Addressing Shape Checking

The most frequent forms of shape checking of obese patients with eating disorders are touching rolls of fat, comparing their body with those of others, and asking reassurance from others about the appearance of their body. Interestingly, the mirror checking typical of normal- and underweight eating disorder patients is rare. Despite this, the procedures and strategies to address shape checking are the same.

Accepting a Healthy Weight

Both therapist and patient should be aware that body weight and shape are under the strict control of genetic factors, and that weight loss is strongly bound by several physiological processes. For this reason a key aspect of treatment is to encourage overweight and obese patients to change the things they can (e.g., lifestyle, moderate weight loss), while accepting with serenity that which they cannot (e.g., the body shape, and the condition of obesity) (Wilson, 1996). This means that patients should be assisted to live positively with a body weight that is significantly greater than that generally described as ideal. Aiming for the abovementioned concept of a healthy weight and the focus on healthy eating and improving physical fitness may help patients to achieve this difficult goal.

Addressing Other Features of the Eating Disorder

As for normal-weight patients, Stage Two (after four weeks of treatment) involves a detailed review of any progress and obstacles to change, with a view to setting up Stage Three, in which the work on developing a healthy lifestyle is continued, and the overvaluation of shape and weight, as well as the external events and changes of mood that can influence eating patterns, are usually addressed. Toward the end of the treatment, when patients begin to experience long periods without undue concerns about their physical appearance, and without adopting unhealthy weight control behaviors, patients are encouraged to implement procedures and strategies to decenter themselves from eating disorder mindset. Finally, in Stage Four, patients are helped to finish the treatment well, and relapse prevention measures are put in place.

Chapter Six

Step 2: Intensive Outpatient CBT-E

Intensive outpatient CBT-E is the second step, in terms of care intensity, of multistep CBT-E. It was recently developed in Italy (Dalle Grave, 2011b; Dalle Grave et al., 2008) to provide an alternative for patients who would benefit from a higher-impact approach than outpatient CBT (non-responders), but whose condition is not sufficiently severe to warrant hospitalization. Hence, this type of treatment adopts most of the procedures and strategies of outpatient CBT-E, but also integrates several developed specifically for these patients.

DISTINCTIVE CHARACTERISTICS OF INTENSIVE OUTPATIENT CBT-E

Unlike traditional intensive treatments for eating disorders, which are aimed at obtaining the maximum possible improvement in eating disorder psychopathology (i.e., the normalization of BMI and a marked reduction in concerns about eating, shape, and weight), intensive outpatient CBT-E, in its latest incarnation, has been designed specifically to address *only* the main barriers to progress in outpatient CBT-E. Once these obstacles have been overcome, the treatment can continue with standard outpatient CBT-E, thereby averting the necessity of hospitalization, a considerable burden on both the health-care provider and the patient. For example, a patient in no immediate danger, but whose inability to address dietary restriction and weight regain or to reduce the frequency of some eating disorder behaviors (e.g., bulimic episodes, self-induced vomiting, excessive and compulsive exercising) after several weeks of outpatient sessions, may be given access to a treatment tailored to address these obstacles, without having to destabilize the patient further by removing the patient from his or her supportive home environment.

INDICATIONS AND CONTRAINDICATIONS

The treatment has been principally designed, as an alternative to the more costly day-hospital, for underweight patients unable to start the process of weight regain with outpatient CBT-E. Unfortunately, deciding when patients need a more intensive level of care is often a therapeutic dilemma—prolonging a less intensive form of treatment without any improvement may increase costs needlessly, and, since the eating disorder psychopathology tends to evolve, it may even risk worsening the clinical severity of a patient's eating disorder, but intensifying a treatment too early may interrupt a patient gradually developing a motivation to change and benefiting from a less intensive and costly treatment. Although the therapist is undoubtedly in the best position to judge progress, even experts may therefore have difficulty in deciding when to draw the line with apparent non-responders. Judging by my own clinical experience with outpatient CBT-E, however, patients who do not start to regain body weight before twelve weeks of treatment are unlikely to do so without more intensive assistance. I therefore suggest that twelve weeks with no significant weight regain is a reasonable cutoff point for outpatient CBT-E, whereupon patients should be offered the intensive outpatient version. That being said, intensive outpatient CBT-E should obviously be implemented earlier in severely underweight patients or in those who continue losing weight during outpatient CBT-E, for example, or after the twelve-week deadline if they are not able to normalize their body weight. Intensive outpatient treatment may also be indicated for patients with very frequent bulimic episodes and self-induced vomiting, even if they are not underweight, when their eating habits do not improve during standard outpatient CBT-E; I suggest after eight weeks. Finally, in patients with long-standing eating disorders who have not responded to several outpatient approaches, or in very underweight adolescent patients who cannot rely on parental support during mealtimes, intensive outpatient treatment may be the most appropriate first step.

As described in detail in chapter 3, intensive outpatient CBT-E is not suitable for patients with daily substance abuse, acute psychotic disorders, and/or severe medical complications that cannot be managed in an outpatient setting.

PREPARATION FOR INTENSIVE OUTPATIENT CBT-E

In typical cases, the preparatory phase has the main aim of helping patients who have not improved with outpatient CBT-E to make the decision to intensify the treatment. The clinician should have a frank discussion with the patient regarding the reasons why outpatient CBT-E appears to be failing. The literature suggests, and my own clinical experience confirms, that the most common barriers to treatment are lack of motivation, clinical depression, significant substance abuse, distracting major life problems, competing commitments, fear of change, rigidity, and difficulties in reducing the frequency of binge eating and purging (Fairburn et al., 2008, pp. 90–93). If the therapist perceives that the barrier(s) cannot be overcome in the context of outpatient CBT-E, he or she should explain to patients why they would benefit from a more intensive, targeted approach to their eating disorder, and that intensive outpatient CBT-E might be a more effective next step.

The clinician should go on to describe intensive outpatient CBT-E in detail, and ask patients to think about the pros and cons of intensifying their treatment. As in outpatient CBT-E, patients should be informed about the aims, duration, organization, procedures, and expected results of the more intensive form, and that although the decision to intensify the treatment is voluntary, it should be considered a priority.

THE INTENSIVE OUTPATIENT UNIT

Centers offering intensive outpatient CBT-E should provide a specialized unit for the purpose, bearing in mind the treatment procedures outlined below. Care should be taken to create a psychologically beneficial, rather than clinical, environment, a place where patients will feel at home. In addition to the standard treatment rooms, the unit will need to be equipped with a kitchen (with a kettle, microwaves, a refrigerator with a large freezer, a sink, and a dishwasher), a dining room where assisted eating can take place, a recreation room, and facilities to enable patients to study.

THE INTENSIVE OUTPATIENT CBT-E TEAM

Intensive outpatient CBT-E needs to be managed by a multidisciplinary team fully trained in multistep CBT-E (see chapter 3), a team that comprises physicians, psychologists, and dietitians. The dietitian addresses the patient's low weight and undereating, preparing and assisting patients during the meals consumed at the office, dispensing food to be eaten outside the unit, and helping patients to plan their weekend meals, and reviewing any problems encountered the previous weekend. The psychologist addresses the overvaluation of shape and weight, and implements the broad CBT-E modules, and the physician assesses and treats any medical complications, prescribing medications as necessary.

GENERAL ORGANIZATION

Intensive outpatient treatment is scheduled to last a maximum of twelve weeks, but can usually be brought to a close beforehand, when patients successfully address the key factors responsible for the lack of progress with outpatient CBT-E (e.g., weight regain, binge eating, irregular meals). In order to maximize the opportunities for assisted eating, in our unit patients generally attend every weekday from 12:45 p.m. to 7:45 p.m., and follow the procedures outlined below (figure 6.1):

- Three supervised meals a day (lunch, snack, and evening meal—severely underweight patients should also be offered the possibility of assisted breakfast).
- Provision of meals to be eaten outside the unit (breakfasts, midmorning snack, weekend meals).
- Two individual CBT-E sessions per week with a CBT psychologist.
- Two individual sessions a week with a CBT dietitian.
- Regular checkups with a CBT physician.

As previously mentioned, the team meets weekly to monitor patients' progress, and can therefore, toward the end of treatment, gradually encourage responders to eat more meals outside the unit, thereby allowing the treatment to evolve into conventional outpatient CBT-E.

CORE TREATMENT PROCEDURES

Many procedures and strategies in intensive outpatient CBT-E are the same as those in the outpatient version (see chapter 5), and will therefore not be described here. Instead, I will concentrate on those that have been adapted or developed specifically for this particular step.

Monitoring of Eating, Weight, and Treatment Course

The patient's monitoring record should distinguish between assisted and non-assisted eating, and in the former the patient needs merely note the name of the meal consumed (e.g., lunch, snack, evening meal), as the dietitian will provide the relevant details. Non-assisted eating should be recorded by the

	Monday	Tuesday	Wednesday	Thursday	Friday
12:45-13:00	Body weight measurement				Body weight measurement
13:00-14:00	Assisted lunch	Assisted lunch	Assisted lunch	Assisted lunch	Assisted lunch
14:00-15:00	Weekly review meeting	Free time for studying or doing other activities	Free time for studying or doing other activities	Free time for studying or doing other activities	Free time for studying or doing other activities
15:00-16:00	Individual session with dietitian (weekend review and meal planning)	Individual CBT-E session with psychologist	Medical examination[1]	CBT-E individual session with psychologist	Individual session with dietitian (weekend preparation)
16:30-17:00	Assisted snack	Assisted snack	Assisted snack	Assisted snack	Assisted snack
17:00-18:30	Free time for studying or doing other activities	Free time for studying or doing other activities	Free time for studying or doing other activities	Free time for studying or doing other activities	Free time for studying or doing other activities
18:30-19:30	Assisted evening meal	Assisted evening meal	Assisted evening meal	Assisted evening meal	Assisted evening meal
19:30-19:45	Food provision for breakfast	Food provision for breakfast	Food provision for breakfast	Food provision for breakfast	Food provision for weekend

[1] Weekly in severe underweight patients (BMI < 16 kg/m^2) and/or with medical complications (e.g. low serum potassium levels), every two or three weeks in those treated with antidepressant.

Figure 6.1. **Organization of Intensive Outpatient CBT-E. Originally published as table 15.1 in *Cognitive Behavior Therapy and Eating Disorders* by Christopher G. Fairburn, 2008. Copyright Guilford Press. Reprinted with permission of The Guilford Press.**

patient in real time, as per outpatient CBT-E, and the patient should be instructed to write down a simple description of what he or she ate or drank, without recording the calorie intake.

In order to check weight trends on weekdays of assisted eating and weekends of non-assisted eating, patients should measure their weight on a scale with 0.5 kg divisions twice a week (Monday and Friday). This will be performed with the assistance of the dietitian for the first eight weeks, and thereafter they will be entrusted with the task themselves. Patients are trained to plot their weight on their weight graph, and write the interpretation of the weight changes in the last column of the monitoring record.

In addition, patients fill out the *Eating Problem Checklist* (see appendix) once a week, reporting the frequency of key eating disorder behaviors (e.g., binge eating, self-induced vomiting, laxative and diuretic misuse) and the intensity of body checking and avoidance, feeling fat, concerns about shape, weight, and eating control they have experienced over the previous week.

Individual CBT-E Sessions with the CBT Psychologist

In intensive outpatient CBT-E, individual sessions are similar to those of conventional outpatient CBT-E, but are conducted more often (twice weekly for the entire duration of the treatment). These sessions focus mainly on helping the patient to accept the rapid changes in eating, weight, and shape that usually occur in intensive outpatient CBT-E, and to cope with mood swings associated with these changes. As treatment progresses, the content of the sessions gradually evolves into addressing the overvaluation of shape and weight, and, in a subgroup of patients, one or more of the external maintenance mechanisms (clinical perfectionism, core low self-esteem, and/or interpersonal problems).

Individual Sessions with the CBT-E Dietitian

The sessions with the dietitian should be fixed for Mondays and Fridays. The agenda of the Monday session is mainly dedicated to going over the weekend entries on the monitoring record, measuring and interpreting the patient's weight, and planning any adjustment of calorie content necessary to maintain a steady weight gain of between 1.0 to 1.5 kg per week. Patients are encouraged to interpret their weight change as if they were therapists, and to suggest modifications to their diet for the following week according to the *Weight Regain Guidelines* discussed at the beginning of the treatment (see below). The CBT dietitian uses the patient's weight interpretation to educate the patient about weight regulation, and to restructure any cognitive bias regarding weight changes and the calorie content of the prescribed diet.

The Friday session, on the other hand, should be devoted to reviewing the progress and obstacles encountered during the preceding week, and to plan the meals for the weekend ahead. Patients are instructed to use proactive problem solving to address the difficulties encountered the previous weekend.

Medical Examinations with the CBT Physician

The CBT physician examines patients with medical complications (e.g., severe weight loss, electrolyte abnormalities, refeeding syndrome, gastrointestinal symptoms) once a week, although in some cases it may be necessary for this to be scheduled more often, at least until they achieve a stable medical condition. Patients being treated with antidepressants are usually examined every two weeks.

Assisted Eating

Intensive outpatient CBT-E has been principally designed for patients who are not able to alter their eating habits in standard outpatient CBT-E. To address this problem, *assisted eating* must be implemented. Patients consume two meals plus one snack each day (lunch, midafternoon snack, and evening meal) with the assistance of the CBT dietitian, who adopts cognitive behavioral procedures to help patients to eat (for details see chapter 10). Patients are encouraged to consider food as if it were medication and to eat mechanically, without being influenced by any external (e.g., food availability) or internal (hunger, anxiety, and thoughts) cues. This new form of eating is encouraged until patients can eat without being influenced by anxiety and preoccupations about control over shape, weight, and eating. Other therapeutic techniques adopted during the meal in this phase are support, education, distraction, and, in patients who are not too preoccupied, decentering from problematic thoughts and urges. During the meals, the therapist also addresses some ritualistic modes of eating (e.g., cutting the food in small pieces) if patients adopt this behavior to increase control over eating. Patients are also asked not to request access to a bathroom for one hour after eating.

Underweight patients establish their goal BMI range (which is generally between a 19.0 and 20.0) collaboratively with the CBT team. In addition, they are trained by the CBT dietitian on the *Weight Regain Guidelines*, which indicate how to modify the calorie content of the diet to maintain a steady weight regain of between 0.5 kg to 1.0 kg per week (see textbox 6.1).

The food services provided to patients will largely depend on the resources available. Food supplied in our unit is either pre-frozen or packaged so that it does not require much preparation and can be handled without any fuss (a feature that permits implementation of assisted eating in a normal outpatient setting). To encourage investment, all foods are given to patients by the CBT dietitian ten minutes before the meals, but are defrosted by the patients themselves. At 7 p.m., the CBT dietician gives patients their food for the following breakfast, and on Friday evenings the prepackaged and frozen foods for the weekend are dispensed. To expose patients to eating food of uncertain calorie content and preparation, two meals a week are assisted outside the unit, in restaurants, pizzerias, or other suitable eating establishments.

Although assisted eating is particularly helpful, and perhaps indispensable, in aiding underweight patients to regain weight, it is also useful in not-underweight patients with binge eating and purging who have not managed to curb this behavior in conventional outpatient CBT-E. In these cases, assisted eating is designed to show them that they can eat a varied diet comprising three meals and a snack without gaining weight, and that they are able to digest these meals without binge eating or purging. Interruption of the binge-purge cycle in the intensive outpatient setting is used as evidence that some processes encouraging this behavior in operation at home will need to be addressed later on during the treatment if setbacks are to be pre-empted (Dalle Grave et al., 2008).

TEXTBOX 6.1. GUIDELINES FOR WEIGHT REGAIN: A PATIENT'S HANDOUT

These are the treatment guidelines drawn up to assist you in meeting weight regain goals. The guidelines are the fruit of many years of experience in treating eating problems, and have been developed to help you gain lasting active control of your own weight.

Please read the guidelines carefully because you will need to use them to interpret your weight graph and to decide on the modifications to your diet for the following week in the weekly review meeting. Remember that in this treatment you have to become an expert therapist on your own eating problem.

How do I interpret my weight?

First you have to interpret your weight. To do this, calculate your BMI, which is your weight (in kg) divided by the square of your height (in meters) (i.e., kg/m^2). Your therapist will show you how to do this.

According to the World Health Organization, BMI is classed as follows (WHO, 1995; 2000):

- BMI of less than 18.5 = Underweight
- BMI of 18.5 to 24.99 = Normal weight
- BMI of 25.0 to 29.99 = Overweight
- BMI of 30.0 or more = Obese

What is my goal weight?

If you are underweight (i.e., you have a BMI lower than 18.5), your weight goal is a BMI of between 19.0 and 20.0. This BMI range can be maintained without dietary restriction, it is not associated with symptoms of being underweight, and permits a fulfilling social life. In other words, it is a low weight that does not contribute to the maintenance of your eating problem.

Only people with a particular constitution are able to maintain a BMI of between 18.5 and 19.0 while remaining healthy (e.g., those whose weight was in this range before the onset of the eating problem and some of their close relatives have a BMI in this low range).

How fast should I be gaining weight?

The optimal rate of weight regain for outpatients is 0.5 to 1.0 kg per week. To obtain this optimal weight regain rate you should follow the following dietary plan:

First week: 1,500 kcal per day (the physician may decide to suggest a diet with a lower calorie content if you are at risk of developing medical complications associated with refeeding).

After the second week you should interpret your weekly weight change in the weight graph and decide on the modifications to your diet, adopting the following guidelines:

- If your weight increases between 0.5 to 1.0 kg per week, you should maintain the same calorie content as the previous week.
- If your weight increases by less than 0.5 kg per week, you should increase the calorie content of the diet by 500 kcals per day.
- If your calorie intake needs to exceed 2,500 kcal, you may choose to get part of this from energy drinks rather than increasing the amount of food you eat (a typical energy drink contains 250 kcal per carton).
- If your weight increases more than 1.0 kg per week, you should decrease the calorie content of your diet by 250 kcals per day.

- When you reach a BMI of 18.5, you should gradually reduce the calorie content of your diet (e.g., 250 kcal per day in comparison with the previous week) to reach and maintain a BMI of between 19.0 and 20.0. You will then go on to follow the weight maintenance guidelines.

Following this plan you will realize that to regain weight at an average rate of 0.5 kg per week, you will need to consume, on average, an extra 500 kcal of energy each day (i.e., an extra 3,500 kcal per week), over and above what you are currently consuming, assuming your weight is currently stable.

The menu plan you will be given conforms, flexibly, to nutritional dietary guidelines for a healthy diet and includes a broad range of foods. The calorie content of the diet is a weekly mean, and it is not rigidly fixed every day.

N.B.: Over the first two to three weeks of weight regain, you may put on more than 1 kg per week. This is due to rehydration (i.e., water retention), as people with eating problems are often dehydrated. Remember that if you increase your level of physical activity, you will need to consume proportionately more energy.

Non-Assisted Eating

In the first weeks of intensive outpatient CBT, patients are instructed to adopt the same eating approach for weekends and breakfast as they do in the unit. On these occasions they should consume the prepackaged and frozen foods given to them in advance by the CBT-E dietitian. In the last four weeks, on the other hand, patients are gradually encouraged to eat all meals outside of the unit, replacing pre-frozen or packaged food with normal meals. When a patient reaches the BMI threshold of 19.0, the CBT dietitian will help the patient to address the residual dietary restraints and rules using the same procedures adopted in outpatient CBT-E (see chapter 5), and to maintain his or her weight following a flexible healthy diet based on national dietary guidelines. In this phase, patients are allowed to self-manage the period after meals and are given free access to bathrooms.

The Involvement of Significant Others

Significant others of adult patients (see chapter 8 for the adolescents' adaptations), as in standard outpatient CBT-E, are asked to participate in three sessions, but only if patients are willing. The aims of these sessions are to discuss how to create a home environment that will facilitate a patient's efforts to maintain the change in eating behavior outside the outpatient unit, and how to use problem solving to address everyday difficulties and family crises.

Maintaining the Changes in Eating outside the Unit

Intensive outpatient CBT has introduced several strategies to help patients maintain the changes in eating outside the outpatient unit. First, in the initial weeks of treatment, patients are provided the same meal packs that they eat in the unit for breakfasts and weekends. This prevents them having to buy and cook food, two situations that typically trigger concerns about eating. Second, patients with binge eating are encouraged to remove from their environment foods that could set off bulimic episodes, and to adopt a regular eating pattern (i.e., eating every four hours, and to resist eating between scheduled meals). Third, sessions with the CBT dietitian focus on accurately preparing and reviewing weekends and eating outside of the unit. Fourth, patients are supported more intensively than in conventional outpatient CBT-E. Fifth, the involvement of significant others is used to create a home environment that is likely to support patients' efforts to change their eating patterns.

These strategies, and the intensive outpatient step itself, have been de-vised to counter the high rate of relapse typically observed in patients after discharge from inpatient eating disorder units. Indeed, relapse is likely to be driven by the patient's removal from the protected, supportive environment of the hospital where the eating and weight changes took place, being "cast back," so to speak, into the environment that undoubtedly fostered the pa-tient's eating disorder psychopathology. Moreover, it is commonplace for major disruption of treatment to occur on discharge, particularly in structures whose outpatient philosophy is not coherent with the inpatient regime. It is evident therefore that these problems are pre-empted by intensive outpatient CBT-E, where eating and weight change occur while the patient is living at home, and individual CBT-E sessions with the same therapist continue, even after the treatment intensiveness has been stepped down (Dalle Grave et al., 2008).

Chapter Seven

Step 3: Inpatient CBT-E

As previously mentioned, the ideal setting for the treatment of eating disorders is a purpose-designed outpatient clinic. This is because outpatient treatment is less disruptive than inpatient or day-hospital care, meaning that the changes made are more likely to last, as patients make them while living in their normal environment (Dalle Grave et al., 2008). However, as some patients do not respond well or at all to outpatient treatments (conventional or intensive) and some cannot be managed safely on an outpatient basis, a more intensive form of care, namely inpatient treatment, may become necessary. Thus, an adapted form of CBT-E, developed at the Department of Eating and Weight Disorders of Villa Garda Hospital (Italy), can be used to treat patients in an inpatient setting, as summarized in this chapter. A comprehensive account of inpatient CBT-E and details of its implementation can be found in the main treatment guide (Dalle Grave, 2012).

RATIONALE FOR EXTENDING CBT-E TO INPATIENT SETTINGS

The rationale behind extending CBT-E to inpatient treatment stems from three main considerations (Dalle Grave, 2011b). The first of these considerations is, as mentioned above, that patients may present with an eating disorder of extreme clinical severity that is not manageable in an outpatient setting. Added to that is a large subgroup of patients who fail to improve with either conventional or intensive outpatient CBT-E. Conventional wisdom would appear to dictate that these latter patients may benefit from a different approach, but, on second consideration, available data on changing the nature of outpatient treatment (e.g., from CBT to IPT or fluoxetine) are by no means conclusive (Mitchell et al., 2002). In the current state of affairs, non-responders and severe cases are generally hospitalized in specialized eating disorder units. Unfortunately, however, most eating disorder units adopt an eclectic approach, not driven by a single unifying theory, that is associated with a high rate of relapse after discharge. The third and final reason for stepping up to inpatient CBT-E is that in some patients the ineffectiveness of outpatient CBT-E might be due to an insufficiency of care intensiveness rather than the nature of the treatment itself.

DISTINCTIVE CHARACTERISTICS OF INPATIENT CBT-E

Inpatient treatment for severely underweight eating disorder patients is often successful in bringing about weight restoration. The problem is that few patients are able to maintain this weight gain once removed from the inpatient setting; instead, a large proportion of patients relapse (Strober, Freeman, & Morrell, 1997; Walsh et al., 2006), and as much as 30 percent to 50 percent of these patients require rehospitalization during the first year following discharge (Herzog et al., 1999; Isager, Brinch, Kreiner, & Tolstrup, 1985; Pike, 1998).

This failure to maintain the changes achieved in the hospital has led to interest in developing post-hospitalization means of preventing deterioration once the patient has been sent home. An initial report suggested that fluoxetine might be useful in this respect (Kaye et al., 2001), but this was not confirmed in a subsequent controlled trial (Walsh et al., 2006). There is also preliminary evidence that a form of CBT may be beneficial (Carter et al., 2009; Pike, Walsh, Vitousek, Wilson, & Bauer, 2003), although this still needs to be substantiated.

Within the framework of CBT-E, a different strategy has been adopted, modifying the inpatient version itself with a view to reducing patients' propensity to relapse on discharge. To this end, in our hospital the traditional multidisciplinary eclectic approach to inpatient treatment has been replaced with a specialized intensive CBT program. This has its roots in CBT-E (Fairburn, 2008a), a treatment that is specifically designed to produce enduring change and appears to have lasting effects when delivered on an outpatient basis (Fairburn et al., 2009; Fairburn et al., 2012). To this end, CBT-E focuses on instilling personalized relapse prevention skills (Fairburn et al., 2008) in addition to modifying the mechanisms thought to perpetuate the eating disorder psychopathology (see chapter 2) (Fairburn et al., 2003).

Inpatient CBT-E includes four additional elements designed to reduce the high rate of relapse that typically follows discharge from the hospital. First, the inpatient unit is *open*—patients are free to go outside (see below). In this way they continue to be exposed to the types of environmental stimuli that tend to provoke their eating disorder psychopathology, while remaining in a stable, nurturing environment set up to deal precisely with their reactions to these stimuli. Second, particularly during the six weeks prior to discharge, a concerted effort is made to identify likely environmental triggers of each patient's eating disorder mindset, ones that the patient might have been sheltered from during his or her stay in the hospital. These are then addressed in turn during the individual CBT-E sessions, wherein the patient is provided with effective preventative and counteractive coping strategies. Third, toward the end of treatment, significant others, i.e., those involved in a patient's daily life, are helped to create a positive stress-free home environment in readiness for the patient's return. The fourth, and perhaps most important, relapse-prevention measure is that inpatient treatment is always followed by a stepped-down CBT-E-based treatment performed in an outpatient setting. This means that the patient's treatment continues in much the same way, and the therapist is on hand to support and monitor the patient through this often difficult transitional phase.

INDICATIONS AND CONTRAINDICATIONS OF INPATIENT CBT-E

Although the main indication for inpatient CBT-E is the failure of well-delivered outpatient treatments, it can be indicated as the first step of care in patients with a high medical risk. Typical cases feature a very low BMI (< 15.0), rapid weight loss (> 1 kg per week) over the course of several weeks and/or marked medical complications (e.g., pronounced edema, severe electrolyte disturbances, ECG alterations, hypoglycemia). Other indications include high frequency and intensity of binge eating and vomiting or driven exercising, severe interpersonal problems, and/or a troubled home life.

In contrast, inpatient CBT-E is not recommended for patients with daily substance misuse, acute psychosis, high suicide risk, and/or medical conditions requiring urgent treatment. Nonetheless, once these acute states have been resolved, these patients can readily be admitted to inpatient CBT-E.

PREPARATION FOR INPATIENT CBT-E

The admission to inpatient CBT-E is voluntary and hinges on a patient's willingness to change and to play an active role in the treatment, which, in order to meet with success, needs to become a priority in the patient's life. For these reasons pre-treatment preparation for the inpatient CBT-E is a fundamental stage. In keeping with the individualized nature of the CBT-E program as a whole, the preparation stage is adjusted according the reason for hospitalization. Thus, non-responding CBT-E outpatients (conventional and/or intensive) are dealt with differently to patients referred by general practitioners or outpatient eating disorder specialists. Indeed, patients in the latter group have already been extensively assessed during the course of their ongoing treatment and therefore do not need to be reassessed for the inpatient CBT-E. In these cases, the main aim of the preparation step is to get patients to agree to treatment intensification. They should therefore be helped to see that outpatient CBT-E is not proving sufficient, and a more intensive intervention may help them make the necessary changes. Once agreement has been reached, patients should receive a detailed explanation of inpatient CBT-E (and should be provided with an information pamphlet) and evaluate collaboratively with the therapist both the pros and cons of intensifying the treatment.

Patients not previously treated by outpatient CBT-E, i.e., those referred by others, will require an evaluation interview as part of their preparation. This will be conducted in a similar fashion to those described in chapter 4, but will usually occupy three sessions (very ambivalent patients may need more). In these cases the aims of the evaluation are as follows:

- To determine whether or not the patient has an eating problem of clinical severity. The assessment also necessarily includes a thorough physical examination, as many referred patients arrive at the consultation in a condition of medical instability.
- To assess whether inpatient CBT-E will be a suitable treatment option (i.e., ruling out the abovementioned contraindications).
- To educate patients about their eating problem and the inpatient CBT-E program.
- To help patients to evaluate the pros and cons of intensive CBT-E. Patients are encouraged to reflect on the short- and long-term effects of their eating problem on their health, psychological function, relationships, and school or work performance, and whether or not their eating problem provides them with something positive that they are afraid to lose.

If patients arrive at the conclusion that inpatient CBT-E represents a good opportunity for them to change, they are placed on a waiting list and are usually admitted four to six weeks later. One week before admission, which is usually planned for a Monday, patients have another session to review the treatment procedures in detail and to re-evaluate and confirm their motivation to change.

THE UNIT

Inpatient CBT-E should be held in a specialized unit for the treatment of eating disorders. Our unit at Villa Garda Hospital, for example, accepts no more than twenty-eight patients, and aims to create a homely atmosphere, being furnished with comfortable, rather than institutional, furniture. Bedrooms house two or three patients and are equipped with a private bathroom, wardrobe, and desks. Patients are encouraged, as in a college, to decorate their room with posters, personal items, and photos. Shared spaces include a dining room, a recreation room, where there is also a kitchen for the cooking group, a computer room equipped with Internet, a living room with digital TV, DVD player, and a selection of DVDs and books. During the day patients may also be allowed access to other areas of the department, such as the gym, the gardens, and rooms set aside for individual and group therapy.

It is particularly important that as well as being homely, the unit is *open*, i.e., patients are free to come and go during the day, provided that they are judged to be in a stable medical condition. Similarly, patients are free to receive visits from significant others whenever treatment sessions are not in progress. In addition to limiting any stigma or discomfort a patient may feel at being "institutionalized," an open unit has the added advantage of not shielding patients from exposure to a wide range of environmental triggers associated with the maintenance of their eating disorder, a fundamental strategy which has the twofold aim of reducing the relapse rate after discharge and minimizing patients' dependency on the unit—two problems often observed in conventional, closed units.

GENERAL ORGANIZATION

Inpatient CBT-E itself lasts thirteen weeks, and is followed by seven weeks of day-hospital. In the day-hospital stage patients sleep at home or, if they live too far from the hospital, in an apartment close to the unit. Like outpatient-based CBT-E, the inpatient treatment is divided into four stages (see figure 7.1), which are highly individualized to take into account the personal formulation developed jointly with the patients upon admission.

- *Stage One (weeks 1 to 4).* The focus of this stage is to engage patients, to educate them about their eating problem, and to construct the personalized formulation of the main maintenance mechanisms, which will provide a framework for the forthcoming treatment. During this stage patients are encouraged to aim for maximum behavioral change, including initiation of weight regain if they are underweight.
- *Stage Two (weeks 5 and 6).* In this stage, a detailed review of a patient's progress and barriers to change is conducted. In addition, as part of the individual CBT-E sessions, the presence of any other psychological problems (viz., clinical perfectionism, core low self-esteem, and interpersonal problems) that might contribute to maintaining the patient's eating problem are assessed.

- *Stage Three (weeks 7 to 17)*. The precise content of this stage is dictated by the nature of the patient's problem, and the treatment therefore becomes very individualized. In typical cases, the overvaluation of shape and weight are addressed, together with any food avoidance behavior and/ or other dietary rules. In this stage, one or more of the additional psychological problems might be also addressed in specific broad CBT-E modules. It is expected that underweight patients reach their target BMI range and start to practice weight maintenance at this point.
- *Stage Four (weeks 18 to 20)*. By this time, the patient's main physical and behavioral problems will have been dealt with, and the focus of this final stage of treatment is therefore on helping patients to prepare the transition to outpatient therapy.

The inpatient treatment program also includes a CBT-oriented family module for patients who are under eighteen years of age (see chapter 8).

Setting	Inpatient																Day-hospital			
Stage	One				Two		Three											Four		
Weeks	1	2	3	4	5	6	7	8	9	10	11	12	13	14	15	16	17	18	19	20
CBT-F	Individual CBT-E sessions (twice a week in the first four weeks and then once a week)																			
	Weekly review meeting (patient, dietitian, psychologist, physician, nurse)																			
	Assisted eating			Unassisted eating (if BMI ≥ 18.5)																
	Group treatment sessions (four times a week)																			
	Physical exercise sessions																			
CBT-B (If additional "external" maintaining mechanisms emerged)				Clinical perfectionism module																
				Core low self-esteem module																
				Interpersonal problem module																
	CBT oriented family module (if < 18 years)																			

Figure 7.1.   General Organization of Inpatient CBT-E. (CBT-F = focused cognitive behavioral therapy, CBT-B = broad cognitive behavioral therapy)

THE INPATIENT CBT-E TEAM

A multidisciplinary team comprising physicians (internists and psychiatrists), dietitians, psychologists, and nurses are responsible for delivering the treatment. All team members are fully trained in CBT-E, and therefore use the same concepts and terms, adopting mutually compatible CBT-E procedures and strategies (see chapter 3). The individual contribution of each staff member will be determined on a case-by-case basis, according to the prescriptions of each personal formulation. In general, the CBT dietitian's primary focus is helping patients to change their eating habits and weight. The CBT psychologist will address the patient's overvaluation of shape and weight, and any additional maintenance mechanisms. The patients' physical health is overseen by the CBT physician, and the CBT nurse is charged with the usual tasks of supervising the administration of medications, assisting patients in weighing, and helping them to manage daily difficulties and major crises. If one of a patient's therapists must be absent for a period exceeding one week, a fully trained replacement must be on hand to ensure continuity of appropriate care.

Other professionals, such as educators, who help young patients to address homework or study, and physiotherapists, who run the exercise sessions, will also operate in the unit. Like the clinical staff, these therapists will also need to be trained in CBT-E.

CORE TREATMENT PROCEDURES

The treatment adopts the main procedures of outpatient CBT-E (see chapter 5), some of which are adapted to suit the inpatient setting, as well as other procedures specifically designed for inpatient CBT-E.

Personal Formulation

In the first week, together with the CBT psychologist, patients build their own personal formulation of their eating problem (see chapter 11). This personalized formulation is used by patients and all team members to identify features to address in the treatment, and will be revised as necessary during the course of the treatment. The aim is to create a bespoke treatment that is perfectly suited to the patient's particular problem.

Monitoring Weight, Eating Habits, and Exercising

Patients in the unit measure their body weight once a week. This is performed in private, and during the period of assisted eating a nurse needs to be on hand to supervise (see below). Patients are instructed to record their weight on a personalized graph and to interpret their change in weight in the last column of the monitoring record. After each weigh-in, patients fill out the *Eating Problem Checklist* (see appendix), answering questions about their frequency of binge eating, weight control behaviors (e.g., dietary restraint, self-induced vomiting, misuse of laxatives and diuretics, driven exercising), body checking and avoidance, and concerns about shape, weight, and eating control over the previous week. The weight graph and Eating Problem

Checklist are then entrusted to the nurse, who will record the new entries in an apposite database to be discussed the same morning at the review meeting (see below).

During unassisted eating, patients measure their weight in the unit once a week, without the assistance of the nurse, and in the last four weeks of day-hospital they will be instructed to use their own bathroom scales at home. All resulting data will be recorded and dealt with as per assisted weighing.

Assisted Eating

The predominant reason why patients are admitted to the inpatient CBT-E is that they have previously been unable to address weight regain or interrupt binge eating and vomiting. This may be due to various factors, including the intensity of preoccupation with food and eating, the fear of losing control over eating and weight, the presence of extreme rituals affecting eating, and the ambivalence to change. Assisted eating has therefore been designed to help patients to overcome these problems.

Assisted eating typically takes place throughout the first six weeks of inpatient treatment, or until patients reach a BMI of 18.5. In this stage of the treatment, patients consume four meals a day (breakfast, lunch, snack, and evening meal) in the dining room, together with the other patients and with the assistance of a CBT dietitian, who uses psychological procedures to help the patients eat. Patients are encouraged to view food as a medicine, and to *eat mechanically*, until they can eat autonomously and appropriately. The main task of the CBT dietitian is to support patients and help them to eat without being influenced by their thoughts on eating. In some case they may also help patients to address some eating rituals (e.g., eating too slowly or cutting food into tiny pieces). Once the assisted meal is concluded, patients must stay in a dedicated room for one hour after eating, without access to a bathroom, so that the urge to vomit after eating can be addressed. It may be helpful to plan distracting activities such as homework in this hour.

One of the principal aims of inpatient CBT-E is to help patients to feel in control during the process of weight regain. Patients are encouraged therefore to become active participants in deciding their goal BMI range (which is generally between 19.0 and 20.0) and the nature of their diet, which should adhere to the *inpatient CBT Weight Regain Guidelines,* which are explained to them by the dietitian the first day of admission (see chapter 11). Generally speaking, the inpatient guidelines are similar to those described for intensive outpatient CBT (see chapter 6, figure 6.1), with the exception that the weight regain goal is higher, at 1.0 kg to 1.5 kg per week (in outpatient CBT-E it is 0.5–1.0 kg per week). This more demanding target is partially motivated by the need to help patients achieve a BMI of 19.0 before the conclusion of inpatient treatment, since available data have shown that a higher BMI at the time of discharge is a powerful predictor of good outcome (Kaplan et al., 2009).

In order to achieve this goal, the energy intake during the first week of treatment is set at 1,500 kcal per day (it might be set lower—i.e., 1,000 kcal per day—in patients with very low BMI and at a high risk of developing refeeding syndrome), being increased to 2,000 kcal per day in the second week and 2,500 kcal per day in the third week. Subsequently, the energy intake is adjusted collaboratively, as in intensive outpatient CBT-E, on the basis of a patient's rate of weight regain. If patients require an intake of over 2,500 kcal per day to achieve adequate gain, they are given the option of doing so using normal food alone or with the addition of high-energy drinks.

Once the patient nears a BMI of 18.5, the energy intake is gradually reduced so that they reach and maintain the body weight within the goal BMI range. Since the treatment is voluntary, neither nasogastric tube feeding nor parenteral nutrition should be used to address undereating or low weight. Instead, if patients are not able to eat planned meals, even with assistance, they will need to be referred for another form of treatment.

In patients admitted due to binge eating and purging that has proved impossible to control on an outpatient basis, assisted eating is designed to show them that they are able to eat a normocaloric diet comprising three meals and a snack per day without gaining the weight that they fear, and that they can eat these meals without bingeing or purging. This will help these patients to understand that some processes that encourage these behaviors are at work in their home environment, and that these will need to be addressed during a later stage of the treatment if relapse is to be avoided.

Non-Assisted Eating

When the period of assisted eating is over, patients are encouraged to eat without aid, and to start eating outside the unit while continuing their weekly weigh-ins and real-time food monitoring. In this phase, patients eating in the unit are free to choose their own food, as in a self-service restaurant, and are given free access to the bathroom. From week fourteen onward, patients live outside the hospital, either at home or in temporary accommodation, eating meals they have planned in advance with the assistance of the CBT-E dietitian and recording them in much the same way as in outpatient CBT-E. Dietary restraint and dietary rules are approached in a day-hospital setting using the strategies and procedures described for outpatient CBT-E.

Before patients are sent home full-time, they are encouraged to spend some weekends and several weekdays at home, thereby gradually building up to consuming all meals outside the hospital. Upon discharge, patients should be able to maintain their weight within a normal range, following

flexible dietary guidelines, and not resorting to extreme weight control behaviors. It may therefore on occasion be necessary to slow down or prolong
this mealtime normalization to deal with any lapses in behavior.

Individual CBT-E Sessions

These are held twice a week for the first four weeks, then once a week in the
subsequent period. The initial focus is on engaging patients in the treatment
and then helping them to accept the rapid changes in weight and shape,
addressing events and emotions influencing eating and the overvaluation of
shape and weight. In some patients, one or more external maintenance mechanisms are also addressed. Finally, with the active participation of the patient, a post-discharge treatment plan is prepared, in order that they achieve a
smooth transition from inpatient to outpatient CBT-E.

Group Therapy Sessions

In addition to individual counseling, patients are scheduled to attend group
therapy sessions. This combination has the advantage of efficiency and also
encourages self-disclosure, mutual support, and learning from patients who
are doing well, while helping patients address issues of secrecy and shame.

Two types of group sessions are scheduled, psychoeducational and CBT-
E focused. The psychoeducational groups are held three times a week and
aim to stimulate discussion of eating disorders and CBT-E strategies for
addressing them. The CBT-E groups are held weekly and focus on three
main topics: (i) addressing events and associated mood-influenced eating; (ii)
addressing dietary restraint; and (iii) addressing overvaluation of shape and
weight.

Weekly Review Meeting

Once a week, the same morning as the weigh-in, patients and their therapists
(i.e., physician, psychologist, dietitian, and nurse) meet together to discuss
the various elements of the treatment and their relationship to one another.
This fundamental review meeting starts by analyzing the patient's interpretation of his or her weight graph. Patients are then encouraged to suggest
changes to be made to their diet based on the weight regain or weight maintenance goal decided upon admission. The personal formulation and Eating
Problem Checklist scores are also analyzed collectively, and the maintenance
mechanisms to be focused on in the following week are also discussed.

Physical Exercise Sessions

Twice a week, patients participate in group physical exercise sessions led by a CBT-E-trained physiotherapist. These sessions should be designed to help the patients: (i) maximize the restoration of muscle mass; (ii) improve fitness; (iii) accept changes in shape; (iv) learn to exercise without thinking about shape, weight, and calorie consumption.

Involvement of Significant Others

With adult patients, significant others are included if the patient is willing for this to happen and if their involvement is likely to facilitate treatment. Significant others are people who have a major influence on the patient's eating. Typically they attend three sessions during the course of treatment and are encouraged to create a positive home environment that will support the patient's efforts to change (see chapter 11). The significant others of patients under the age of eighteen years need to be more involved, and should participate in an additional treatment module consisting of eight family sessions and two family meals in the unit (see chapter 8).

Daily Management Difficulties

In CBT-E group sessions and in individual CBT-E sessions with the psychologist, patients are trained to cope with events by applying proactive problem-solving techniques and procedures designed to modulate mood changes with functional means of modulating mood. However, if the application of these strategies is not at first sufficient to enable the patient to overcome his or her difficulties without aid, the CBT nurse should be trained and on hand to help patients to address these problematic moments.

Maintaining Change after Discharge

Inpatient CBT-E has been designed with the problem of relapse after discharge in mind, and has accordingly introduced the following elements to maximize the chances that the changes made in the unit will be maintained after the patient is sent home:

- The unit is open, meaning patients are exposed to authentic environmental triggers during the treatment.
- The treatment is focused both on modifying the mechanisms thought to perpetuate eating disorder psychopathology and on developing personalized relapse prevention skills.

- There is a day-hospital treatment phase near the end of the stay, during which patients must face some of the difficulties that they will encounter after discharge while still having the support of their therapy team. During the days spent at home, patients are encouraged to note all the triggers of eating disorder psychopathology they encounter. Some of these triggers may encourage body checking (e.g., too many mirrors in the house), others may increase shape dissatisfaction (e.g., clothes that are too tight, having previously been worn while underweight), dieting (e.g., diet books, a member of the family who diets or is very thin or has an eating disorder, pro-ana websites) or negative emotions that foster binge eating or dietary restraint (e.g., interpersonal difficulties with family members). Once the triggers have been identified, patients are actively involved in thinking about which things in their environment must be changed in order to minimize the risk of relapse (e.g., getting rid of mirrors and/or unsuitable clothes, improving living space, way of shopping and/or preparing food, or dealing with friends, school, or work, etc.).
- During the final few weeks of treatment, patients spend progressively more of the day at home, again while still being able to count on the support of the hospital.
- Significant others are involved in treatment and are helped to create a positive environment for the patient's return home.
- Toward the end of treatment, considerable effort is put into arranging suitable post-discharge outpatient treatment, preferably with CBT-E, so continuity of care is guaranteed. The ideal arrangement is for outpatient-based CBT-E to start prior to discharge so that the transfer is seamless.

Chapter Eight

Multistep CBT-E for Adolescents

A version of CBT-E adapted for adolescents has been described by Cooper and Stewart (2008). This chapter outlines some further adaptations of CBT-E for this age group (from thirteen to seventeen years of age), as well as how to adapt intensive outpatient and inpatient CBT-E to cater to their needs.

RATIONALE BEHIND MULTISTEP CBT-E FOR ADOLESCENTS

There are several factors that make multistep CBT-E particularly suitable for adolescents (Cooper & Stewart, 2008). First, the treatment adopts an individualized approach, which is easily adaptable to the needs of adolescents at different developmental stages of their life. Second, the pursuit of control, autonomy, and independence are issues of major relevance to younger patients, and they therefore respond favorably to a treatment such as CBT-E, which is designed to enhance their sense of control, catering to their need to develop autonomy and independence. Third, the clinical features of eating disorders in adolescents are similar to those observed in adults, and they should therefore benefit from a similar type of treatment. Fourth, the transdiagnostic nature of CBT-E is a fundamental characteristic of treatments for adolescents, who often receive a diagnosis of eating disorder NOS. Fifth, CBT-E includes several strategies for engaging patients in the treatment, a feature that is vital for the management of adolescents who, by nature, are usually very ambivalent toward treatment. Finally, CBT is effective in treating other psychological problems in teenagers, which strongly indicates that CBT-E, using CBT procedures and strategies, is suitable for this age group.

DISTINCTIVE CHARACTERISTICS AND NEEDS OF
ADOLESCENT PATIENTS

Adolescents with eating disorders have several distinctive features and needs (see for a detailed description Cooper & Stewart, 2008), which should be carefully considered when delivering CBT-E at all intensiveness steps of care.

Clinical Features

The clinical features of an adolescent with eating disorder generally mirror those observed in adults, although a higher proportion of teenage patients report only the overvaluation of eating control per se, and do not report the fear of weight gain or the concerns about shape and weight typical in adults. The classification of eating disorder in adolescents is identical to that adopted for adults (i.e., anorexia nervosa, bulimia nervosa, and eating disorder NOS), with the most common diagnosis in this age group being eating disorder NOS; at the other end of the spectrum, binge eating disorder is a rarity (Eddy, Celio Doyle, Hoste, Herzog, & le Grange, 2008).

The Egosyntonic Phase of Eating Disorder

Many adolescents with eating disorder are completely unaware of having an eating problem (this is the term we use with patients and parents), and for this reason are often difficult to engage in the treatment. This lack of awareness is due primarily to the egosyntonic nature of the eating disorder psychopathology, and is compounded by the adolescent's difficulties in perceiving the negative effects of the eating problem on his or her life. Egosyntonicity, also observed in adult patients with long-standing eating disorders, is particularly accentuated in adolescents because their attempt to control shape, weight, and eating is reinforced on several fronts (Garner et al., 1997). A typical positive cognitive reinforcement, which also operates in adult patients despite the negative impact of the eating disorder on their lives, is the feeling of triumph, mastery, general self-control, and superiority that the adolescents derive from controlling their eating. This explains why adolescent patients in the early stages of an eating disorder usually feel that nothing is going wrong, and that they are happy, proud, healthy, and satisfied. To them, weight loss is a goal, an achievement, a virtue, a source of positive pleasure, and a delight to the senses.

Furthermore, adolescent eating control, far more so than in adults, tends to be reinforced by several social factors. For instance, in the early phases of weight loss, they may have received positive comments from significant others due to their ability to control their eating and the attractive thinness achieved. Hence, it is not uncommon for adolescent patients to seek, and then cling to, an *anorexic identity,* determined by the association of the need to be popular with the presence of socially desirable traits (Garner et al., 1997).

In some adolescent patients, eating control and weight loss may be a way to attract the attention and affection of parents perceived as absent, and in others it may be a way to affirm their identity and autonomy from their parents. It is also worth stating that excessive weight loss often produces a return to a pre-pubertal body shape, thereby enabling the avoidance of perceived aversive stimuli (e.g., fears associated with sexuality, high expectations regarding performance, autonomy from parents, and family conflict; Crisp, 1997). Although from a clinical perspective this may (negatively) reinforce the overvaluation of shape, weight, and eating control, the patient's perception of positive gains brought about by this behavior needs to be carefully considered together with the adolescent, and the treatment should always involve a detailed exploration of the dysfunctional developmental function of the patient's eating disorder.

Medical Complications

The medical complications associated with eating disorders tend to be more severe in adolescents with respect to adults. Adolescent girls in particular are more vulnerable to the effects of malnutrition and weight loss, as their organs are not yet fully developed. Indeed, if the weight restoration is delayed or incomplete, the physical damage may be irreversible. In particular, the following potential medical complications will require special attention (Katzman, 2005; Nicholls & Bryant-Waugh, 2009):

- *Osteopenia and osteoporosis.* The onset of eating disorder often coincides with the period of bone growth, before patients reach their bone peak mass (usually at between seventeen and twenty-two years of age). Available data suggest that the loss of significant bone mass is detectable after six months of weight loss (Mehler & Andersen, 2010). Moreover, if weight restoration is not brought about promptly, bone mass deposition is compromised and permanent osteoporosis develops, increasing the risk of fracture in adulthood.
- *Growth arrest or retardation.* This complication occurs when the onset of anorexia nervosa precedes complete pubertal development. If weight is not restored before the ages of sixteen to eighteen (when epiphyseal fusion usually occurs), the process may be irreversible.

- *Delayed or absent puberty.* Like growth arrest or retardation, this complication develops when the onset of anorexia nervosa occurs before pubertal development. Delayed or absent puberty is characterized by impaired maturation of the sexual organs, which, if weight restoration does not occur by the ages of sixteen to eighteen years, may become permanent.

The above medical complications, often very severe and potentially permanent, justify a lower threshold for a more active intervention in younger adolescent patients with anorexia nervosa. Indeed, if weight regain in adolescent patients does not occur with standard outpatient treatment within a reasonable time frame, hospitalization in a specialist eating disorder unit should be seriously considered. On a positive note, however, there is a large body of evidence that suggests adolescent patients tend to respond better to treatment than adults (Fairburn, 2005).

Psychosocial Complications

Eating disorders in adolescence are associated with distinctive and severe psychosocial complications. Hence it is common to see developmental psychological regression and complete parental dependency in these patients. In the most severe cases, patients become socially isolated, becoming disaffected with most of their former interests, and the persistence of the disorder may even damage the development of their identity. For these reasons, the treatment of adolescents should not only address the eating disorder psychopathology, but also give priority to the patients' psychosocial development. Common developmental issues to be addressed are developing a sense of identity, learning to become independent, improving interpersonal relationships, and adjusting to the changes associated with puberty (Cooper & Stewart, 2008).

Another important area to include in the treatment is peer relationships, as these, if they are problematic, seem to play a central role in the development and maintenance of the eating disorder in the young. Some theorists on the psychosocial factors implicated in the development of anorexia nervosa suggested that girls, in particular, with poor peer relationships and low self-esteem, may pursue thinness in a bid to improve their perception of self-worth and win the approval of their peers (Striegel-Moore, Silberstein, & Rodin, 1993). Thus therapists should always take into careful consideration the distinctive psychosocial problems associated with eating disorders in adolescents. The intervention should be adapted to cater to the cognitive and emotive development of teenagers, and should aim to foster the development of their autonomy, personal responsibility, social communication skills, assertiveness, and conflict resolution strategies, teaching them how to exert appropriate control, not only over their eating, but also over other aspects of their life.

Parental Involvement

Involving parents in CBT, and therefore CBT-E, for adolescent patients is recommended for several reasons (Garner et al., 1997):

- Parents have the responsibility and the right to make important decisions regarding the treatment of their teenage children, and treatment cannot be commenced without their informed consent.
- Controlled studies have provided some empirical evidence that involvement of the family is a positive factor in the treatment of anorexia in adolescents (Lock et al., 2010).
- Some statistical data also indicate that the parents' reaction to the symptoms of the adolescent with an eating disorder may positively or negatively influence the outcome (van Furth et al., 1996).
- Adolescent patients usually live at home with parents, who can therefore be of direct assistance in helping them to address the process of weight restoration and family meals.
- Parents' own behavior may be having an impact on their children's eating habits, and they therefore need to be brought into the loop.

ASSESSING AND PREPARING ADOLESCENT PATIENTS FOR MULTISTEP CBT-E

Engaging Adolescents

Although adolescent patients are often only dimly aware that they have a problem, and are often in a very egosyntonic phase of their eating disorder upon referral, CBT-E clinicians commonly experience that an appropriately delivered approach procedure may help to engage the majority in the treatment. First and foremost, parents are asked for their consent to the CBT-E practitioner initially seeing the adolescent alone. This one-to-one approach will facilitate the exploration of the adolescent's perspective on consultation and the nature of his or her problems, and lay the foundations for a sound therapeutic relationship (Cooper & Stewart, 2008). Another key aspect of engaging adolescents in treatment is to dedicate time to listening to their standpoint on their eating problem and the treatment itself, since their opinions on these issues will be rarely, if ever, sought elsewhere.

Thus the first evaluation session should begin by asking patients if they came freely to the consultation or felt pressured to attend by their parents. The therapist is likely to find that very few adolescents come to the consultation of their own free will, and will therefore be underequipped with the determination to address their eating problem. For this reason, the assessing clinician should not fail to tell patients that they understand their difficult emotional state deriving from their being in a place they do not want to be, and should ask whether they agree that the main purpose of the interview is to exchange information about any problems they may have. In most cases, this non-threatening goal is accepted by even very ambivalent patients, who are reassured by the news that they will not be forced to start treatment straightaway.

Another CBT-E strategy for engaging adolescent patients is emphasizing that the therapist will be operating entirely on *their* behalf, rather than as agents of their parents (Cooper & Stewart, 2008). This can be emphasized by the provision of a clear explanation of what treatment will entail directly to the adolescent patients, and the assurance that they themselves will be responsible for decisions concerning its progress.

It cannot be understated that for many adolescent patients the negative effects of the eating disorder are often irrelevant, because they perceive only positive effects of eating, shape, and weight control. In these cases, like in ambivalent adults, engagement can be facilitated by a joint exploration of whether the control of eating, shape, and weight is a *healthy choice*, or whether it has become a *problem* that has got out of hand (see chapter 4 for details). The aim of this discussion is to induce a *state of dissonance* around the belief regarding the nature of their control over eating, shape, and weight, which may help bring them round to the idea that they do indeed have an eating problem and that the treatment of such is the only sensible step.

A final consideration when seeking to engage adolescents is that the evaluation of the pros and cons of treatment should be focused more on the immediate future (six months to a year) rather than on the long-term ends (five years or more), as the latter are more difficult, if not impossible, for young adult patients to envisage (Cooper & Stewart, 2008). In order to further motivate adolescent patients, the assessing clinician should try to focus their attention on the negative effects that will ensue if their behavior continues (e.g., missing school, not being able to take school tests, not being able to go on vacation, missing out on the prom, losing their place on a team, losing friends, etc.).

Establishing the Nature and Severity of the Eating Problem

The procedure used to assess the development and the current status of the eating problem in adolescents is similar to that described for adults in chapter 3. The adult version of the EDE-Q is suitable for those aged sixteen or over, and a modified version is also available for use with younger patients (Carter, Stewart, & Fairburn, 2001). Unlike adults, however, an adolescent's weight status should be assessed using BMI centile cards, which classify young people aged two to eighteen years into the following categories (www.cdc.gov/growthcharts):

- Under the 5th percentile = underweight.
- Between the 5th and 84th percentiles = normal weight.
- Between the 85th and 94th percentiles = overweight.
- Equal to or greater than the 95th percentile = obese.

In adolescents, it is also important to inquire about past weight and height, in order that the growth curve after the onset of the eating problem can be assessed—photographic evidence may provide the therapist with a general idea of weight history if clinical data is unavailable. Historical data needs to be taken into account because, as described above, undereating and being underweight in adolescence can have permanent consequences on growth. Finally, as in adults, the patient's physical state needs to be accurately assessed, to check for the presence of any eating disorder repercussions that might pose an immediate medical risk and therefore necessitate urgent hospitalization. The assessing physician should also always be on the lookout for any atypical features that might indicate an ongoing medical condition.

Engaging Parents or Other Family Members

It is CBT-E practice to avoid a separate parental interview in the evaluation sessions, because it may compromise the process of engaging an adolescent patient if their parents are taken off to discuss them "behind their back" (Cooper & Stewart, 2008). Nevertheless, as active, accountable participants in their child's life, parents do need to be included in special family sessions, so that they can be apprised of the whys and wherefores of the treatment. Thus, once the patient's trust has been gained, his or her consent for the therapist to meet briefly with the parents alone can be sought. As with adult patients (see chapter 4), the assessing clinician should provide detailed information about the eating disorder, the prescribed treatment, and the role the parents may be expected to play. It must also not be forgotten that parents can have a key influence on a patient's commitment to starting treatment, and could therefore be called upon to further this end. For this reason, it is advisable to suggest that parents help their daughter or son to evaluate the pros and cons of starting the treatment, taking care to stress that they approach this in an inquisitive rather than authoritative manner. It is also important to take on board the parents' views of the eating problem, to discern to what extent they are prepared to get actively involved in the treatment, and to discuss any personal or marital difficulties they may be experiencing that may be having an incidental effect on their child's eating disorder.

Deciding on the Level of Care

As in adults, outpatient treatment is the first CBT-E step recommended for the majority of adolescent patients with an eating disorder for two main reasons: (i) it enables young patients to remain in their family environment, attend school, see friends and, at the same time, (ii) it addresses their eating disorder psychopathology in the context of the environmental and interpersonal factors that contribute to maintaining it. However, in some adolescents the onset of the eating disorder is acute and often associated with a rapid weight loss and severe medical complications, which may threaten their life. In other cases, parents may not be able to tolerate or cope with the eating behavior of the adolescent, leading them to react with criticism and hostility, a behavior that is likely to further intensify the psychopathology of the patient. Moreover, some adolescent patients do not respond at all to outpatient CBT-E. In all these cases, a more intensive CBT-E treatment (i.e., intensive outpatient CBT-E or inpatient CBT-E) may be necessary.

If a patient is not at high physical risk but has failed to improve with outpatient CBT-E, intensive outpatient CBT-E is the preferred option (see chapter 6), as this is a form of treatment that allows patients to receive an intensive level of care, addressing the environmental mechanisms maintaining their eating disorder, while continuing to attend school, have contact with friends, and live in the family household. However, if patients are at high physical risk or the family environment is very disturbed, inpatient CBT-E should be taken into serious consideration. It should be stressed that multistep CBT-E is not appropriate for patients under thirteen years of age, due to their level of cognitive development. Instead, these patients often benefit from a family-focused approach, such as the Moudsley method of family-based treatment (Lock et al., 2001), an empirically supported outpatient-based method for helping adolescent patients regain weight.

THE CBT-E FAMILY MODULE

In outpatient multistep CBT-E, patients under the age of eighteen years and their significant others participate in a *family module* consisting of one session with the parents alone—whose content and rationale should be explained to the patient beforehand to avoid jeopardizing the trust that has been built up—and eight sessions with the adolescent together with the parents. These are to last fifteen minutes each and should be scheduled for the time slot immediately after the patient's individual sessions.

The parents-only session should be fixed for the first week of treatment (between the two individual CBT-E sessions), and be dedicated to the assessment of the family environment and to educating parents on the eating disorder of their child. The aim is to discern the presence of any potential family factors that could hinder the patient's efforts to change. The following areas are jointly evaluated with parents and dealt with accordingly:

- The parents' knowledge about eating disorders in general.
- The parents' interpretation of the patient's eating disorder behavior. Typical dysfunctional interpretations reported by parents are thinking that the eating problem is self-induced, a kind of hunger strike or form of self-destruction, which may be the consequence of their poor parenting skills.
- The parents' reaction to the patient's eating disorder behavior. Typical dysfunctional reactions are criticism, excessive care and control, anger, guilt, collusion with the eating disorder behavior, and avoidance of the problem.
- The effects of the parents' reactions on the adolescent's behavior. For example, criticism may produce a change of mood, triggering a bulimic episode in the child, while excessive care may intensify the eating control of the daughter or son as a way of maintaining the parents' attention.
- The presence in the home environment of factors that encourage dieting and concerns about shape and weight. For instance, the therapist should ask parents about the number and type of mirrors, the number and type of weighing scales, the type of magazines read by family members, whether any other family members are following a diet, adopting rigid and extreme dietary rules, or giving excessive importance to shape and weight.

Education is undertaken interactively and simultaneously with the assessment. Parents should be given the following general information:

- The causes of eating disorders are not yet clear, although they do seem to derive from a complex and not yet fully understood interaction between genetic and environmental factors.
- The adolescent is not anorexic but has an eating problem. His or her dysfunctional behavior is the consequence of a characteristic mindset that operates in people with eating problems.

- The eating problem is maintained by means of several mechanisms that perpetuate it, and addressing these is the primary goal of treatment. To explain this concept, the therapist should outline the cognitive behavioral theory of the maintenance of eating disorders to parents, and explain the adolescent's personal formulation.
- Many patients recover completely from their eating problem, and there is no reason to think that this will not happen to their son or daughter.
- Parents may unwittingly contribute to the maintenance of the patient's eating problem or, in contrast, may decide to foster the process of recovery, and this is the reason for their involvement in the treatment. They should be made aware that typical reactions that contribute to maintaining the eating problem are criticism, excessive care and control, anger, collusion with the eating disorder behavior, and, at the other end of the spectrum, avoidance of the problem.
- Parents are also encouraged to create a positive home environment that is likely to support the patient's efforts to change (e.g., by removing bathroom scales and surplus mirrors). Once again, parents should be encouraged to involve their child in this process rather than appearing to foist their decisions upon them.

In the second individual session of week one, the therapist trains patients in interpreting the weekly weight change and in *meal planning*, using the *outpatient CBT Weight Regain Guidelines* (see textbox 6.1). The therapist also explains how the diet menu plan works and provides patients with several daily menus of different calorie content (of 250 kcal increments from 1,500 kcal per day to 3,500 kcal per day), adapted from the exchange system (American Diabetes Association, 2003), from which to choose according to their needs. The menus, identified with a letter of the alphabet (e.g., Menu A: 1,500 kcal, B: 2,000 kcal, C: 2,500 kcal, D: 3,000 kcal, etc.), all follow the national dietary guidelines for a healthy but flexible diet, and include a broad range of foods. Moving away from the conventional idea of calorie counting, likely to be counterproductive in patients in whom such a measure would only compound the problem, the calorie content of single food items are not reported. Likewise, the calorie content of the daily diet is not rigidly fixed, a weekly mean instead being used as a point of reference.

After the patient has been fully apprised of the meal content, the therapist and patient meet with the parents to discuss the ins and outs of meal planning, with the aid of the *outpatient CBT Weight Regain Guidelines*, previously explained to the patient. In addition, the following information about *family meals* is shared:

- Parents, as in most families, should be responsible for buying, preparing, and serving the food, without adopting rules dictated by the eating problem of their child, and sticking to the appropriate menu planned for the week.
- The majority of meals should be consumed with all the family together as a unit.
- Dysfunctional thoughts about eating should not be criticized, as they are the expression of the eating problem. Parents should instead encourage their son or daughter to eat (mechanically) without being influenced by the eating disorder mindset.
- Patients should be gently dissuaded from practicing any atypical methods of food intake and rituals to control eating (e.g., separating fat and sauce from food, eating too slowly or too fast, drinking a lot during meals, hiding food in a handkerchief, making strange mixtures of foods, leaving most of the pulp in the fruit peel).
- Parents should avoid manipulative criticism (e.g., *"Eat for us; aren't you ashamed of upsetting us in this way?" "We have made a lot of sacrifices for you. The least you can do is eat this meal I've prepared." "You are killing us with your behavior. You are so cruel"*). In difficult situations during meals, parents should use empathy and supportive phrases (e.g., *"We know that the process toward recovery is hard, but we are here to help you. Try to eat mechanically without being influenced by what you think or feel"*).

A second session with parents, together with the adolescent, is fixed after the fourth individual CBT-E session in the second week of treatment. This family session is dedicated to reviewing meal planning and the family meals, and to generate solutions (using proactive problem-solving procedures involving both parents and their child) for any problems that emerged during the week. A further family session is fixed at the end of week 4 in Stage Two with the dual aims of reviewing the progress and the obstacles encountered during Stage One and designing Stage Three (see chapter 5). Subsequent family sessions are scheduled for weeks 8, 12, 20, and 40.

When the patient reaches his or her target weight, parents are informed that the treatment will now focus on addressing residual extreme and rigid dietary restraint, and meals should progressively be consumed as a family without the eating problem rearing its head. In this phase of treatment, parents can encourage their child to invite his or her friends out for meals and to accept invitations to parties.

THE FORMULATION, REAL-TIME MONITORING,
AND WEIGHING

The construction of the personal formulation and the procedures for real-time monitoring and weighing-in are identical to those described for adults (see chapter 5). Indeed, actively involving adolescent patients in creating their personal formulation, monitoring their behavior, and interpreting their weight change is highly engaging, and helps them to feel in control during the treatment.

TARGET WEIGHT

While for adult patients the aim of CBT-E is to reach a BMI of 19.0 to 20.0, with adolescents the aim is to achieve full physical recovery (i.e., restoration of menstruation, for example, and normal physical functioning), especially as partial recovery could cause permanent damage to their physical development. In female patients a pelvic ultrasound carried out when they are approaching their pre-morbid BMI centile may help to assess their pelvic maturity and therefore the need for possible further weight gain (Lai, de Bruyn, Lask, Bryant-Waugh, & Hankins, 1994).

OTHER ASPECTS OF EATING DISORDER PSYCHOPATHOLOGY

The other aspects of adolescent patients' eating disorder psychopathology are addressed using the same strategies and procedures employed in adults. However, in many cases the intervention is focused only on the overvaluation of control over eating per se, because, as previously mentioned, many adolescent patients do not report the overvaluation of shape and weight. If treatment is successful, adolescent patients will achieve periods free from concern about shape and weight and eating control faster than adults. If this positive outcome occurs, it is at this point that adolescent patients should learn about mindsets and how to control them (see chapter 5 for details).

EXTERNAL MAINTENANCE MECHANISMS AND
COEXISTING CLINICAL DEPRESSION

For the reasons described above, treatment of adolescents, more often than in adults, includes the interpersonal and core low-self-esteem modules of the broad CBT-E. These modules, as for adults, should always be associated with the work carried out on the core eating disorder psychopathology.

The management of coexisting clinical depression is more controversial. SSRI antidepressant medications are associated with few side effects in adolescents, but they may trigger agitation and abnormal behavior in certain individuals. Hence the pros and cons of pharmacological treatment should be carefully evaluated, considering the increased risk of suicidal thoughts or behavior in children and adolescents treated with SSRIs. Indeed, fluoxetine is the only medication approved by the FDA for use in treating depression in children aged eight and above. Should the CBT physician decide to prescribe an SSRI medication, adolescent patients must be closely monitored, especially in the first few weeks of treatment, for any worsening of depression, emergence of suicidal thinking or behavior, or unusual behavioral changes such as sleeplessness, agitation, or withdrawal from normal social situations (National Institute of Mental Health, 2011).

ADAPTATIONS OF INTENSIVE OUTPATIENT CBT-E FOR ADOLESCENTS

Intensive outpatient CBT-E for adolescents is similar to that for adults, outlined in chapter 6, except for the addition of the family module, an adapted version of that described above for outpatient CBT-E, in which parents of patients under the age of eighteen years participate with their child. In general, the first family session, which includes the CBT dietitian, parents, and patients, is arranged for the Friday of the first week, and focuses on how to address weekend meals. Although discussions about the preparation of food are usually mitigated during the first eight weeks by the use of the pre-packaged and frozen foods provided by the outpatient center, parents need to be trained to assist in the patient's *consumption* of these weekend meals, adopting the procedures described above.

The subsequent week also features a family session with the CBT dietician to review the difficulties encountered during weekend meals. Any issues are addressed using a proactive problem-solving approach, and both family members and the patients are encouraged to generate solutions for improving the management of family meals. In most cases, only a few additional family sessions with the dietician are necessary in intensive outpatient treatment, because if the patients are unable to consume the meals appropriately during weekends, a more intensive step (namely inpatient CBT-E) needs to be considered. Other family sessions with the CBT dietitian are arranged when patients start to eat regular food at home, with a view to discussing with parents the best way to prepare meals. In general, parents are encouraged, as in most families, to take charge of food shopping, preparation, and serving, without bending to the eating problem dictates expressed by their daughter or son. The food provider must plan a weekly menu based on national dietary guidelines, and parents should encourage social eating with other people outside the family unit.

ADAPTATIONS OF INPATIENT CBT-E FOR ADOLESCENTS

Inpatient CBT-E for adolescent patients is similar to that adopted for adults (i.e., same format, stages, and duration), and includes the same core procedures. However, the treatment has been modified to include the general CBT-E adaptations for adolescents described above, as well as some procedures designed specifically for the inpatient setting. In particular, the inpatient CBT-E unit should include designated spaces for adolescents. Young patients should sleep in separate rooms from adults, and a study room should be provided. In addition, students should receive tuition from a teacher, either directly or via Internet. The unit should also provide a kitchen where parents may cook and eat a meal with their son or daughter. In the inpatient phase, adolescent patients need to be supervised outside the unit by an adult, who may be appointed by parents if they are not available themselves. In the day treatment phase, if the family home is too far from the unit, the family should rent an apartment where at least one adult, preferably a parent, should live with the patient.

Unfortunately, it is inevitable for inpatient CBT-E to interrupt the peer relationships that patients have in their home environment, which in most cases can lead to a worsening of their insecure sense of identity. Fortunately, however, the patient is unlikely to be the only adolescent in the inpatient CBT-E unit, meaning that they have the opportunity to develop new peer relationships with people who really understand what they are going through. Moreover, the availability of computers equipped with communications software, coupled with the fact that they have the opportunity to continue studying during the treatment (see below) may help the patients to maintain stabilizing contact with their classmates and significant others.

Patients who have to be hospitalized for a long period of time should nevertheless be encouraged to continue following their school curriculum. To this end, like other hospitals in Italy, Villa Garda runs a project called *School in the Hospital*, set up by the Italian Ministry for Education, University and Research (MIUR) (www.pso.istruzione.it), which offers all youngsters hospitalized for over thirty days the opportunity to continue with their studies. The scheme includes both face-to-face lessons with a teacher using national curriculum textbooks and lessons conducted via web using webcam technology. The School in the Hospital project helps patients not to fall behind in their studies and facilitates their eventual reintegration into the traditional school context, two problems that may predispose patients to setbacks after discharge.

Once a week, adolescent patients also attend CBT-E groups specifically designed for their age range, rather than the group therapy reserved for adult patients described in chapter 7. The adolescent group sessions are structured in a similar way to adult groups, but are specifically adapted for teens. For instance, homework assignments are simplified, particular focus is placed on problem-solving skills, and therapy sessions feature extensive use of experiential learning (e.g., role-plays).

The Family Module

The transition to outpatient treatment is generally less problematic in adolescent patients than in adults, as they tend to spend all of the day treatment period either at home or in an apartment with their parents, and some environmental triggers (e.g., performance at school) are addressed during the program. However, ending treatment well is also essential for adolescent patients and the procedures used are similar to those described in chapter 7.

Although many adolescent patients achieve complete remission at the end of the inpatient program, they are encouraged to continue to attend the CBT-E outpatient clinic so as to continue the work undertaken during hospitalization, and thereby avert setbacks. If no signs of relapse arise in the first two to three months after discharge, the treatment may be considered successful and wound up accordingly. In most cases, however, it is better if patients are monitored for at least six months following discharge in order that they are helped to deal with stressful situations without reactivating their eating disorder mindset. However, if patients start to lose weight after discharge, outpatient CBT-E may even continue as long as twelve months because several months may be spent engaging them in the process of weight regain.

II

Case Studies

Chapter Nine

Case Study A: Outpatient CBT-E

This case illustrates how outpatient CBT-E was adapted to treat a professional sportswoman affected by an eating disorder. The outpatient CBT-E applied in this particular clinical case draws extensively on my knowledge and clinical experience with this form of treatment and, although I endeavored to adhere to the main procedures and strategies described in the CBT-E manual (Fairburn et al., 2008, pp. 145–193), as the patient was treated in a real-world setting, some deviation may be noted. To conceal the patient's identity, several details of the case have also been modified, and selected transcripts have been adapted for brevity.

CASE DESCRIPTION

Veronica is a competitive artistic gymnast. Her athletic career began at the age of fourteen and was constellated by numerous achievements and medals. At the age of eighteen, however, while she was training for an important competition, she suffered acute lower back pain, which hampered her training. The same week, her coaches decided to implement daily group weigh-ins for all the gymnasts on her team, telling them that they needed to lose weight in order to improve their performance. Veronica reported that the moments preceding the weigh-in were very distressing for her, and that she ceased to enjoy training altogether. Indeed, she reported that her coaches reacted with anger and punishments (e.g., increasing the duration of the training session) if she failed to lose weight. Veronica was not given any suggestions, professional or otherwise, regarding dietary guidelines for losing weight, and stated that "the coaches were only concerned about taking food from our hands when they discovered we were eating snacks." On several occasions Veronica also remembers the coaches checking the athletes' rooms and bags to see whether they were "hiding" food. This series of events led Veronica to look on training, gym sessions, and anything related to the world of gymnastics as a nightmare.

In a bid to avert the coaches' criticism, she started restricting her food intake during her evening meals, leaving part of her meal on the plate, and began to avoid ingesting carbs completely. However, these dietary rules failed to produce any weight loss, and Veronica therefore decided to start self-inducing vomiting after lunch. The loss of liquids arising as a consequence of the persistent vomiting and the associated transient loss of weight was very much appreciated by her coach, who complimented her on her commitment. This reinforced Veronica's use of vomiting as a means of controlling her weight, and this extreme weight control behavior became progressively more frequent, even after the intake of small amounts of food. After a few weeks of this practice, Veronica experienced objective bulimic episodes, bingeing on large amounts of cookies and chocolate before falling asleep in the evening. She also started to buy large amounts of food at the supermarket, especially sweets and chocolate. She remembers this period as one of the most terrible of her life. She felt as if the world was falling apart around her: her lower back pain persisted, her eating problem was getting the upper hand, her social life was becoming ever more limited, and her training performance was getting progressively poorer.

Despite her less than optimal physical fitness at this time, she participated in a very important competition, and was very disappointed to find that she had placed far below her usual rank. After the competition, Veronica's back pain intensified and her sports physician recommended she refrain from training for one month to recover. She also made a failed attempt to stop purging at this time, and the persistence of objective and subjective bulimic episodes, combined with the interruption in her training, led to a weight gain of 3 kg, despite the dietary restraint, the frequent daily self-induced vomiting, and the sporadic misuse of laxatives. This weight change led Veronica to stop weighing herself altogether, and instead to spend large amounts of time naked in front of the mirror checking the shape of her legs and stomach. She also remembers frequently comparing her body shape to those of other gymnasts. Avoiding objective measurement of her weight, she used the feeling of bloating and fullness after eating and the size of certain garments to obtain feedback about the changes in her body weight and shape.

After she recovered from the lower back pain and resumed training, she realized that her performance had markedly deteriorated. She became desperate and afraid that her sporting career was slipping away from her. The coach, noticing the changes in Veronica's performance and psychology, called her aside and asked what was going on. Veronica confided in him, recounting her use of vomiting, bulimic episodes, and profound distress. The coach was very understanding and suggested that she discuss the problem with the team's sports physician, who then referred Veronica to us for specialist eating disorder treatment.

Textbox 9.1 shows Veronica's case summary and textbox 9.2 shows the abbreviation guide for the transcripts.

TEXTBOX 9.1. CASE A SUMMARY

Personal information and home life

- Age: Nineteen years
- Occupation: Elite gymnast
- Marital status: Single, unmarried
- Home life: Lives alone
- Social class: Middle

Eating problem onset

- Age: Eighteen years
- Weight at the onset of the eating problem: 44 kg
- Behavioral precursor: dieting and vomiting. Reasons for dieting: losing weight to meet her coach's expectations

The twelve months before the onset

- Events that may have triggered the control of eating, shape, and weight: coach pressurizing her to lose weight, being weighed in front of teammates, increasing pressure to improve her athletic performance, lower back pain

The first four months after the onset

- The dietary rules and vomiting were experienced as an easy and positive way of controlling her weight, and hypothetically improving her athletic performance. Positive comments received for being able to lose weight

Since then

- After four months: onset of subjective and objective bulimic episodes, intensification of dietary restraint, limitation of social life, deterioration of training performance
- After eight months: poor performance at a very important competition
- Nine to twelve months: interruption of training to recover from lower back pain, persistence of objective and subjective bulimic episodes with daily self-induced vomiting and sporadic misuse of laxatives, and an increase in body weight of 3 kg; weight avoidance and intensification of mirror and shape comparison checking
- After twelve months: recovery from lower back pain and resumption of the training; performance far lower than her habitual standard

Current state of the eating problem (last four weeks and last three months for DSM diagnosis).

- Current weight: 44 kg
- Current height: 144 cm
- BMI: 21.2
- Frequency of menstruation: One in the last three months
- Weight changes: Gained 3 kg over the last three months
- Dietary restraint: Present
- Self-induced vomiting: sixteen episodes in the last four weeks (sixty in the last three months)
- Excessive exercising: Present
- Objective binge eating: twelve episodes in the last four weeks (thirty in the last three months)
- Subjective binge eating: eight episodes in the last four weeks (thirty in the last three months)
- Smoking, substance and alcohol misuse: Absent
- Weight avoidance: Present
- Shape checking: Present
- Shape avoidance: Absent
- Fear of weight gain: Present
- Preoccupation with shape, weight, and eating control: Present
- Feeling fat: Present
- Feeling full: Present (after meals)
- Physical health: Not impaired
- Psychosocial functioning: Impaired
- Athletic performance: Impaired
- DSM-IV diagnosis: Bulimia nervosa (307.51)

Personal and family medical history

- Past and current medical and psychiatric comorbidity: None
- Current medications: None
- Family medical and psychiatric history: Aunt with a probable eating disorder in adolescence; mother with body dissatisfaction, despite being in the normal weight range

Physical Examination

- No apparent physical complications

TEXTBOX 9.2. ABBREVIATIONS IN SELECTED TRANSCRIPTS

V = Veronica; AC = Assessing Clinician; T = Therapist; C = Coach

ASSESSING AND PREPARING THE PATIENT FOR OUTPATIENT CBT-E

Objectives

- Assessing the patient's attitude toward the interview.
- Assessing the nature and the severity of the eating problem.
- Preparing patient for the outpatient treatment.

The assessment and the preparation for the treatment were performed over two sessions by a clinician expert in both psychological assessment and CBT-E. Veronica came to the first evaluation interview accompanied by her coach. The assessing clinician welcomed Veronica in the waiting room and invited her into the office, asking the coach to wait outside.

Assessing the Patient's Attitude toward the Interview

In the first part of the interview, the assessing clinician evaluated how Veronica felt about the interview, in particular if she came to the consultation freely or with reluctance.

[. . .] Selected transcripts:

> AC: Did you come to this evaluation interview of your own accord?

> V: Sincerely, I don't know what to say. In part it was my decision, but in part my coach and my mother convinced me.

> AC: Veronica can you tell me the reason that led you to make the decision to come to this consultation?

> V: Umm . . . I really do not know the exact reasons and I don't know if this is the right place. I only know that I am tired and I can't train as well as I would like.

> AC: Right . . . and what do you think may have induced your mother to encourage you to come to this consultation?

> V: She sees that I have been very sad and agitated over the few last months.

> AC: And what about your coach?

> V: He is worried about my performance, which has been very poor over the last year.

Assessing the Nature and Severity of the Eating Problem

The focus of the first part of the evaluation session was to assess the development, nature, and severity of Veronica's psychopathology. This was concluded with the collaborative measurement of Veronica's weight and height, with her wearing indoor clothes but no shoes.

[. . .] Selected transcripts:

> AC: Veronica do you agree that the aim of this consultation is to exchange information about your potential eating problem and perhaps to discuss any available treatments?

> V: Ok.

> AC: Good. Do you remember the onset of your difficulties?

> V: It all began when I turned eighteen. In that period I had a physical problem.

AC: What problem was that?

V: I had a very annoying pain in my lower back that stopped me training properly . . . and in addition my coaches decided to check the weight of all the gymnasts on my team every day so that we would be better prepared for an important competition.

AC: Can you explain better?

V: The coaches weighed us in front of each other and pushed us to lose weight.

AC: Was it the first time that this had happened?

V: Well . . . we are athletes and they are always telling us to watch what we eat, but . . . it was the first time that they had been so insistent.

AC: Did you receive a dietary counseling from a sports dietitian?

V: No . . . we self-managed our diets.

AC: Coming back to the daily group weigh-ins—how did you feel about this experience?

V: At first I thought that it might help me to improve my performance. But then, it upset me because the coaches were often critical when our weight rose, and made lots of comments.

AC: Can you give me some examples?

V: A typical comment was: "How do you think that the competition judges will score athletes that look like twirling barrels?" or "Hurry up, the competition is coming up in a few months, and with your weight you will have no chance of success."

AC: I think that it must have been a very stressful situation.

V: Yes . . . in addition, the coaches, if they saw us eating snacks during breaks from training, snatched them away from us. They also began checking our bags and rooms searching for food . . . so it was a nightmare.

AC: I understand. And how did you react?

V: The first thing that I thought about when I woke up in the morning was our daily weigh-in. So I decided to cut out several foods.

AC: Which foods did you start avoiding?

V: In particular pasta, bread, sweets, and red meat.

AC: Did you lose any weight after adopting these dietary rules?

V: No, my weight was stable . . . and my coaches were ever more critical . . . so one day I made myself sick after lunch . . . and my weight was one kilogram less than on the day before. This was the start of me doing this to control my weight.

AC: And the coaches?

V: They stopped criticizing me.

AC: How long did this go on for?

V: Only a few weeks . . . in fact after few weeks my appetite increased . . . the more I vomited the more I ate. In the evenings I started to eat entire boxes of cookies that I had bought at the supermarket before returning home.

AC: I am sorry to hear that.

[. . .]

Preparing the Patient for Treatment

Providing Education on the Eating Problem

The assessing clinician drew up a provisional formulation of Veronica's eating problem including the main maintenance mechanisms reported by her in the first part of the evaluation session. In particular, the assessing clinician explained the relationship between dietary restraint and binge eating; the partial effect of vomiting on calorie absorption and its effect on increasing the frequency of binge eating; the overvaluation of shape, weight, and eating control; and the perpetuating nature of her eating problem. In addition, he emphasized the negative impact of the eating problem on her athletic performance.

Providing Detailed Information about the Treatment

The assessing clinician gave Veronica detailed information about the treatment and an informative handout on outpatient CBT-E. He also discussed the issue of continuing training and competition.

[. . .] Selected transcripts:

AC: Well. Let's go over what the treatment involves.

V: Ok.

AC: Cognitive behavioral therapy is the most effective treatment available for your eating problem. With this approach, about two-thirds of patients completing the treatment program achieve excellent results.

V: Hmm . . .

AC: If you engage in the treatment and you give it priority, there is no reason why you should not fall into this group.

V: Er . . . can you give me more details about the treatment?

AC: The treatment is individualized and focused mainly on the factors maintaining *your* particular eating problem. In other words it mainly deals with your present and future, rather than looking back at your past.

V: And what about the cause of my eating problem?

AC: That will only be addressed if necessary. However, the treatment will be tailor-made to your specific needs, and you and your therapist will both need to become experts on your particular eating problem and the mechanisms fueling it.

V: How long is the treatment? I know that psychotherapy may last years.

AC: Since the treatment is focused principally on the processes maintaining your eating problem, it has a short and fixed duration. It is scheduled to last twenty weeks and will involve twenty fifty-minute individual sessions. The first eight sessions will be held twice a week, the subsequent nine sessions once a week, and the last three every two weeks.

V: Ok.

AC: It is also important that the treatment is not interrupted, because we will work from session to session to erode the mechanisms maintaining your eating problem. Interruptions of the treatment are dangerous because you may lose what we call the "momentum." Constancy is particularly important in the first six weeks of treatment, and gaps between sessions in the following weeks will never be longer than two weeks. We have to bear this in mind when we decide on the best moment for you to start the treatment.

V: Well, this might be a good period. I have no competitions coming up.

AC: Another point to stress is that it is in your best interest that all our sessions start and finish punctually.

V: That won't be problem. I'm always on time.

AC: Good. It is also a good idea for you to come fifteen minutes before the appointment so you have time to prepare yourself for the session. You should also let us know in advance if you won't be able to attend.

V: Ok.

AC: The idea is that you and your therapist will work together, much like an athlete and her coach, to overcome your eating problem.

V: I'm an expert on this kind of collaboration [smiling].

AC: You and your therapist will agree on specific homework for you to do between sessions. The homework assignments are an integral part of your treatment and you should therefore make them a priority. What you do between sessions will go a long way to ensuring that you benefit from treatment.

V: I understand. I need to play a very active part in the treatment.

AC: Yes, it is crucial. The treatment will be hard but it will be worth it— the more effort you make, the greater the rewards will be.

Confirming the Homework Assignment

At the end of the first evaluation session, the assessing clinician asked Veronica to do three homework assignments for the following evaluation session: (i) considering the pros and cons of undertaking outpatient CBT-E; (ii) reading the information handout on outpatient CBT-E; and (iii) creating a list of questions about the treatment to discuss with the therapist.

Involving the Coach in the Treatment

There are at least three main reasons why involving the coach(es) of athletes with eating problems in the CBT is a good idea (Thompson & Trattner Sherman, 2012). First, coaches have significant power and influence over their athletes, and often have more contact with them than their significant others; second, involving coaches allows the therapist to have more control over the coach's power and influence; and third, coaches are in a prime position to facilitate treatment with their encouragement and support. Therefore, at the end of the first evaluation session, the assessing clinician asked Veronica if she would agree to the coach being informed about her eating problem and the treatment she might undertake. Veronica consented, and the assessing clinician explained to the coach the principal processes maintaining her eating problem, the structure and the aim of the treatment, and the important role the coach could play in encouraging and supporting her. He also asked the coach to cease making any comments about Veronica's eating and weight, to refrain from conducting group weigh-ins in the future, and to focus on Veronica's training and performance rather than her weight.

The second evaluation interview was fixed one week later. Veronica, although ambivalent, and not fully convinced of the need to address her eating problem, decided to start the program.

OUTPATIENT CBT-E

Stage One: Session 0

Objectives

- Engaging the patient in the treatment and the idea of change.
- Assessing the nature and severity of the psychopathology present.
- Jointly creating a formulation of the processes maintaining the eating problem.
- Explaining what the treatment will involve.
- Setting up real-time self-monitoring.
- Setting the homework assignments.
- Summarizing the session and scheduling the next appointment.

Engaging the Patient in the Treatment and Change

Engaging patients in treatment is very challenging, and must bear the particular needs of the patient in mind. For example, although there were some features of Veronica's eating problem that she did want to change (e.g., binge eating), there were others she was less sure about discarding (e.g., extreme and rigid dietary rules, self-induced vomiting, excessive exercising). Her ambivalence was also increased by fears associated with the incidental effects on her athletic performance (e.g., fear of losing her competitive edge and athlete status) should she relax her extreme weight control behaviors. To address Veronica's ambivalence, in addition to following the general CBT-E guidelines used to engage patients in the treatment (e.g., being empathetic and engaging in manner, involving the patient actively in the creation of the personal formulation, instilling hope, inquiring about any concerns that patient may have), the therapist placed particular emphasis on analyzing the pros and cons of potential change on her athletic participation and performance. As she was medically stable, and for the following psychological reasons, Veronica was also encouraged to maintain training (Thompson & Trattner Sherman, 2012):

- It allows the athlete to maintain a sense of attachment by continuing to be part of a team.
- It makes it easier to monitor the patient's symptoms and condition.
- It encourages the patient to continue doing an activity that is his or her primary source of self-esteem.
- It allows the patient to maintain an important sense of identity (as a sports participant).
- It facilitates implementation of the necessary eating changes.
- It can be used to determine whether the patient really wants to continue practicing his or her sport.

[. . .] Selected transcripts:

T: We should also discuss your training.

V: Why?

T: An eating problem tends to worsen sports performance and, if it becomes very severe, it is not advisable to train or compete.

V: Really?

T: Yes. Do you want to keep training and competing?

V: Of course!!!

T: Good. I don't think that there is any reason that you shouldn't at the moment. You should know, however, that there are certain conditions to this, namely that you are not underweight, you are in treatment and progressing, and that your participation in sports is not symptomatic.

V: What do you mean by my sports participation not being symptomatic?

T: I mean that some athletes with an eating problem may overdo training primarily to change their shape and weight rather than to improve their sports performance.

V: Er . . . that is partly true in my case.

T: Do you know that the exercise you do over and above your requirements for training actually causes your performance to deteriorate and serves to maintain your eating problem?

V: No, I didn't know that.

T: Sports performance is also impaired by poor nutrition and by the dehydration and electrolyte imbalance brought on by vomiting.

V: I've experienced that. I'm really tired all the time and not able to train as hard as I wish.

T: Healthier individuals are able to perform better for longer. So, when evaluating the pros and cons of change you should consider the effect of your eating problem not only on your health, but also on your sports performance, and on the potential benefits of overcoming it.

V: For me my athletic performance is the driving force in my life. I will try to change, even if I am really afraid of failing.

Assessing the Nature and Severity of the Patient's Psychopathology

The CBT-E therapist conducting the treatment was not the person who conducted the initial interview, and the former met Veronica for the first time at this initial session. This meant that a second assessment needed to take place in order that the therapist could hear directly from Veronica the nature of her eating problem. Even though some overlap with the first assessment interview was inevitable, the second assessment was set up to focus primarily on treatment rather than diagnosis. In particular, the aim was to use an evaluation of Veronica's present status and the main processes maintaining her eating problem, with a view to creating a personalized formulation to guide her forthcoming treatment program.

Jointly Creating a Formulation of the Processes Maintaining the Eating Problem

The next step was the creation of Veronica's formulation. Once this had been done, the therapist went on to discuss its implications with her. The main point he emphasized was that the treatment should focus on not only the things that she wanted to change (e.g., binge eating), but also the mechanisms maintaining these things (e.g., dietary restraint, excessive exercising, overvaluation of shape and weight). At the end of the session, the therapist gave Veronica a copy of her formulation (see figure 9.1) and asked her to review it before the next appointment and to modify it as she saw fit.

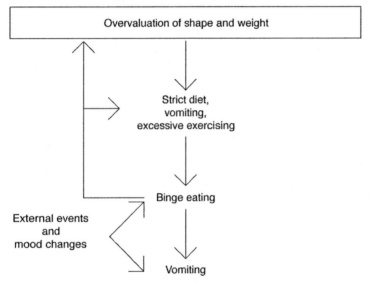

Figure 9.1.   Veronica's Provisional Personal Formulation

[. . .] Selected transcripts:

T: This formulation shows the main things that are maintaining your eating problem.

V: Hmm . . . this means that I have to deal with these things to overcome my eating problem?

T: Yes! If you change these things you will overcome your eating problem.

V: All these things?

T: Yes, we need to address all of them—otherwise you will be at risk of relapse.

[...]

T: In treatment we will start by addressing your eating habits and excessive exercising, and then we will move on to addressing your overvaluation of shape and weight.

V: That sounds like a good plan.

T: Take this copy of your formulation—I suggest you have a think about it before our next session and make any modifications you think are necessary.

V: Ok.

Explaining What the Treatment Will Involve

The therapist reviewed what the treatment would involve with Veronica, repeating much of the information provided during the first evaluation session (see above).

[...] *Selected transcripts:*

T: Veronica, do you have any questions or concerns?

V: Er ... is my eating problem severe enough to need treatment?

T: We discussed before how your eating problem has impaired your athletic performance and your psychological and interpersonal functioning. Without treatment you are unlikely to recover from this damage, which, should you not face up to it, can only get worse and affect every other aspect of your life.

V: Right. I understand.

Setting Up Real-Time Self-Monitoring

As real-time self-monitoring—recording behaviors, thoughts, feeling and events the moment they occur—is one of the key procedures of outpatient CBT-E, the patient needs to be made aware of this fact. In Veronica's case, the concept and the practice were introduced in session 0, fine-tuned in session 1, and continued throughout the course of the treatment. The thera-

pist gave Veronica twenty blank record sheets, together with written instructions detailing how to complete them (see Fairburn et al., 2008, pp. 57–61 for
details).

[. . .] Selected transcripts:

T: Self-monitoring is one of the most important procedures in this treatment, as important as attending the sessions themselves. It is a tool that
will help you to become an expert on your eating problem and will be
instrumental in helping you to overcome it.

V: What is the point?

T: It has two main purposes. The first is to illustrate how your eating
problem works. For this reason you should report what you are doing,
thinking, and feeling on this monitoring record (the therapist shows Veronica a blank monitoring record sheet) in real time. If you do this, we can
find out the details of your eating problem and better understand what to
do to overcome it. Second, it will help you to change. Monitoring in real
time will enable you to gain control of some behaviors that now seem
automatic and uncontrollable.

V: Ok, I understand.

T: Let's take a look at this sample monitoring record to see how it should
be done. You should use a new monitoring record every day. In the first
column you should note the time when you eat or drink anything. In the
second column you should note *what* you eat or drink—just write a simple description of what you eat or drink, not the calorie content. Meals
should be marked in brackets. Is that clear? Do you have any questions?

V: No, it is clear.

T: In the third column you should note *where* you ate or drank, while in
the fourth column you should place an asterisk adjacent to any episodes
of eating or drinking that you felt were excessive.

V: Ok.

T: The fifth column is for noting any episodes of vomiting (V), when you
take laxatives (L, with the name and number of pills taken), or do any
exercise (E, type and duration).

V: Do I have to write down my training, or only any exercise out of the training?

T: For the first week I suggest you to note down both types of exercise. Then, we will decide how to proceed.

V: Ok.

T: The use of the last column, "context and comments," will vary during the treatment. For the first week you should use it as a diary to note events, thoughts, and emotions that influenced your eating.

V: But recording all the food I eat will increase my obsession with food!

T: That may happen. However, any increase in your preoccupation with food will only last a week or so, and monitoring will help you to understand the things you need to change to overcome your eating problem.

V: Can't I do without these monitoring records? I have to train several hours a day, and I won't have time to write down everything I eat.

T: I know that you have a very busy schedule. However, if you do this monitoring thoroughly and well, you will have a high probability of improving your training and competition performance.

V: Hmm . . . ok, I will try to do it.

T: Do you have any questions?

V: No, everything's clear.

Setting the Homework Assignments

Homework assignments, or "next steps" in CBT-E terminology, are also integral to treatment, and the eating problem cannot be overcome without patient compliance in this. Hence, in the final moments of session 0, the therapist made sure to explain this to Veronica and gave her two homework assignments: (i) to start real-time self-monitoring immediately; and (ii) to review her personal formulation for at least fifteen minutes before the next session. The therapist asked Veronica to write down these two homework assignments on a next steps sheet.

Summarizing the Session and Scheduling the Next Appointment

The session, as in all the others, was closed by summarizing collaboratively its content, reminding Veronica of the homework, and booking the appointments for the first four weeks. The next appointment was scheduled after three days.

Stage One: Session 1

Objectives

- Initiating in-session weighing.
- Reviewing self-monitoring.
- Setting the agenda.
- Working through the agenda.

    1. Attitudes toward the treatment.

    2. Reviewing the formulation.

    3. Educating about weight checking.

    4. Educating about weight, goal weight, and weight change during treatment.

- Setting homework, summarizing the session, and arranging the next appointment.

Initiating In-Session Weighing

In-session weighing involved the therapist and Veronica collaboratively checking her weight, with indoor clothes and without shoes, on a scale with 0.5 kg intervals. Her weight was then spoken aloud in kilograms and plotted on Veronica's personalized weight graph. In-session weighing was also used as an opportunity to educate Veronica about the issues of weight checking, body weight, and optimal body weight for sports performance (see below).

[. . .] Selected transcripts:

   T: Your weight is 43.5 kg.

   V: Yes.

   T: Can we put this number on your weight graph?

   V: Ok.

T: As you can see, the vertical axis shows weight in kilograms, while the horizontal axis shows the number of weeks. There are also two lines marking the limits of the range of healthy weight—this corresponds to a BMI of between 20 and 25.

V: Erm . . . so I am in the healthy weight range.

T: Yes you are. We will plot your weight on this graph once a week, and you will then go on to interpret any variation.

V: Ok.

Reviewing Self-Monitoring

The therapists reviewed Veronica's real-time monitoring record with her in detail to reinforce her collaboration. In session 1 this review had two main aims: (i) assessing the quality of Veronica's monitoring; (ii) assessing the information obtained about Veronica's eating habits. The therapist did not address the problem identified while reviewing the recording, but included it in the session agenda (see below).

[. . .] Selected transcripts:

T: Veronica, how did your monitoring go?

V: Well, as I told you last time I was skeptical about doing it. But since you told me that it is a very important procedure, I started to record the food I ate the evening after our first session, following your instructions.

T: Did you find it useful?

V: It's strange but, although I was skeptical, I realized that it was useful . . . writing what I eat and drink gives me more control.

T: Did you record in real time?

V: Most of the time . . . but once I ate with a friend of mine and I didn't record what I ate . . . I was embarrassed to start writing it down in front of her.

T: I understand. In the future, why don't you take a note in a little notebook and then write it on your monitoring record when you get home.

V: Ok, I'll do that next time.

T: Let's take a look together at your monitoring records (see figure 9.2).

V: Ok.

(. . .)

T: I see that you do not eat midmorning. Don't you ever have a snack? Why not?

V: I can't stop my training . . . and I want to have an empty stomach while I am exercising.

T: I see that you have marked the meals with brackets. Very good!

V: Thank you.

T: What do you think about your lunch?

V: Ok, I know I should eat more . . . but I feel better eating only a small can of tuna with a slice of bread—so I feel light and maintain my weight under control.

T: Do you always eat lunch in the changing room?

V: Yes, during weekdays. On Saturdays I eat something at the bar, and on Sundays I often have lunch at my parents' home.

T: I see that during the afternoon you drink two cappuccinos. . . .

V: Yes I do. Is that too many? Will it make me fat? Liquid foods do not make me feel full and even though I know that they do contain some calories, it doesn't seem the same as eating, However, I don't take sugar.

T: I see that you skipped your afternoon snack—do you often skip afternoon snacks?

V: Yes, because if I start eating solid foods I know I won't be able to stop. Also I wouldn't know what to eat—I don't like fruit, and sweets make me fat. So it is better to avoid eating altogether . . . and then these are foods that I binge on.

Day.................... Monday ....   Date.................... October 16th ....

Time	Food and liquids consumed	Place	*	V/L/E	Comments
7:00	2 croissants 1 coffee without sugar	Kitchen			Training 9-12 am
1:15	1 small can of tuna ½ slice of sandwich loaf 1 coffee without sugar	Changing room			I feel fine. Training 2-4 pm
4:30	1 cappuccino with sweetener	Bar			
5:30	1 cappuccino with sweetener	Bar			I can't stop. Fortunately they are sugar-free
6:30	1 apple 1 bag of gumdrops	Car			
7:00	50g chicken breast 1 cup of salad and tomatoes with oil and vinegar	Kitchen			
9:00	2 apples 10 chocolate candies 8 slices of sandwich loaf 1 can of tuna 1 ice cream	Dining room	*		I am still hungry. I ate some fruit. It is not enough. I must eat something else. It always ends up the same way. I am disgusted with myself. It will be impossible to train well with all this food in my stomach

Figure 9.2. Veronica's First Monitoring Record. Adapted from figure 5.3 in *Cognitive Behavior Therapy and Eating Disorders* by Christopher G. Fairburn, 2008. Copyright Guilford Press. Reprinted with permission of The Guilford Press.

T: I see that you also used one asterisk.

V: Yes, I used the asterisks, as you suggested, when I ate something without control. Here, for example, I had a binge and I marked it with an asterisk.

T: Well done. You did a great job. This is a very good start. We will learn a lot about your eating problem and what is maintaining it. What we have to do now is to analyze together the way to make your recording even more useful—so we can obtain as much information as possible from it. For example, the next time you should mark with an asterisk every single food you ate without control. In this way a binge will be characterized by a chain of asterisks.

V: Why?

T: Because, sometime the binge is triggered by your breaking some dietary rule, and the use of asterisks may help us to understand how this happens.

V: I don't understand.

T: For example, I see that in this binge you started by eating two apples, but then you ate chocolate candies, several slices of bread, one can of tuna, and an ice cream.

V: Yes, I planned to eat only two apples, but then I ate a chocolate bar and I completely lost control.

T: If this happens again, only mark the foods you didn't plan to eat with an asterisk, i.e., those after the apples.

V: Ok. Now it is clear.

T: When you ate the chocolate bar and the other foods, did you know that you were going to vomit?

V: Yes. When I lose control, I say to myself that I can eat until I am full, then I can get rid of all the calories by vomiting.

T: A final question. Would you eat an entire pack of cookies, if you were not going to vomit?

V: No! Of course not!

Setting the Agenda

The agenda of the session, and of those to follow, was set collaboratively with Veronica based on information from four main sources: (i) the homework from the previous session; (ii) the issues identified during the monitoring record review; (iii) items that Veronica wanted to discuss; (iv) new topics based on the particular stage of the treatment.

Working through the Agenda

Attitude toward the treatment. Since attitude toward the treatment influences the outcome, the therapist asked Veronica directly for her views on the treatment.

[. . .] Selected transcripts:

T: Veronica, how do you feel about having started the treatment?

V: Um . . . on the one hand I'm happy I made this decision. I hope to get better, and to improve my sports performance, which is currently very poor. But . . . on the other hand, I am afraid that if I stop dieting and vomiting I will get fat. I am a gymnast . . . I can't get fat.

T: I understand your ambivalence. However, as I already explained, the best way to control your weight is to overcome your eating problem, to stop binge eating and using extreme methods of weight control, and to adopt a healthy diet.

V: Yes, I believe you, but I am still afraid.

T: In any case, the only way to test your predictions about the consequences of stopping your extreme weight control behaviors is to try to change. If you are unsatisfied with the outcome, you may always go back to extreme dieting and vomiting to control your weight.

V: No, I want to eliminate these behaviors.

Reviewing the formulation. The therapist then went over Veronica's formulation with her to understand her opinion of the diagram, and to resolve any misunderstanding.

[...] Selected transcripts:

> T: Veronica, did you have a think about the formulation we constructed last session?

> V: Yes, I did.

> T: Is it clear?

> V: Yes, it is quite clear.

> T: Did you change anything?

> V: No. I think we included all the main features of my eating problem.

> T: Good. However, this formulation is not set in stone—we may need to change or enhance it when we acquire more information about the mechanisms maintaining your eating problem.

Educating about weight checking. The therapist then went on to educate Veronica about how to interpret variations in her weight. He explained that weight naturally fluctuates during the day, and from day to day, as a consequence of the state of hydration, bowel content, glycogen body content, and menstrual status, with weight tending to increase in the second part of the menstrual cycle due to water retention. In this way he helped her see that weight variation cannot be interpreted on the basis of a single reading. He also added that frequent weighing increases preoccupation about physiological fluctuations and favors dietary restriction following a perceived increase in weight. He explained that, at the other end of the scale, avoidance of weight checking is problematic too, because one is not aware of any *real* changes in body weight and therefore the adoption of healthy methods of weight control tends to be delayed. The therapist suggested to Veronica that checking her weight once a week and interpreting its variation every four weeks would be the best way to have a clear picture of any changes in her weight. Finally, the therapist asked Veronica not to weigh herself between the weekly in-session weigh-ins, but that if she did, she should record the event in the last column of her monitoring record.

[. . .] Selected transcripts:

T: To interpret your weight you should focus on any variation over a four-week interval, because how heavy you are is influenced by your state of hydration, which may vary day by day, and your menstrual cycle, as hormone levels change throughout the month.

V: Do you mean that when my coach weighed me every day, he measured the daily variation in my body water?

T: Yes. To have an accurate estimate of the variation in your body weight you should look at the variations every four weeks. Take a look at this graph showing the changes in weight of a patient. At the start of treatment her weight was 52 kg; after a week 51.5 kg, in the second week 52.5 kg, the third week 52.5 kg, and the fourth week 52 kg. If we were to interpret her weight on a week-by-week basis, it would appear that her weight decreases in the first week, increases in the second week, is stable in the third, and decreases again in the fourth. However, if we trace a line between the baseline weight and that of the fourth week, we can see that in reality her weight fluctuated but was essentially stable.

V: Right.

T: This clearly illustrates that rather than having an exact weight, it is better to accept a weight *range* of two to three kilograms to allow for natural weight fluctuation.

V: I understand the concept, even if it is not easy for me to consider my changes in weight as simple fluctuations.

Educating about weight, goal weight, and weight change in the treatment. Finally, the therapist educated Veronica about her body weight, BMI, and goal weight, leading to an inevitable discussion about the relationship between body weight and sports performance, and the weight change during treatment.

[. . .] Selected transcripts:

T: Veronica, how much do you know about the factors controlling body weight?

V: Um . . . it depends on what we eat and consume.

T: In part that is true, but both the control of eating and our energy expenditure is regulated by physiological mechanisms.

V: What do you mean? Do our genes regulate our weight?

T: Yes. This explains why it is difficult to change weight in the long term.

V: That's exactly what I've found.

T: A convenient way of representing body weight is body mass index, or BMI, which is the weight in kilograms divided by height in meters squared.

V: I know this measurement. My BMI is 21.4.

T: Exactly. A person is defined as normal weight when they have a BMI of between 18.5 and 24.9. So, according to this classification, you are . . .

V: I am normal weight . . . but I am a gymnast—I need to be very light to optimize my performance.

T: Where did you get this information?

V: My coach, and other athletes.

T: Most coaches and athletes believe that the leaner you are, the better you will perform. But the research tells a different story—the data indicates that losing too much fat may worsen sports performance.

V: Really?

T: Yes, an athlete achieves the best performance with an optimal nutritional state, a healthy diet, and suitable training. Leanness is not essential, and is often counterproductive. For example, looking at your performance over the years—how heavy were you when you got the best results?

V: I was the same weight I am now. But then my results worsened, and this was the reason my coach made me lose weight.

T: Have you considered that it was not your weight that led to a deterioration in your performance?

V: Well . . . it's possible. In reality, it isn't as if my normal performance worsened—other young gymnasts started competing alongside me and I lost my position in the rankings.

T: Very interesting. And when you lost weight by dieting and vomiting, did you improve your performance?

V: No, I completely failed the competition. I had no strength or concentration and I made a lot of mistakes.

[. . .]

V: What will happen to my weight at the end of the treatment?

T: It is difficult to say now. In most cases, patients do not change their weight, while some patients lose weight and others may gain a little. It is not possible to predict exactly what will happen to you.

V: I don't want to put on weight!

T: Well, in order to have better control of your weight, you need to get control over your eating, and this is the aim of the treatment. I suggest you postpone the decision about a specific weight range until your eating behavior is be stabilized.

V: I agree, but I do not want to gain weight.

T: The goal is to maintain a weight that requires nothing more than slight dietary restraint—as you know, strict dieting maintains preoccupations about food and eating and increases the risk of binge eating (shows Veronica the specific part of the formulation).

Setting Homework, Summarizing the Session,
and Arranging the Next Appointment

At the end of session 1, the therapist gave Veronica two homework assignments: (i) improving self-monitoring; and (ii) refraining from weighing herself at home. After that, he summarized the session, and they arranged the next appointment.

[. . .] Selected transcripts:

T: Veronica, let's summarize what we have done in this session. We started with in-session weighing and learned about your weight chart. We then reviewed your self-monitoring performance—we saw that you had done a great job and we discussed how to make it even better.

V: Yes, how to use the asterisks and how to record when I eat with friends.

T: Exactly. Then, we discussed your ambivalence about starting treatment, but we concluded that the best way to test your predictions about the consequences of stopping the extreme weight control behaviors is trying to change.

V: Yes.

T: We also discussed the need for leaving at least four weeks between interpretation of any changes in your weight, in addition to the risks of too frequent weight checking or weight avoidance. Then we discussed your weight, BMI, weight fluctuations, and the optimal weight for a sportswoman. Finally, we agreed that for the next appointment you should do your best to improve your self-monitoring and to endeavor not to weigh yourself at home.

Implementing the Rest of Stage One

Objectives

- Educating the patient about the eating problem.
- Establishing "regular eating."
- Addressing the patient's style of eating.
- Addressing purging.
- Addressing excessive exercising.
- Involving significant others.

Educating the Patient about the Eating Problem

Although Veronica was an athlete competing at a high level, she was poorly informed about the relationship between extreme and rigid dietary rules and binge eating, and the effects of vomiting on calorie absorption. To educate Veronica about her eating problem, the therapist provided her with a copy of *Overcoming Binge Eating* (Fairburn, 1995), a cognitive behavioral-oriented self-help book providing information about eating problems for not-underweight individuals. He encouraged her to read it, to put checks next to the sections that seemed to apply to her, crosses next to those that did not, and question marks alongside parts that were not clear; she was asked to do this for the next session, and to bring the book along, so that the therapist could help her review her thoughts and questions.

Establishing "Regular Eating"

Regular eating implies that patients should be eating three planned meals and two planned snacks a day, and avoid eating between meals and the snacks. Regular eating is the foundation on which the other changes are built. In patients like Veronica who binge eat, it usually produces a rapid reduction in the frequency of bulimic episodes, leaving only those that are termed "residual bingeing," which are addressed in Stage Three. The reduction of bulimic episodes reinforces the adherence of patients to the treatment, and is usually associated with an improvement in mood. It has been suggested (see Fairburn et al., 2008, pp. 75) that the reduction of the frequency of bulimic episodes is dependent on two main mechanisms, namely: (i) it reduces dietary restraint, in particular delayed eating; and (ii) it provides structure and control to the eating pattern.

[. . .] Selected transcripts:

> T: Veronica, a fundamental strategy for improving eating control is regular eating. It consists of eating three planned meals and two planned snacks every day, and not eating between these meals and snacks.

> V: But I don't know what I should be eating!

> T: For the moment, it is not important *what* you eat, only that you eat every three to four hours. In other words, your day should include a breakfast, a morning snack, lunch, an afternoon snack, and an evening meal. In addition, you should avoid eating between these meals and snacks. This new eating pattern should take precedence over other activities.

> V: But I can't eat during training!

> T: Don't you have any breaks during training?

V: Almost never. I only stop when the coach is explaining the exercise to me. It would be unthinkable to stop to eat. I would be sick, and, anyway, I don't even know if the coach would let me eat!

T: Let's address the two problems you just raised—first, that you have no breaks, and second, that you do not know what to eat. Do you think there are any other obstacles to your eating regularly?

V: Sure—if I ate so frequently I would put on a lot of weight.

T: Well, your monitoring records show that during the afternoon you tend to drink cappuccinos, tea, and eat candies. Do you think this behavior is helpful?

V: I can't avoid it. I need it. I know it's wrong . . . but is this why I can't lose weight?

T: Let's try to plan meals and snacks on the basis of your training schedule. Maybe you should consider eating very soon after you finish a workout. I also suggest you that you plan in advance what to eat. For example, if I call you at any time of the day, you should be able to tell me what you are having for the next meal.

V: Ok, I might have breakfast at seven, as I do now; a snack at ten, lunch at one, a snack at five in the afternoon, and dinner at eight. And what should I eat?

T: In this phase of the treatment, it is more important *when* you eat than what you eat. However, here is a statement by the American Dietetic Association on Nutrition and Sport Performance (Rodriguez, DiMarco, & Langley, 2009). Can we read some of their recommendations together?

V: Yes. Yes! I am very interested.

T: As you can see, the statement suggests that athletes should avoid skipping meals and allowing themselves to become overly hungry. They also recommend that during heavy training or doing multiple daily workouts, athletes may need to eat at least three meals and three snacks per day, and to drink a variety of fluids, especially water before, during, and after exercise.

V: That's similar to your advice.

T: They also state that a low energy intake will not let you sustain athletic training, and that athletes should not deprive themselves of their favorite foods or set unrealistic dietary rules or guidelines. Instead, dietary goals should be flexible and achievable, and similar to those recommended for the general population. The statement also emphasizes that athletes should remember that all foods can fit into a healthful lifestyle, and discourages labeling food as "good" or "bad."

V: . . . meaning that I shouldn't avoid carbs.

T: Yes, the statement says that carbohydrate restriction has been shown to be detrimental for athletic performance, and suggests that 60 percent of your calorie intake should come from carbs, such as whole grains, cereals, and legumes.

V: Can you give me a diet plan?

T: I don't think it is a good idea. As you see from your formulation, rigid dietary rules encourage binge eating. I suggest you read these guidelines and experiment a little. For example you might include vegetables and fruit with some carbs at every meal, and eat some protein in at least one of the main meals. Then, together we will assess how you feel, and whether this new way of eating is affecting your performance. Do you agree?

V: Ok, I'll try. I hope to succeed and I hope that eating in this way will help me to avoid binge eating but especially not to gain weight. But if I feel the urge to binge, what can I do?

T: Regular eating in this way will help you to reduce the urge. However, I suggest you prepare a response card where you write things you can say and do to help you overcome the urge to eat. Do you have any ideas?

V: I might say that if I binge I will train badly and . . .

T: Good. You might also say to yourself that the urge to eat is like a wave and that to get over it you have to ride it out. We call this strategy "urge surfing."

V: I like this suggestion!

T: Can you also think of anything to do that will allow you to move away from places where there is food and distract yourself from the urge to eat?

V: Erm . . . I might call a friend, take a walk, or listen to music.

T: Good. Write the things to say and to do on a memo card and keep it with you. If you have the urge to eat between your planned meals, take it out, read it, and try to apply the things to say and do at once.

V: Ok, I'll do it.

[. . .] Selected transcripts from regular eating review:

V: I skipped my afternoon snack. It's too difficult, and I'm too afraid to eat. If I start to eat I won't be able to stop and I'll binge, and I have to train.

T: I understand that it is difficult for you. Can we evaluate the pros and cons of having an afternoon snack?

V: Ok. The pros are, as suggested by the dietary guidelines for gymnasts, reducing tiredness, improving concentration, and decreasing the risk of binge eating. The cons are putting on weight, feeling fat, not digesting, and training badly because I feel full. The coach will not let me have a break and . . . I don't want to ask him to stop the training session because he might think that I'm lazy and do not want to train hard.

T: Let's analyze these pros and cons.

V: Maybe I should do an experiment to see if changing my way of eating makes me have these problems and put on weight. The possible advantages are interesting . . . the problem is that I am really afraid to change.

T: What do you think if we involve your coach to help you in this difficult change?

V: It might be useful.

T: If you agree, you might invite him to the next session so that we can address this issue together.

V: Ok. I'll ask him to come.

T: What should we discuss with him?

V: Um . . . we might explain to him the reason for having a snack break during training.

T: I agree. What do you think if we also explain to him the importance of regular eating and the main recommendations in the statement from the American Dietetic Association on Nutrition and Sport?

V: I agree.

Addressing the Patient's Style of Eating

The therapist also initiated steps to address Veronica's *style* of eating, in particular the absence of a formal lunch when she had afternoon training, suggesting that she avoid eating in the changing room and resorting to candies or cappuccinos during the day.

[. . .] Selected transcripts from regular eating review:

T: Veronica, a good strategy for improving control over eating is to eat in a formal way, sitting at a table. The meals should have an easily identifiable start and end.

V: It is not what I do for lunch when I have afternoon training.

T: I know . . . and often, as I can see from your monitoring records, you binge on these days. Do you think it is possible to eat these meals in a formal way?

V: I don't know. Maybe I could go to eat with the other gymnasts in a place close to the gym.

T: That is a good idea. And what about the candies and cappuccinos? I don't see them in this week's monitoring record.

V: I stopped eating candies and cut out several cappuccinos after including the afternoon snack in my diet.

Addressing Purging

Veronica had both compensatory (after objective bulimic episodes) and non-compensatory self-induced vomiting episodes (after subjective bulimic episodes). The therapist did not address the compensatory vomiting, as it was decreasing spontaneously as Veronica's eating habits improved. However, he did address non-compensatory purging directly, since this does not usually disappear with the remission of objective bulimic episodes, as it is a form of weight control, similar to dieting.

[. . .] Selected transcripts:

T: Veronica, I see from your monitoring records a single asterisk and that you sometimes vomit after eating a small amount of food. For example, here you vomited after eating three cookies.

V: Yes, I make myself sick to eliminate the excessive calorie intake when I feel that I eat something I shouldn't, as in this case.

T: This behavior is problematic. First, it makes no sense in terms of calorific balance to vomit to eliminate such a small amount of calories as there are in three cookies. Do you know how many calories these three cookies contained?

V: Yes, a total of 120 calories.

T: And how many calories in excess do you have to eat to increase your body weight by one kilogram?

V: I don't know.

T: About 7,000 calories.

V: Wow . . . So, it *is* nonsense.

T: Yes. In addition, the use of non-compensatory vomiting reinforces your unhealthy eating habits, and prevents the remission of your eating problem. I suggest you stop this behavior immediately. A good strategy is to write in the monitoring record in real time when you eat something unplanned, including the asterisks, and ride out the urge to vomit by applying the strategy of things to say and do that we have already discussed.

V: Ok, I'll try.

Addressing Excessive Exercising

In addition to her intense training regime, Veronica practiced 1.5 hours of jogging on Sundays, both to maintain her body in constant activity and to compensate for the perceived excessive calorie intake that unfailingly occurred every Saturday. She also spent extra time in the gym after her scheduled training.

[. . .] *Selected transcripts:*

> T: Veronica, I wish to discuss with you the pros and cons of jogging on Sunday and doing extra training during the week. Let's start with the pros.
>
> V: Well, the pros are that I keep my body active, and especially that I make up for my excesses of Saturday night.
>
> T: And the cons?
>
> V: Well, I don't know . . . sometimes I feel very tired, and I think it is probably a bad idea not to let my body rest for at least one day a week.
>
> T: Yes, you are right. Overtraining may cause fatigue and underperformance, often associated with frequent infections and depression, which can affect your training and competitive edge.
>
> V: I've had these problems in the past.
>
> T: Overtraining happens when there is a chronic state of insufficient recovery as a result of excessively prolonged and/or intensive exercise. Do you think that exercising beyond the training schedule might be having some negative effects on your eating problem?
>
> V: Well, I don't know. It keeps my mind focused on controlling my weight and eating.
>
> T: Yes. In addition, viewing exercise as an effective means of weight control tends to relax your rigid control on food intake, making you lose control.
>
> V: Yes, I agree.
>
> T: Ok. Why don't you try to interrupt any form of exercise that isn't in your training program and then see what effect this will have on your athletic performance and eating control?

V: Ok, I'll give it a shot.

T: And if you get the urge to exercise, you should use the "Things to say and do" card. You might also consider planning your Sundays in advance—think of something fun you would like to do that your excessive exercising has prevented you from doing in the past.

Involving Significant Others

As described above, after three weeks of treatment, Veronica and the therapist agreed to involve her coach in the treatment. An extra session was scheduled for this purpose after a regular one and was organized in the following way: (i) a therapist-led introduction explaining the aims of the session; (ii) Veronica's description of the treatment rationale and her progress so far; (iii) airing of the coach's questions and doubts; and (iv) a three-way discussion on how the coach might practically help Veronica to improve her way of eating.

[. . .] *Selected transcripts:*

T: Do you think it would be possible for Veronica to have a small snack break during the morning and afternoon training sessions?

C: I don't see any problem with that.

V: Really?

C: Yes. I understand that regular eating is essential for you to overcome your eating problem and, as a consequence, to improve your performance.

T: Very well. So I suggest planning the training session in such a way that Veronica can have a one-hour break to have both the time to eat a small snack and to digest it without negatively impacting her performance.

Stage Two (Weeks 5–6)

Objectives

- Conducting a joint review of progress.
- Identifying emerging barriers to change.
- Reviewing the personal formulation.
- Deciding whether to use the broad or focused form of CBT-E.
- Designing Stage Three.

Stage Two of CBT-E is a transitional stage planned in such a way as to introduce and prepare the maintaining mechanisms to address in Stage Three. The aims of this stage were to help Veronica reach a balanced evaluation of the progress achieved so far, and, at the same time, to improve her understanding of the obstacles to change and the main maintaining mechanisms that would be addressed in Stage Three. Veronica filled out the EDE-Q (Fairburn & Beglin, 2008) and CIA (Bohn & Fairburn, 2008) so that she could objectively assess with her therapist her improvement over the first four weeks of treatment. This assessment is vital because the degree of reduction in the frequency of binge eating and vomiting is the most significant predictor of treatment outcome.

Conducting a Joint Review of Progress

[. . .] Selected transcripts:

> T: Well, this is session nine and we have now begun Stage Two of the treatment. This is the right moment to review, not only the progress you have made, but also how you feel regarding the therapy. Do you feel satisfied with what you have achieved?

> V: Well . . . I feel a little better; however, I still binge sometimes, and I still feel exhausted during training.

> T: At this stage of treatment, residual bingeing is normal, as we still have not addressed several mechanisms maintaining your residual binges. However, I see from the EDE-Q that you have markedly reduced the frequency of bulimic episodes and vomiting. This is a very good start.

> V: Really?

> T: Yes. The data on this treatment indicates that a reduction in the number of bulimic episodes and vomiting is a potent predictor of a good treatment outcome.

> V: Good. This gives me some hope.

Identifying Emerging Barriers to Change

The second aim of Stage Two was to identify obstacles to treatment. This included an assessment of Veronica's attitude toward the treatment itself and the use of the procedures introduced in Stage One. This analysis showed that Veronica was actively involved in the treatment and had no particular difficulties in using the procedures of not weighing herself outside the sessions and eating regularly. However, during the course of Stage One, some of

Veronica's attitudes and behaviors in the sports domain led the therapist to suspect that her eating problem was compounded by a clinical perfectionism issue.

[. . .] Selected transcripts:

T: In some cases, successfully overcoming an eating problem can be hindered by the presence of clinical perfectionism. This is a term used to describe people that have tend to overvalue *achievement*, pursuing personally demanding standards in valued areas of life, such as sports performance.

V: But I am a gymnast! I need to pursue high standards in my field!

T: Of course! I'm not talking about your goal of winning competitions, rather the overdependence of your sense of self-worth on sporting prowess and meeting excessively demanding standards in training and competitions, despite the adverse consequences.

V: It's true. My self-evaluation is mainly dependent on how much I train and the results I attain in the competitions. But sports are my life. In this period I am down because my sports performance is poor.

T: I understand. Let's analyze in detail the main features of clinical perfectionism.

V: Ok.

T: Do you think that your standards in training are extremely high and inflexible?

V: Um . . . maybe . . . yes.

T: Do your colleagues put in as much effort as you do?

V: No, most of the gymnasts only follow the training schedule set by their coach . . . in fact, some of my fellow athletes have suggested I should train less and chill out. But you know, they are essentially my competitors and probably just get jealous if they see me improving my performance.

T: When they recommended that you train less and be more relaxed, did they refer to something in particular?

V: They were talking about my Sunday jogging and my extra training sessions in the gym to improve my sports performance.

T: Do you really think that these extra and extreme efforts are useful for improving your sports performance?

V: Um . . . I don't know. I had the eating problem, and maybe the deterioration in my performance depends on the vomiting . . . I don't know.

T: Ok. Does your coach know all the exercise you do in addition to the planned training?

V: He knows that I stay in the gym after the end of formal training, but he does not know that I jog on Sundays.

T: If he knew, would he think it's a good idea?

V: Erm . . . I don't think so.

T: Are you often concerned about your performance?

V: Yes. These concerns occupy most of my time.

T: Even when a competition is still a long way off?

V: My concerns are intensified when the competition is close, but they are also present during regular training.

T: Do you often check your performance?

V: I don't understand.

T: Sorry, I didn't explain myself properly. Performance checking means gauging how your performance is going.

V: Ah! Now I understand. Yes, after a routine I mentally go over my performance several times looking for mistakes. In addition, if I make a visible mistake I repeat the routine from the beginning.

T: Do you do any other type of other performance checking?

V: Umm . . . sometimes when I am alone in the gym I do the routine as if I was in a competition to check how ready I am.

T: Is your judgment of your athletic performance usually similar to that of your coach?

V: No, no. My coach is usually less strict than me.

[...]

T: It seems that you have clinical perfectionism expressed in two main domains: the achievement of extreme standards in gymnastics, and the control of shape, weight, and eating.

V: Yes, I agree, but I don't see the problem.

T: The clinical perfectionism is problematic because your efforts to meet the standards are so extreme that, instead of improving your performance, you deteriorate it.

V: Can you explain this concept better?

T: For example, following rigid and extreme dietary rules favors the development of binge eating and worsens your control over your weight. Not only that, but overtraining, i.e., doing such a lot of exercise that you exceed your recovery capacity, may lead to injury, stop you making progress, and lose strength and fitness. Remember also that if you get injured you won't be able to train.

V: Yes, it's true—it's what happened to me.

T: Also excessive body and performance checking is problematic. For instance, too frequent body checking amplifies the physical defects you perceive, increasing your body dissatisfaction and causing you to intensify your extreme weight control behaviors such as strict dietary rules, exercising, and vomiting. In the same way, too frequent performance checking selectively focuses on mistakes or goals that have not yet been achieved. The consequence is intensification of your concerns and the dissatisfaction with your performance, leading in turn to you intensifying your commitment and the intensity and duration of training.

V: I see—it's a vicious cycle.

Reviewing the Personal Formulation

Going over Veronica's progress and the obstacles to treatment also provided an occasion to review her personal formulation, to which was added her clinical perfectionism and its mode of interaction with her eating problem.

Deciding Whether to Use the Broad or Focused Form of CBT-E

Veronica and the therapist agreed to address clinical perfectionism in an additional Stage Three module, and as a consequence, that the broad form of CBT-E would be appropriate.

Designing Stage Three

Stage Three is the central part of the treatment in that it addresses the key maintenance mechanisms behind the patient's eating problem. In this case, the therapist and Veronica decided that the following main maintenance mechanisms would need to be addressed: her overvaluation of shape and weight together with her clinical perfectionism, her dietary restraint, and the events and moods influencing her eating. The therapist suggested that Stage Three be commenced by tackling her overvaluation of shape and weight, as this is usually a particularly time-consuming process. They also agreed that after one week, the procedures and strategies Veronica would use to address dietary restraint would be introduced, and subsequently those for dealing with events and moods influencing eating.

Stage Three (Weeks 7–14)

Objectives

- Addressing the overvaluation of shape and weight and clinical perfectionism.
- Addressing dietary restraint.
- Addressing events and associated mood changes.
- Learning to control the eating problem mindset.

Addressing the Overvaluation of Shape and Weight and Clinical Perfectionism

Veronica's overvaluation of shape and weight and clinical perfectionism were addressed throughout the entire course of Stage Three. The procedures and strategies used to tackle these two clinical features were the following: (i) identifying the overvaluation and its consequences; (ii) promoting the importance of other domains of self-evaluation; (iii) addressing body shape and performance checking; and (iv) addressing feeling fat.

[. . .] Selected transcripts — identifying the overvaluation and its consequences:

> T: Now I suggest we discuss a complex and abstract topic: how people evaluate themselves.

V: Go on. . . .

T: Generally, people judge themselves on the basis of various factors in various areas of life. For example, how their relations with others, like their parents, spouse, or children, if they have any, are going. Other common domains of self-evaluation are performance at work or school or sports, and personal interests. Usually, if things are going well in the areas of life a person uses to judge their self-worth, they feel good. Accordingly, if things go badly they tend to feel bad.

V: That's clear.

T: To identify the life domains that are important for us, we must pay attention to the intensity and the duration of our feeling bad when things don't go well in that domain.

V: Are you referring to my reaction when my sports performance goes badly?

T: Yes, but also to your reaction when you have a binge eating episode or a slight increase in body weight.

V: Um . . . maybe it is so.

T: A good procedure to help us understand our self-evaluation system is to draw a pie chart. The pie chart in general represents our self-worth as a whole, and the various slices of the pie represent the areas of the life that are important for us—the bigger the slice, the more importance we give to it. Will you draw your own pie chart now? Remember that to estimate the proportion of the pie occupied by the slice, you will have to think about the intensity and duration of your negative reaction when things go badly in that specific area of your life.

V: Ok, I'll try (Veronica draws her pie chart on a piece of paper).

T: Veronica, looking at your pie chart, what conclusions can you draw?

V: Well . . . the slices representing gymnastics and my body are the biggest. Maybe the slice representing my shape and weight is too big, but that one really does show how much importance I give to gymnastics. However, my shape and weight is also important because I must be light.

T: Ok. For homework, I'd like to ask you to review your pie chart every day, and to redraw it on the back of your monitoring records, changing the dimensions of the slices on the basis of your behavior and experiences.

V: Ok.

[. . .]

T: Did you do the pie chart homework?

V: Yes, I did.

T: Did you encounter any difficulties?

V: No. However, the last pie chart is very similar to those I drew in the previous session.

T: Well, I suggest we analyze the consequences of having a pie chart like this. What do you think?

V: Umm . . . I don't know. Maybe if things go badly in one of these areas I feel bad.

T: Yes. This is the first problem. It is very risky for you to base your self-esteem on only one or two domains—it's like putting all your eggs in one basket—if things go wrong in these areas, your sense of self-worth inevitably collapses.

V: You are right, but I am an athlete. It is normal for me to self-evaluate on the basis of the results I achieve.

T: It is in part true. However, try to think ahead, to the point in your life when you will no longer be able to have a sports career.

V: Don't say that! I'm terrified about this happening. I will just be a normal person.

T: Isn't this a form of self-evaluation?

V: Um . . . maybe so.

T: Do you see any other risks?

V: Well, it is clear that this system limits the time I spend with my friends.

T: Yes, I agree. We term this effect "marginalization" of other important areas of life, such as maintaining friendships, having a family, or other interests. All these areas are usually very important for developing a stable and balanced system of self-evaluation.

V: I agree. I often feel alone.

T: Another problem I see in your pie chart is that the areas of gymnastics and shape and weight are very problematic.

V: Why?

T: In some areas, such as "sports" or "body shape," it is impossible to get constant success. For example, you have won several competitions, but you are not yet satisfied. You also have an excellent figure, but you are still extremely dissatisfied with it because you think you are not thin enough.

V: Yes, That's true.

T: I see that you are sad.

V: I am a little confused.

T: Don't worry—discussion of this issue often generates negative reactions. But it can be very useful for your future.

V: Yes, I understand, but how can I get out of this situation?

At this point the therapist draws a broad formulation for Veronica, in which the main maintenance mechanisms of her overvaluation of shape, weight, achievement, and sports success are included (see figure 9.3). This broad formulation helped the therapist to explain that there are two main strategies for developing a pie chart with more slices without one being too predominant. To increase the *number* of slices, efforts need to be made in other areas of the life (e.g., taking up a new hobby), and to decrease the *dimension* of the two predominant slices, in this case to reduce the importance Veronica attributed to her shape, weight, and sporting achievement, it will be necessary to address the main expressions that maintain this state of mind (i.e., shape checking and avoidance, performance checking, feeling fat, and dietary restraint).

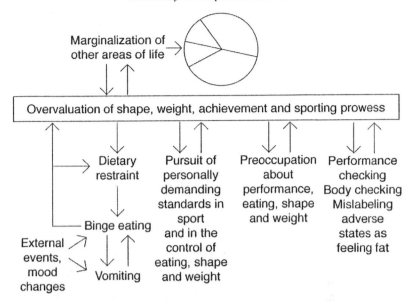

Figure 9.3. **Veronica's Revised and Extended Formulation**

[. . .] Selected transcripts—promoting the importance of other domains of self-evaluation:

T: A key strategy for reducing perfectionism and the overvaluation of shape and weight is promoting the importance of other domains of self-evaluation.

V: I understand the theory, but in practice it is not easy. For many years I have dedicated most of my time and energy to pursuing high gymnastic standards. I really wouldn't know what else to do.

T: I understand your difficulties. However, you might consider any activities or interests that you have always wished to cultivate but you never got around to, or, if you are short of ideas, why not try something that your teammates do in their free time? To overcome your overvaluation of achievement and sports success, it is advisable that the activities are not performance focused, but done just for fun.

V: Er . . . I would like to dedicate more time to photography. It has always been a passion of mine, but I have never done it seriously. I'd also like to dedicate more time to watching movies, concerts, and plays.

T: Well, why don't you try to find a photography course and plan your week so that you have time to see some movies or shows that you are interested in? Maybe with some friends?

V: Yes, it's a good idea.

T: I'd also advise you to do other things that are sometimes seen as "a waste of time," for example, reading a book or a magazine, listening to music, or contacting friends.

V: Ok. I'd like to do all these things.

T: Good. Try to record any of these activities you do in the last column of your monitoring record, so that next session we can go over any obstacles you may meet and look for solutions. If you encounter any difficulties, you should use the proactive problem-solving procedures we discussed.

V: Ok.

At the same time as encouraging Veronica to adopt other domains of self-evaluation, the therapist also explained the main expressions of her overvaluation of shape and weight, and of her clinical perfectionism. The first step was to educate her on the subject of body and performance checking, giving her several examples. He then asked Veronica to record these behaviors in real time for two twenty-four-hour periods.

[. . .] Selected transcripts—addressing body checking:

T: Veronica, in the last session we discussed the role of body checking in maintaining your eating problem and I asked you to record any instances you noticed in the last column of your monitoring records for two periods of twenty-four hours. Did you encounter any difficulties in doing this homework?

V: It was complicated to record the various episodes of body checking in real time. However, I tried to do my best.

T: Very good. Do you have any comments about your monitoring?

V: Yes, I do much more body checking than I'd thought.

T: Can we review your monitoring records? We agreed to record a training day and a rest day.

V: Yes.

T: Let's take a look at the training day. I see that you looked at yourself in the mirror immediately after you woke up.

V: Yes, I always do it.

T: Which part of your body did you scrutinize?

V: My stomach and legs.

T: Why do you check your stomach and legs?

V: To check if my stomach is flat, and if my legs are toned.

T: What was the effect of the checking on your mood?

V: Generally, in the morning, it is not too bad . . . I am never satisfied, but it is the moment of the day when I am happiest with my appearance.

T: I also see that you checked your body in the mirror before and after training.

V: Yes, I do that all the time, too.

T: On these occasions, how did you feel after checking your body?

V: I felt very fat because I had eaten badly.

T: What do you mean by eating badly?

V: I had cookies for breakfast.

T: I see that you put the asterisk on your monitoring record.

V: Yes, because I ate too many cookies.

T: So, if I understand correctly, you were thinking about the breakfast you had eaten when you checked your body in the mirror?

V: Yes.

T: Which mirror did you use to check your body?

V: The one in the changing room at the gym.

T: Did you look at any specific part of your body?

V: As usual, I checked my stomach and legs.

T: Do you ever look at any other part of your body?

V: No, only my stomach and legs.

T: Did you also look at your body in the mirror after training?

V: Yes, I did.

T: And on this occasion, how did you feel?

V: A little better than before, but I had trained very hard.

T: In your opinion, what had changed with respect to the previous time you checked your body in the mirror?

V: I had trained very hard.

T: Then, I see, you had a bingeing episode in the evening.

V: Yes, I was thinking about all the food I had eaten during the day . . . I felt so big, and thought that there was nothing else I could do, apart from bingeing and vomiting.

T: Ok. That is clear. Let's have a look in detail at what happened.

V: Ok.

T: At breakfast you checked your body and you felt ok. Then, you checked your body before training and you felt worse, because you had eaten too many cookies at breakfast. Finally, you felt better after the training because you trained hard.

V: Yes, that's how it went.

T: Do you really think that the shape of your body can change so rapidly, and that eating some cookies or doing some training has an immediate effect on the shape of your stomach and legs?

V: Effectively, described in this way, it seems absurd.

T: In addition, when you look at your body in the mirror you only check your stomach and legs. In your opinion, does this way of observing your body give you an objective view?

V: I don't know.

T: Generally, what we see in the mirror depends on the way we look at our body. In other words we find what we seek.

V: In what sense?

T: For example, if you only look at your stomach and legs in detail and with a critical attitude, you are bound to amplify your perception of defects. You also never look at your entire body, and you do not check the parts of the body you like. In addition, sometimes you check your body when you are in a negative frame of mind, and this seems to worsen your perception of your body shape.

V: I agree. So the conclusion is that I must pay attention to how I use the mirror.

The therapist and Veronica then established collaboratively how to use the mirror in a *functional* way. This included *when* (e.g., before going out and not before or after training), *how* (e.g., looking at the entire body, not focusing attention on specific parts, and noticing the surrounding environment to get a more accurate idea of physical proportion), *why* (e.g., observing if clothes are on straight), *where* (e.g., using only one mirror at home and not checking the body in other reflective surfaces such as shop windows or, in this case, the changing room mirror). They also agreed that Veronica would attempt to refrain from all the other forms of shape checking, for example, measuring the circumference of her legs or pinching the subcutaneous fat. Finally the therapist asked Veronica to record all the episodes of dysfunctional body checking and their effects in her monitoring record in real time.

[. . .] Selected transcripts — addressing body checking:

T: Veronica, how has your management of mirror checking been going?

V: It's hard, but I'm working on it.

T: What difficulties did you encounter?

V: Sometimes I have the impulse to look at my body in the mirror, but I try to think back to what we discussed about healthy mirror use.

T: It might also be useful for you to write the reason for not doing mirror checking on a memo card so you can consult it when you have the impulse to do it.

V: Ok.

T: What could you write?

V: Umm . . . I could write that it's not worth mirror checking because it increases my body dissatisfaction and it worsens my mood.

T: Good . . . and have you managed to use the mirror in a functional way?

V: I am doing my best to look at my entire body and the surrounding environment. It's a different way of looking at myself. I have to say that sometimes I haven't even seen my body as bad. But I will not declare victory too soon.

T: I understand your prudence. Nevertheless, I predict that if you continue to use the mirror in this positive way, your body dissatisfaction will progressively decrease.

The therapist and Veronica, after addressing the shape checking, started to tackle her feeling of being fat. The therapist informed Veronica that feeling fat is often the consequence of mislabeling negative mood states such as sadness, or aversive physical states like feeling full or bloated, and can be brought on by body checking. He invited Veronica to record episodes when she had an intense feeling of being fat in real time in the last column of her monitoring record, and also to write down any triggers she noticed.

[. . .] Selected transcripts—addressing feeling fat:

T: Veronica, did you record any instances of feeling fat?

V: Yes I did. Here are my monitoring records.

T: What made you feel that way?

V: I was concerned about eating because I was planning to have a plate of pasta for lunch: a food that I generally avoid eating. I got anxious and immediately felt fat.

T: What does this suggest to you?

V: That it was my anxiety that led me to feel fat.

T: Yes . . . otherwise it is not understandable why you felt fat before eating.

V: Yes. It's absurd.

T: I see that the feeling of being fat increased in the afternoon.

V: Yes, after eating the pasta; I could not resist looking at the shape of my stomach in the mirror, and this was the consequence.

T: What lesson have you learned from this analysis?

V: Body checking intensifies my feeling fat.

T: Very good. Today we have learned that when you feel fat there is always something else behind it, and that feeling fat is not the same thing as being fat.

As very similar psychological mechanisms were involved, the therapist and Veronica addressed the clinical perfectionism at the same time as the over-valuation of shape and weight.

[. . .] Selected transcripts—addressing clinical perfectionism:

T: Perfectionism, like your eating problem, is maintained by some specific behaviors.

V: Are you referring to performance checking?

T: Yes. Performance checking increases dissatisfaction with performance and, in some cases, may impair training and also worsen performance. In the end, it tends to reinforce negative self-evaluation.

V: The mechanism is quite similar to that of body checking.

T: You are right. Do you agree to record your performance checking and the efforts you make over and above what is set for you by the coach to improve your performance?

V: I agree. For me improving performance is vital.

The monitoring record showed that Veronica used the following performance checking behaviors: repeating an exercise over and over; rehearsing the exercise in the mind focusing only on the mistakes; and watching teammates' routines, focusing only on the parts they did well. Veronica identified the following excessive efforts: doing extra training for one and a half hours after the planned session; doing sit-ups at home after training; and running on Sundays.

[. . .] Selected transcripts—addressing clinical perfectionism:

T: Veronica, did you consider the negative effects of making excessive efforts to improve your sports performance?

V: I have always thought that to improve my sports results I must train in this way.

T: Did your results improve over the last year?

V: No. They got worse.

T: I think we have to analyze this aspect in detail, perhaps using a sportsman as an example.

V: Ok.

T: A marathon runner has to plan his training for the next Olympic marathon. He has two options. The first is to train every day with a gradual increase in long-distance mileage without any days of rest. The second is to train by alternating long-distance running, speed work, and periods of recovery. In your opinion, which option is the best?

V: I understand what you are getting at. I would say the second option.

T: Why?

V: Because it includes period of training and recovery so that the marathon runner will be less tired.

T: I agree. The negative consequences of excessive efforts in training are tiredness and deterioration in performance. It also increases the risk of injuries. A perfectionist athlete usually reacts to the worsening of performance by self-criticism, bringing about negative emotions.

V: Yes. This is what happens to me.

T: It seems that your self-criticism leads to two negative consequences. The first is increasing your efforts in training, because you attribute your poor competitive performance to insufficient training rather than overtraining. The second is binge eating to modulate the negative emotions associated with your failure to achieve your performance goals. In this case it is evident how the perfectionism and the eating problem interact.

V: Yes. That's right. I often get home very frustrated with my poor performance and I binge to comfort myself.

T: How do you suggest you could address your excessive training efforts?

V: Umm . . . Maybe I should stick to my coach's training plan, without doing any more—but I am afraid to do less exercise!

T: I can imagine. However, I predict that, like what happened with the regular eating, you will be very frightened at first, but then your fear will decrease when you realize that your performance will not be worsened and might even improve.

V: Ok. I want to try.

[. . .]

T: You reported on the monitoring record that you became very upset during an exercise.

V: Yes. I lost my balance when I landed on the mat. I repeated the exercise but it kept getting worse.

T: Did you get angry?

V: Yes . . . very.

T: Did you judge yourself on the entire routine?

V: No, only the last part when I lost my balance.

T: This way of judging your performance is termed "selective attention" meaning that you only focus on the mistakes.

V: I understand; like my selective body checking.

T: Selective attention increases performance dissatisfaction because it focuses the attention only on the part of the exercise that went wrong and triggers self-critical thoughts.

V: Yes, this often happens to me.

T: What is your reaction to these self-critical thoughts?

V: I continue to rehearse the exercise.

T: Even if you are tired?

V: Yes.

T: And what is the outcome?

V: Sometimes I complete the exercise well, but other times I continue to make mistakes and I finish my training completely exhausted and depressed.

T: It is like a patient of mine with a perfectionism expressed in the "study" domain who would not allow himself to move on to the following paragraph until he had memorized the first one perfectly. To do this, he reread the paragraph over and over until, exhausted, he gave up and decided to close the book. With this method he very often did not complete reading the entire chapter.

V: This also happens to me—I rehearse a part of my routine repeatedly, and if it doesn't go according to plan I stop training.

T: This is a behavior associated with perfectionism termed "excessive performance checking."

V: Yes, I understand . . . but how can I stop this negative behavior?

T: I suggest you do this homework assignment: after every routine, write both the parts you do well and those with mistakes in the last column of your monitoring record. Then, give yourself a score from zero to ten for the *entire* performance, where zero is a routine full of mistakes, and ten one without any. I also suggest you involve your coach in this exercise, asking him to score your performance from zero to ten.

V: I think that is a very good idea. In this way I can understand if the way I judge my performance is too severe.

T: Then, if your coach agrees, you might get him to video your routine so that you can get a more objective view of your performance.

V: Ok.

Addressing Dietary Restraint

Extreme and rigid dietary rules played a central role in maintaining Veronica's binge eating episodes and concerns over eating. To address the dietary rules, the therapist adopted the following procedures: (i) helping Veronica to see the dietary restraint as a problem; (ii) educating her on dietary restraint; and (iii) suggesting to her some strategies for identifying and addressing her dietary rules, and for reacting functionally should she break them.

[. . .] Selected transcripts:

T: In Stage One and Two we addressed regular eating, that is, eating three meals and two snacks and not eating between meals. You also made efforts to eat normal portions of food.

V: Yes.

T: Now we should address your residual dietary rules.

V: Do you think I am eating too much? My weight is stable.

T: The problem is not the calorie intake, but the rigid and extreme rules you apply to control eating. We call this dietary restraint. Do you have this problem?

V: Yes . . . I am still very strict with myself, and I restrict my diet. However my weight is stable, and I think that if I relax my eating control I will gain weight.

T: Your weight is stable because you alternate undereating with binge eating. Doing so, although you vomit after every bulimic episode, your calorie intake matches your energy expenditure.

V: Yes, I know . . . with vomiting I eliminate only a part of the calories ingested.

T: Why is it crucial to address dietary restraint to overcome the eating problem?

V: Because I will be never free.

T: What would it mean to be free?

V: Er . . . for example, not thinking constantly about eating or avoiding all the food that makes me fat.

T: Do you think that these concerns might interfere with your life in general?

V: I think so. Several times I have bowed out of social occasions because I wouldn't be able to stick to my dietary rules.

T: Well, in addition, extreme and rigid dietary rules contribute to maintain your bulimic episodes. Do you have any idea why?

V: Sure! When I eat a food I should avoid, I lose control and binge.

T: Right! Avoiding some foods is an eating problem maintenance mechanism. Another mechanism is adopting extreme and rigid dietary rules, such as never eating carbs for dinner. These rules, as they are so strict and excessive, are extremely difficult to follow, and sooner or later it is inevitable that you will break them. Then, when you break a dietary rule you give up eating control completely and binge.

V: Yes, I recognize this mechanism. I oblige myself never to eat carbs for dinner. But I see a piece of bread on the table and I can't resist. I eat it without thinking, and then I immediately feel fat and binge.

T: It is clear that these types of dietary rules prevent you from stopping bingeing. So the first step is to identify all your dietary rules. Can we take a look at your monitoring records?

V: . . . on this occasion I had lunch at my grandmother's house. She cooked pasta with a lot of olive oil, as usual. The bread was on the table and I lost control . . . I ate all the food she had prepared, including a cake. Then, when I got home I continued to eat.

T: What was the dietary rule you broke?

V: Not eating bread and pasta at the same meal. Is this not a correct way of controlling weight?

T: This rule is a problem because is very strict. If you break it, as happened here, you lose control and you binge, and then you try to eliminate the calories ingested by vomiting.

Then the therapist suggested Veronica do a homework assignment, identifying the residual dietary rules, recording them on the monitoring record, together with the probable consequences of breaking them. The subsequent sessions were focused on helping Veronica to address the dietary rules identified, and evaluating the consequences of breaking them. In addition, the therapist asked to her to identify all the foods she avoided for fear of gaining weight or triggering a binge. He then suggested that she divide the avoided foods into four groups, ranked one to four on the basis of the degree of fear they provoked, and then to gradually introduce them to her diet, starting with the least frightening foods in group one. Veronica was also instructed to write the word NEW in her monitoring record next to every previously avoided food introduced to her diet.

[. . .] Selected transcripts:

V: I have been eating five cookies with milk for breakfast all week, but yesterday I ate seven . . . I tried to resist because I can't train after a binge, but I lost control. I drank a lot of milk and I ate the entire box of cookies. Why has this happened to me, since I had already been eating the cookies for a week? I was not avoiding them.

T: Well, it is clear that this binge was not triggered by the avoidance of a food. Can we analyze this interesting event? How do you prepare the cookies to eat for breakfast?

V: I take them one at a time from the box and count to five.

T: Do you do this every morning?

V: Yes, every morning I eat five cookies.

T: Why just five cookies?

V: Because it is the right dose.

T: Why do you have to eat the same number of cookies every morning?

V: Because I am sure that I am eating the right number of calories and I know I won't eat too much.

T: Don't you think that this is too rigid a dietary rule?

V: Yes, I know . . . but what can I do?

T: First of all, you might try to eat a different number of cookies every morning.

V: That's impossible! For example, if I ate seven cookies I'd feel guilty . . . it would be too much.

T: I suggest that, until you learn that eating a few extra cookies has no effect on your weight, you put three folded up slips of paper with three different numbers representing the number of cookies to eat in a jar. Then, before breakfast you might take one note at random and eat the number of cookies written on the paper. You should also remember that to gain one kilogram you have to eat 7,000 calories more than those you usually consume, and that two cookies have no more than 60 to 80 calories.

V: Yes, you are right, and I like the idea of the random selection. It will allow me to eat more cookies without feeling guilty and losing control.

Addressing Events and Associated Mood Changes

Veronica's eating habits were also influenced by external events, in particular her sports performance, and the associated mood changes. This association became more evident with the progressive reduction of dietary restraint. When Veronica had negative emotions she binged, both to distract herself from the concerns about her sports performance and to modulate the negative emotions she experienced. To address this maintenance mechanism the therapist showed Veronica how to use two procedures. The first was proactive problem solving to address the events that may trigger mood changes before/ as they occur. The second was the use of functional methods to modulate mood and to cope with the change of mood without resorting to bingeing.

[. . .] Selected transcripts:

T: Veronica, last session we discussed how to use problem solving in a proactive way to deal with the events that might influence your eating. I also suggested you read the section of the book *Overcoming Binge Eating* (Fairburn, 1995) that describes the application of this procedure. Did you use it?

V: Yes, I did a couple of times to address my performance checking, which, as you know, focuses my attention on the mistakes, making me sad and angry with myself . . . two negative emotions that trigger a binge.

T: Did you write the problem-solving steps in your monitoring record?

V: Yes, I did. Here is the day.

T: I see that you chose the solution of checking the performance of an exercise only twice and then passing on to another exercise. Did it work?

V: Yes, it was useful. I did not develop negative emotions and I did not binge.

[...]

V: Last night I was a little down and tired.

T: Did you apply any strategies for addressing changes of mood?

V: As we discussed in the last sessions, as soon as I noticed a change in my mood, I went away from the kitchen and into the living room. Then I said to myself that it is just an emotion and that I am able to manage my mood changes without bingeing. I took a warm bath and relaxed. Then I read a book and went to sleep. Other times on occasions like this I binged, but yesterday I maintained control. I am proud of this.

T: Very good. Try to apply these strategies every time you notice a change of mood.

The Effects of These and Other Cognitive Behavioral Interventions

The procedures and strategies applied in the treatment produced a progressive erosion of the principal expressions of Veronica's overvaluation of shape and weight and eating control (i.e., body checking and avoidance, feeling fat, dietary restraint, excessive exercising, binge eating, and vomiting), and athletic performance (i.e., excessive efforts, performance checking). This effect was enhanced by her increasing the importance of other domains for her self-evaluation and addressing the change of eating associated to events and mood changes.

[...] Selected transcripts:

V: I feel like a totally different person, like I've been reborn. It's as if I had been wearing a mask for the last few years and now I've taken it away. I feel that I can perform better in what I need to do without the anxiety and fear that I used to feel. I feel really light, not only physically, but also emotionally. When I see my body, I can't say that I like it, but I see it in a more detached way. The most important thing is that I feel liberated. When I go to train I don't have that sense of oppression and sadness that characterized recent years. I go to the gym with more enthusiasm and I find it pleasurable to train. In a certain sense, it's as if I have returned to the same enthusiasm that I had when I started doing gymnastics.

Exploring the Origin of the Excessive Overvaluation

Toward the end of Stage Three, the therapist explored with Veronica the potential origin of her overvaluation of shape and weight. They concluded that doing competitive gymnastics, the need to have a thin and toned body, and her perfectionism might have been potential risk factors involved in the development of her eating problem, while critical comments from her coach regarding her shape and weight, the group weigh-ins in the gym and associated negative moods, her lower back pain, and her dissatisfaction with her athletic performance may have triggered its onset. Finally, they decided that her eating problem was maintained initially by the positive feeling of being in control and by the positive comments from the coach, associated with the use of dieting and other extreme weight control behaviors, and later by the maintenance mechanisms described in her extended formulation.

This analysis helped her to understand how the eating problem had developed and was reinforced, helping her to feel less guilty, and to normalize her experiences. In addition, the analysis helped her to understand the self-perpetuating nature of her eating problem and that its positive functions perceived in the first part of its development had vanished by the end.

Learning to Control the Eating Problem Mindset

Toward the end of Stage Three Veronica experienced prolonged periods without concerns about shape, weight, and eating control, and she had a mindset compatible with the situation she faced. For example, when she was out with friends on a Saturday night, she was not thinking about what to eat or not to eat or her shape and weight. In this stage, the therapist helped Veronica to control the eating problem mindset by introducing three main strategies to her: (i) identifying the events triggering the eating problem mindset; (ii) recognizing the first signs of the eating problem mindset; (iii) decentering from the eating problem mindset.

[. . .] Selected transcripts:

T: Did you think about the events that might reactivate your eating problem mindset?

V: Yes, I did. There are many possible events.

T: Can you give me some examples?

V: Some are related to my eating and weight, for example, bingeing or my body weight changing. Others are related to my sports performance, for example, getting criticized by my coach or not winning a competition. Others are related to my emotions and interpersonal relationships—for example, arguing with a friend.

T: Very good. I suggest that you add to this list any event that might make you restrict your diet, for reasons other than losing weight—for example, having to reduce food intake during an illness.

V: Yes, I agree.

T: It is important to pre-empt these events using proactive problem solving.

V: I use this procedure a lot and it works.

T: However, sometimes you can't prevent the events and the reactivation of your eating problem mindset. In these cases you need to recognize the first signs of its reactivation. Have you noticed what the first signs of reactivation of your eating problem mindset are?

V: Er . . . maybe doing body checking in the mirror and restricting my diet . . . or having a binge . . . or increasing the time dedicated to training.

T: Good. In these cases, or even better, when it *occurs* to you to restrict your diet or take measures to control your weight, you should try to decenter immediately from your eating problem mindset by doing exactly the opposite.

V: What do you mean "doing the opposite"?

T: I mean, for example, instead of dieting, eat regularly.

V: I understand.

T: The key strategy is to decenter immediately from the mindset. Otherwise the mechanisms maintaining the eating problem kick into action again and it becomes very difficult to shut them off.

Stage Four (Weeks 15–20)

Objectives

• Addressing concerns about the end of the treatment.

- Phasing out treatment procedures.
- Ensuring that progress is maintained.
- Minimizing the risk of relapse in the long term.

Stage Four includes three sessions every two weeks (sessions 18, 19, and 20). The structure of the sessions is similar to that in the previous ones, but the focus is more oriented toward the future than the present.

Addressing Concerns about the End of the Treatment

[. . .] Selected transcripts:

T: Veronica, are you worried about finishing your treatment?

V: On the one hand yes, but on the other I am happy, particularly considering the results I have achieved.

T: You have to remember that even if the therapy has ended, your progress will continue if you continue to apply the procedures and strategies you have learned.

V: I hope so.

T: I have seen lots of patients continue to improve after the treatment ends. In particular, when I see them again after twenty weeks, they report a progressive reduction in concerns about shape and weight.

V: That's comforting. I hope it will also happen to me.

T: Even though it might seem strange, it will not be possible to see how much you have improved without interrupting the treatment—there comes a time when every novice swimmer has to take the armbands off. This is the right moment for you to start applying all the things you have learned without my help.

V: I agree.

T: However, in twenty weeks' time we will have a review session to see how you are getting on and discuss any problems you had to face during that period.

Phasing Out Treatment Procedures

In session 18, the therapist asked Veronica to stop self-monitoring, both because it is inappropriate to use this tool indefinitely, and to see the effect of suspending self-monitoring while she was still in treatment. Veronica was relieved to stop monitoring, and its interruption did not produce any negative reaction. In session 18 the therapist also suspended the in-session weighing, and suggested to Veronica that she check her weight at home once a week on a specific day, and to continue filling out her weight chart.

Ensuring That Progress Is Maintained

[. . .] Selected transcripts:

> T: Veronica, which residual maintenance factors do you think are necessary to address without my help over the next twenty weeks?
>
> V: Er . . . I don't know.
>
> T: Well, to help you decide, let's make a list of the problems we addressed during the treatment. Let's start with dietary restraint.
>
> V: Ok. I introduced several avoided foods, like bread and pasta, but I am still avoiding sweets. I should them include in my diet.
>
> T: Good. And what about your overvaluation of shape and weight?
>
> V: Now I feel ok about my body. However, I will do my best to maintain other interests and not focus only on my sports performance and body. I also have to make sure I don't compare my body or performance with that of my teammates and that I don't focus on my stomach and legs when I look at myself in the mirror.
>
> T: And when you feel fat?
>
> V: I will try to understand what triggered this sensation.
>
> T: Very good. And what about the residual binges?
>
> V: Luckily I haven't binged in a long time.
>
> T: Do you remember how to address residual binges?
>
> V: Yes I do. I should consider them an interesting phenomenon from which I can learn the reasons that triggered them.

T And then?

V: Umm . . . maybe I should apply problem solving to prevent other binges?

T: Very good. Do you remember the principal triggers involved in your residual binges?

V: Yes, I do. When I break a dietary rule or when I have a change in mood.

T: Which strategies should you apply to address these triggers?

V: First of all I have to follow flexible dietary guidelines. Second, when I notice a mood change I have to go away from food, accept the emotion, and do something to distract myself.

T: Good. Finally, I advise you to practice identifying the early signs of the eating problem mindset activation and decentering from it by doing the opposite.

V: Yes, I will.

Minimizing the Risk of Relapse in the Long Term

Minimizing the risk of relapse in the long term is the key intervention of Stage Four. Textbox 9.3 shows the Veronica's maintenance plan, in which she included both the problems that she had to focus on over the following twenty weeks and the principal procedures and strategies she should use to prevent long-term relapse.

TEXTBOX 9.3. VERONICA'S MAINTENANCE PLAN

Problems which I have to focus on over the next twenty weeks

Dietary restraint

- I will not avoid carbs, and I will also try to introduce sweets, which I am still avoiding

---

Excessive and compulsive exercising

- I will avoid residual excessive training, and I will follow the training program laid out by my coach

Weight maintenance

- I will continue to check my weight once a week on Mondays
- I will try to maintain my weight between 42.5 and 45.5 kg
- If my weight falls below 42.5 kg on two consecutive readings I will contact my outpatient therapist

Concerns about shape and weight

- I will address the residual mirror and comparison body checking (with my teammates)
- If I feel fat, I will try to identify the triggers and label them
- I will work to increase the time dedicated to life interests other than gymnastics and body control

Strategies to minimize the risk of setbacks

- I will avoid dieting, and especially carb avoidance
- I will avoid dysfunctional body checking
- I will avoid excessive sports performance checking
- I will avoid making excessive efforts to improve my athletic performance
- I will use proactive problem solving to address the problems that may trigger binge eating
- I will try to accept my changes in mood and to modulate my mood without bingeing. In these circumstances I will listen to some music, read a book, or take a warm bath

Circumstances that might increase the risk of setbacks

- Poor sports performance
- Sporting injuries
- Interpersonal problems
- Weight gain
- Negative mood

Early warning signs of a lapse

- Avoiding carbs
- Having a binge
- Restarting body checking
- Avoiding weighing
- Restarting excessive exercising

Dealing with triggers and setbacks

- I will identify triggers
- I will prevent triggers with proactive problem solving
- I will label setbacks as a lapse and not a relapse
- If I have a setback I will immediately get back on track and I will do the opposite of what my eating problem mindset makes me want to do

Follow-Up

During the follow-up period Veronica maintained her weight, adopting healthy dietary guidelines in a flexible way. She reported no occurrence of bulimic episodes, self-induced vomiting, excessive exercising, or excessive preoccupations with her shape and weight. Although she did not reach the results she had before her eating problem onset, her sports performance improved. Finally, she started dating a fellow sportsman.

Table 9.1 shows her clinical state during the course of treatment, and at twenty- and forty-week follow-up sessions.

Table 9.1. Veronica's clinical status before outpatient CBT-E, after outpatient CBT-E, and at twenty- and forty-week follow-ups

	Before treatment	After four weeks of treatment	End of treatment	Twenty-week follow-up	Forty-week follow-up
Weight (kg)	44.0	43.5	43.5	44.0	43.5
BMI (kg/m^2)	21.2	21.0	21.0	21.2	21
EDE-Q					
Global	5.4	4.2	0.3	0.2	0.4
Dietary restraint	5.2	4.4	0.4	0.0	0.2
Eating concern	4,8	3.6	0.2	0.4	0.4
Weight concern	5.9	4.4	0.4	0.2	0.4
Shape concern	5.8	4.3	0.4	0.4	0.6
Objective bulimic episodes[a]	8	4	0	0	0
Subjective bulimic episodes[a]	8	3	0	0	0
Self-induced vomiting[a]	16	4	0	0	0
Laxative misuse[a]	0	0	0	0	0
Diuretic misuse[a]	0	0	0	0	0
Driven exercise[a]	28	28	0	0	0
CIA	37	34	25	10	10

Notes: EDE-Q = Eating Disorder Examination Questionnaire; CIA = Clinical Impairment Assessment
[a]Number of episodes over the past twenty-eight days

Chapter Ten

Case Study B: Intensive Outpatient CBT-E

The case presented here illustrates the procedures and strategies applied in *intensive outpatient* CBT-E, showing how it can be used to help a patient who does not improve with standard outpatient CBT-E. Several details of the case have been modified to protect the patient's identity, and selected transcripts have been adapted for brevity.

CASE DESCRIPTION

Simona, a seventeen-year-old girl, was referred for CBT-E treatment by her family doctor. She lives in a small village with her parents and a twelve-year-old brother. Her father is fifty years old and works in an office, and her mother is a forty-year-old housewife. At the time of referral, Simona was attending the fourth year of high school, got good results, and described herself as a dynamic person who pursues excellence in everything she undertakes. She reported having two close friends, who, however, she had seen less and less over recent months.

She had always been of normal weight for her height, and generally weighs around 50 kg. She reports having been unconcerned about her weight or figure throughout her secondary school career, despite having often been teased about the shape of her abdomen by two classmates, who also criticized the body shapes of other girls. However, during her current year of high school, a male classmate made negative comments about her stomach at the swimming pool. Simona describes feeling very hurt by this episode, and for the first time in her life she experienced an intense dissatisfaction with her body shape. A few months after this event, she lost 3 kg as the consequence of severe gastroenteritis, associated with fever, vomiting, diarrhea, and loss of appetite. Upon her return to school, Simona, for the first time in her life, received positive comments about her figure and her ability to lose weight. This praise prompted Simona to start dieting so that she could lose even more weight and obtain a flat abdomen. She started by eliminating sweet foods, pasta, and bread, and began restricting her portion sizes and skipping meals when she was home alone. Later on she started hiding food and throwing it in the trash when nobody was watching, in addition to walking for several hours a day and standing rather than sitting while studying or watching television.

After two months of this behavior she reached a body weight of 45 kg and her periods stopped, but this did not worry her. On the contrary, she felt euphoric, and had an overall sense of well-being deriving from her feeling of control over her eating and weight. Nevertheless, she was still unsatisfied with the shape of her abdomen, which she still perceived as fat. At this stage she continually asked her parents for reassurance about her physical appearance, and checked her body frequently by pinching the flesh on her abdomen. She also repeatedly scrutinized her body completed naked in front of a full-size mirror.

Observing her rapid weight loss and violent mood swings, Simona's parents became very concerned about the health of their daughter, but all their efforts to persuade her to relax her strict dietary rules failed. Simona become progressively more introverted, refusing to discuss her eating behavior and weight and shape concerns with either of her parents. She also experienced frequent episodes of mood swings, irritability, and anger, and became socially isolated. Disturbed by her behavior, Simona's parents forced her to see a female psychologist, who was not, however, specialized in the treatment of eating disorders. Nonetheless, after her initial reluctance, Simona developed a trusting relationship with her therapist. Unfortunately however, the treatment she was given focused solely on analyzing Simona's anxiety associated with the comments from boys and her relationship with her parents, but did not address the issues of eating and weight control. Accordingly, this approach produced no improvement in Simona's eating problem psychopathology, and after four months of therapy her weight had decreased still further to 37.5 kg, corresponding to a BMI of 15.2. This weight loss was associated with an intensification of her concerns about shape, weight, and eating control, and deterioration in her school performance, as a consequence of her difficulties concentrating and memorizing information. At this point the family doctor, after examining Simona, asked her parents to consent to her referral to an outpatient unit specialized in CBT-E for eating disorders, where she came to our attention.

Textbox 10.1 illustrates Simona's case summary.

TEXTBOX 10.1. CASE B SUMMARY

Personal information and home life

- Age: seventeen years
- Occupation: student
- Marital status: unmarried
- Home life: Resides with both parents and a twelve-year-old brother
- Social class: Middle

Onset of eating problem

- Age of onset: sixteen
- Weight at onset: 50 kg
- Behavioral precursor: dieting
- Reasons for dieting: losing weight to change the shape of the stomach

The twelve months before the onset

- Events that may have triggered the control of eating, shape, and weight: negative comments about her body shape by schoolmates; gastroenteritis with a loss of 3 kg and positive comments by her schoolmates about the weight loss

The first two months after the onset

- She felt euphoric and had a global sense of well-being deriving from the feeling of having control over her eating and her weight

Since then

- Three to four months: Progressive intensification of concerns about the shape of the stomach associated with frequent and unusual body checking; adoption of extreme and rigid dietary rules and progressive weight loss—her body weight decreased to 45 kg; cessation of menstruation

- Five to eight months: Individual psychotherapy focused on interpersonal relations; persistence of dietary restriction and excessive exercising with a progressive weight loss to 38 kg. She become introverted, with frequent mood swings, episodes of anger and irritability, and social isolation

Current state of the eating problem (last four weeks and last three months for DSM diagnosis)

- Current weight: 37.5 kg
- Current height: 157 cm
- BMI: 15.2 (3rd percentile)
- Frequency of menstruation: 0 in the last three months
- Weight changes: Lost 5 kg in the last three months
- Dietary restraint: Present
- Self-induced vomiting, objective binge eating, subjective binge eating: Absent
- Excessive exercising: Present
- Smoking, substance or alcohol misuse: Absent
- Weight checking: two to three times every day
- Shape checking: Present
- Shape avoidance: Absent
- Fear of weight gain: Present
- Preoccupation with shape, weight, and eating control: Present
- Feeling fat: Present
- Feeling full: Present
- Physical health: Impaired
- Psychosocial and functioning: Impaired
- School performance: Impaired
- DSM-IV diagnosis: Anorexia nervosa (307.1)

Personal and family medical history

- Past and current medical and psychiatric comorbidity: None
- Current medications: None
- Family medical and psychiatric history: Negative for eating disorders, psychiatric disorders, and obesity

Physical Examination

- Bradycardia (heart rate 48 beats/min). Hypotension (85 mm Hg systolic). Cyanotic and cold hands and feet. Dry skin. Orange discoloration of the skin on the palms and soles

TEXTBOX 10.2. ABBREVIATIONS IN SELECTED
TRANSCRIPTS

S = Simona; AC = Assessing Clinician; P = Psychologist; D = Dietitian; M =
Mother; F = Father.

ASSESSING AND PREPARING THE PATIENT FOR OUTPATIENT CBT-E

Objectives

- Assessing the patient's attitude toward the interview.
- Determining the nature and the severity of the eating problem.
- Preparing the patient for the treatment.
- Starting the treatment well.

The assessing clinician first met Simona alone, without her parents, and adopted the procedures and strategies described in chapter 8. Simona was not favorably disposed toward the evaluation session, and was very angry as she had been obliged by her parents and family doctor to attend. She was also upset because she had not been consulted further to the decision to make the appointment. Nevertheless, she agreed to share information with the assessing clinician, and described the onset and the development of her eating problem in detail. She also gave an accurate picture of her current status, and the negative consequences that her eating problem was having on her mood, interpersonal relationships, school performance, and health. Despite this perspicacity, she had difficulty accepting the idea that her weight loss and extreme concerns about eating control, shape, and weight were a problem that needed to be addressed, as the following transcript shows.

[. . .] Selected transcripts:

> AC: Simona, I know that it is a difficult question, but do you consider the diet you follow and the resulting weight loss as a healthy choice or a problem?
>
> S: Um . . . I can't say that it is a healthy choice, but I prefer to be thin, even if I do have some problems.
>
> AC: What problems do you have?

S: Well, my periods have stopped, and I can't concentrate on my studies.

AC: You also told me that your mood and desire to socialize have changed.

S: Yes, I have mood swings, I'm very irritable, and . . . I'm not interested in seeing my friends anymore.

AC: Are you happy about these things?

S: No, but if this is the price I have to pay to be thin, I can accept it.

AC: It seems to me that your eating control and weight loss have a very positive function for you, is that right?

S: Yes, I like my stomach . . . even if it is not yet as flat as I would like.

AC: Do you think that this control also has a positive *psychological* function?

S: I do not know . . . maybe I feel stronger.

AC: So, if I understand correctly, your weight loss has had both positive and negative consequences.

S: Yes . . . but I prefer to be thin and I do not want to put on weight.

AC: Simona, do you feel that your control of eating and shape is still a choice?

S: Yes, it is a choice.

AC: In what way is it a choice; which conditions are necessary for a choice?

S: Um . . . I choose what to eat . . . it is a choice.

AC: There are two main conditions that allow us to say that an individual is making a choice. Do you know what they are?

S: The possibility to choose between two or more options?

AC: Yes, and the other?

S: I don't know.

AC: Freedom, or free will, is the second condition necessary for making a choice. Do you feel free to eat, or are there some psychological processes that influence your choice?

S: I am not free. I am afraid to eat . . . I can't eat. You are right—maybe it has become a psychological problem . . . but I do not want to put on weight.

Having led Simona to the conclusion that she might have an eating problem, the therapist engaged her in drawing up her provisional formulation and explained the main maintenance mechanisms that had emerged during the interview. Particular emphasis was placed on the starvation symptoms relevant to her case (e.g., a reduction in basal metabolic rate, preoccupation with food, social isolation), and she was shown how these had intensified her need to control her eating, creating a self-perpetuating state that had become ingrained and out of control. Initially, Simona reacted with amazement, and agreed that she was entrapped in these mechanisms, but then she went on to state that she had no intention of undertaking the outpatient CBT-E treatment that the assessing clinician proposed.

At this point the assessing clinician invited Simona's parents into the evaluation session. He explained to them the main points that had been discussed with Simona, and, as the mother was openly very critical toward Simona's attitudes and behaviors, gave them a detailed overview of the Minnesota study, explaining the implications of starvation symptoms and the fact that many behaviors (e.g., eating rituals), emotional states (e.g., extreme concerns about food), and psychological reactions (e.g., mood swings, irritability, and episodes of hunger explosion) are caused by malnutrition and weight loss. The assessing clinician also explained how the outpatient CBT-E program he advised was organized, and that they should discuss with Simona the pros and cons of signing up, taking care to stress that ultimately the decision to start therapy would be up to their daughter. The parents were somewhat skeptical that Simona would choose to start treatment autonomously, but verbally accepted the assessing clinician's recommendations. At the end of this session, the assessing clinician prescribed routine medical exams and gave Simona a pamphlet describing the main features of CBT-E, reminding her to write down the pros and cons of starting treatment as a homework assignment.

The second evaluation session was scheduled a week later, and on this occasion, Simona was more favorably disposed toward the interview. As her medical test results showed only a moderately reduced white cell count, hypoestrogenic status, and no particular contraindication to outpatient treatment, her attitude toward this was once again evaluated. Although Simona had not completed her homework assignment, namely writing the reasons for and against starting treatment, she nonetheless agreed to sign up to the outpatient CBT-E program, principally to avoid being harried by her parents. The assessing clinician therefore arranged with Simona her appointments for the first four weeks and encouraged her to make the treatment a priority, stressing the importance of starting well.

OUTPATIENT CBT-E

Stage One (Weeks 1–4)

Objectives

- Helping the patient to think afresh about the eating problem.
- Starting the process of weight restoration.

Stage One comprised eight forty-five-minute, one-to-one sessions. The majority of these sessions were attended by Simona alone, with parental involvement limited to a single one-hour assessment session during the first week of treatment and three fifteen-minute sessions scheduled immediately after individual sessions with Simona in weeks 1, 2, and 4.

Helping the Patient Think Afresh about the Eating Problem

The first individual session in Stage One was focused on getting Simona to look at her eating problem with new eyes, drawing up her provisional personal formulation in order to illustrate the processes maintaining it. This was followed by a detailed analysis of the pros and cons of tackling her eating problem, and in particular the process of weight gain. Although she was poorly motivated to address her eating problem, Simona showed good compliance, always doing the homework she was asked to do and unfailingly arriving to the sessions on time. After the second session, she rationally accepted the need for weight regain, and was educated by the therapist on meal planning for a weight regain of between 0.5 and 1 kg per week (see chapter 6, textbox 6.1, and chapter 8 for details). At the same time the therapist started to address her eating disorder psychopathology, in particular her feeling full, excessive exercising, and morbid fear of putting on weight.

As Simona lived at home with her parents, these were necessarily involved, even at this early stage. The aim of the initial, hour-long, parental session was to identify family factors liable to hinder Simona's attempts to change. From this session it emerged that her mother was very critical and used verbal threats during the meal in a misguided attempt to encourage Simona to eat. In addition, her father constantly made negative remarks about her relatively emaciated state, calling her a bag of bones. As this state of affairs was likely to interfere with any progress, the subsequent parental sessions were dedicated to educating Simona's parents on the dangers of criticizing or mocking Simona about her eating and physical appearance. They were also trained how to prepare food according to the prescribed eating plan, and to assist Simona at mealtimes (see chapter 8 for details).

Starting the Process of Weight Restoration

Despite Simona's apparent willingness to accept weight regain, her weight failed to increase over the first four weeks. Although she had extreme difficulty, she was able to follow Menu B of the meal plan (about 1,500 kcal), but was unable cope with the idea of the greater intake that would enable her to gain the proposed minimum of 0.5 kg per week. Furthermore, her concerns about shape and weight had become more oppressive, and she had resorted to compensatory exercising to cope with the anxiety associated with eating. Her parents, interviewed at week 4, described Simona's abnormal physical activity, which was practiced at unusual times, i.e., in the evening after the dinner, and in unusual ways, such as walking for hours around the rooms in their apartment. Digging a little deeper, the therapist discovered that although Simona's parents had been informed about the need to avoid criticism and mockery, and that some of her behaviors were the consequences of her eating problem mindset, they continued to be very aggressive and hostile during meals. In fact, the parents confessed their exasperation and inability to tolerate the family situation any longer, and expressed the desire that Simona be hospitalized urgently, both to save her life and to protect her younger brother from the stressful atmosphere arising from Simona's condition.

Stage Two (Weeks 5–6)

Objectives

- Conducting a joint review of progress.
- Identifying emerging barriers to change and reviewing the formulation.
- Deciding whether or not to intensify the treatment.

Conducting a Joint Review of Progress

Simona began the treatment with a poor awareness of having a problem, but during the course of Stage One she gradually began to accept that her concerns about shape and weight were excessive, and that the eating problem was having repercussions on all aspects of her life. At week 5, she openly stated the wish to overcome her eating problem, but also that the fear of eating and weight gain was too strong, and that she felt that the tensions within her family were not helping her to change and to address meals.

Simona's ambivalence to change was also hampered by her rigid mindset, which was probably accentuated by the psychological consequences of being underweight.

[. . .] Selected transcripts:

P: Simona, four weeks have passed since you started treatment. I think now is the right time to for us to take stock of the situation. Let's start by reviewing your progress.

S: I haven't made any progress! I haven't put on any weight. It isn't easy for me to change my eating behavior and I am terrified of gaining weight.

P: Are you sure that you have not progressed?

S: Well, if better knowledge of my eating problem is progress, I have made some, I suppose. Now I understand that many problems I have are the consequences of my low weight.

P: I agree, you worked pretty well at constructing your personal formulation. You also weighed yourself only once a week in my office. Don't you consider this progress?

S: Yes, this is definitely progress because when I weighed myself several times a day I was always thinking about the variations in my body weight and on how to reduce the number of calories I eat.

P: Also, you have always been punctual to the sessions, and you have done your homework pretty well, in particular the self-monitoring.

S: I am a punctilious person—I don't like to be late, and I always do all my homework.

P: Do you think that recording in the monitoring record helped you in any way?

S: Er . . . yes, I think so. Recording what I eat, and my thoughts and fears, helped me to understand that my diet is very strict and that I am too obsessed with food and my fat stomach.

P: This is an important step forward. And what about your motivation to address your eating problem?

S: I am afraid to say this, but I am really tired of paying constant attention to what I eat, counting the calorie content of the food, and refusing my friends' invitations. I am coming round to the idea of change, but, even if I realize, as you suggested, that a calorie is a calorie, and that you need to eat 7,000 calories to put on one kilogram, I am still afraid of losing control and getting fatter and fatter if I relax my control over eating.

P: It is clear that you are in a state of ambivalence. On the one hand you are starting to realize the need to overcome your eating problem, and on the other you are afraid to change.

S: Yes.

Identifying Emerging Barriers to Change and Reviewing the Formulation

During the first four weeks of outpatient CBT-E, several powerful barriers to change emerged, namely body checking, excessive exercising, and the continued strain in the family relations, and Stage Two therefore continued with a discussion of these, together with a review of Simona's formulation.

[. . .] *Selected transcripts:*

P: At this point it would be useful for us to discuss the things that are making it difficult for you to change. Let's start by having a look at your personal formulation to see if we can identify any barriers to change.

S: [Looking at her formulation] . . . well, I still restrict my diet, I am still underweight, and I am terrified of weight gain.

P: Yes, that's true. Are there any other problems that emerge from the formulation?

S: Umm . . . feeling full after every meal is still present. It is a painful sensation that I can't stand.

P: We discussed that feeling full after eating small amounts of food is the consequence of dietary restriction and being underweight—two factors that slow gastric emptying. Feeling full is also experienced by people who do not have an eating problem, but they do not worry about it because they know that is a transitory phenomenon due to the presence of food in the stomach.

S: While for me it is a signal that I have eaten too much.

P: Do you remember the strategies I suggested you use to address feeling full?

S: Yes, first I have to say to myself that feeling full is not a sign of having eaten too much, because I have slow gastric emptying. Another thing I have to remember is that feeling full is not a sign of being fat—it is due to the presence of food in the stomach and it's a temporary phenomenon.

P: I also suggested that you not wear too tight clothes, and that you avoid checking the shape of your stomach during eating.

S: Yes, you are right, but sometimes I wear tight clothes on purpose so I feel full quicker and have an excuse to stop eating. I also check my belly continuously during eating . . . I can't help myself.

P: These are important barriers that we have to address. Don't you agree?

S: Yes, I do.

P: I see from your monitoring records that you have intensified exercising. Now you walk continuously, and you have also started jogging.

S: Yes, before starting the meal planning, I was in control. Now I feel full and I have to compensate for all the food I eat on my diet. When I walk, clean my room, or jog I feel calm, especially after eating.

P: Excessive exercising is another important barrier to change. Do you know why?

S: I consume calories and I do not regain weight.

P: Yes, it's true. It is a significant barrier to weight regain, and severely underweight conditions may damage your health. It also maintains your concerns about eating because you give yourself permission to eat only if you exercise afterward.

S: And if I stop exercising and start to put on weight without control?

P: I think you have this fear because you have never really tried to stop your excessive exercising. Remember that it is not easy to put on weight. You need to eat at least 7,000 calories more than those you consume to put on one kilogram. You should try cutting down on your exercising as an experiment.

S: Yes, I know, but I am terrified—I will lose control over my weight and I'll get really fat.

P: I think that behind your difficulties in addressing dietary restriction and exercising there are other barriers. Can we analyze them?

S: Yes, sure.

P: Let's start with your family meals.

S: This is a big problem. I don't trust the way my mother cooks. I think she uses a lot of condiments to increase the calorie content of the food I eat. So, after every meal I do some exercise to compensate for the excess of calories and fat I eat.

P: Do you think that there are other problems in your home environment that represent obstacles to change?

S: Yes, I do. My father keeps calling me "bag of bones" and "stupid anorexic," and telling me I'm wasting away, during mealtimes too. My mother is always very critical and hostile about my way of eating. Both continuously repeat that they are fed up with my paranoia about food. They don't understand anything. They spoke with you but they did not change their attitude.

P: And how do you react to this criticism?

S: I get very irritated. Sometimes I stop eating and go for walk. Other times I slam the plates down on the table and scream at my parents that they do not understand me. Then I go to my room to cry.

Deciding Whether or Not to Intensify the Treatment

The main problems emerging from the above review were the absence of weight gain during the first four weeks of treatment, together with the presence of significant barriers to change. These were related both to Simona's eating disorder psychopathology, that is, the morbid fear of weight gain, the rigidity accentuated by the severe state of being underweight, the excessive and compulsive exercising, the feeling full early that was preventing her from increasing her calorie intake, and her family environment, in particular parental criticism and mockery. As these factors would be difficult, if not impossible, to overcome in the context of outpatient CBT-E, intensification of treatment seemed to be the best step forward. For this reason the therapist suggested intensive outpatient CBT-E and explained to Simona how she would benefit. The therapist informed Simona about the aims, duration, organization, procedures, and expected results of this type of CBT-E (see chapter 6), and asked her to think about the pros and cons of this more intensive approach. At session 10 of outpatient CBT-E, Simona decided voluntarily to sign up for intensive outpatient CBT-E. This choice was made easier by the fact that Simona, albeit with extreme difficultly, had gotten through the school year and was free to attend the intensive outpatient unit.

[. . .] Selected transcripts:

P: From the review we did of Stage One, it appears that you have made some important progress; I believe you are now aware that you have a problem and are coming around to the idea of tackling it. However, there are still very significant barriers preventing you from getting better.

S: Yes, it's true.

P: If I understand correctly, the barriers are both environmental—the way your mother cooks and the way your parents react to your eating and physical appearance—and internal—you fear losing control over your weight.

S: Yes, I agree.

P: One possible way of overcoming these barriers would be to intensify your treatment.

S: In what way?

P: You could start intensive outpatient treatment. This means that you would attend the clinic every weekday from 12:45 p.m. to 7:45 p.m. in this unit, eating three supervised meals a day: lunch, a snack, and an evening meal. You would also have two individual sessions per week with me, two individual sessions a week with a dietitian, who I will introduce you to, and regular checkups with the physician who assessed you before you started treatment.

S: That sounds very intensive. Can you give me some information about the meals?

P: Yes, of course. In intensive outpatient treatment, meals are consumed with the assistance of the dietitian. Food provided in our unit is either pre-frozen or packaged so that it does not require much preparation and can be handled without any fuss. You will receive all foods from the dietitian ten minutes before meals, and you will heat them up yourself in our kitchen. In addition, the dietitian will take you out to eat to a local restaurant twice a week.

S: How might this procedure help me?

P: There are several ways. First, you will be assisted by a specialized therapist who will help you to apply some psychological strategies to help you eat with less anxiety, for example, eating mechanically and without being influenced by your eating problem mindset. Second, you will not have to listen to the comments your parents make, which, as we discussed before, are a powerful barrier to you making the change. Third, you will be actively involved in interpreting your weekly weight changes, and in planning changes in the calorie content of your diet in order to achieve a weekly weight regain of between 0.5 kg to 1.0 kg per week.

S: And what about the weekends?

P: On Friday evenings, the dietitian will give you your prepackaged, frozen meals for the weekend. This procedure has two aims. The first is to test whether you can implement at home the strategies for addressing meals that you have learned during assisted eating. The second is to eliminate one of the barriers to change that you described—your lack of trust in the way your parents cook your food.

S: Yes, I understand. And what about the time after the meal?

P: After meals, you will stay in a recreation room for at least one hour with an assistant who will help you keep your mind off your meal by organizing some activities incompatible with compensatory behaviors such as exercise.

S: So, won't I be allowed to take a walk after eating?

P: No, but you should look at this as a good opportunity to try the experiment we talked about—stopping your excessive compulsive exercising for a while, which, as we reviewed, is one of your most powerful barriers to change.

S: Isn't it possible to wait a few weeks? I don't want to stay here all day! Please . . . my parents will certainly be glad if I stay here. They are only interested in me putting on weight. They will force me to do this treatment.

P: It's probably true that they will be less anxious if they know you are consuming your meals here, but this may make them less inclined to criticize you. However, remember that the treatment and your therapists will be working in *your* interest, not on behalf of your parents. You alone can decide whether to intensify treatment or not. Take this pamphlet with you—it describes the intensive outpatient treatment. Have a look at it, and for the next session try to write the pros and cons of intensifying your treatment on the back of your monitoring record, thinking in particular about the effects your eating problem is having on your life. I also encourage you to discuss this opportunity with your parents, but don't forget that ultimately the decision will be yours.

S: Ok, thank you. I appreciate that I have to decide.

[. . .]

P: Simona, did you manage to evaluate the pros and cons of intensifying treatment?

S: Yes, here is the table of the pros and cons [Simona shows the therapist her monitoring record].

P: Can you read it out loud?

S: The cons are that I am afraid of stopping exercising and getting fat. The pros are that for me it is impossible to change at home. I do not trust my mother. She isn't precise when she cooks my meals, and the atmosphere at home is too tense. I also realized this week that I can't go on in this way. I am very upset, I skip snacks and avoid any condiments, and I am always standing up. This is no way to live.

P: These are good reasons to try a more intensive treatment. Here the atmosphere is calm, you will be assisted by a dietitian during meals, and the food is prepackaged so you will know exactly what you are eating. You will also see that when you regain some weight and interrupt your extreme weight control behaviors, you will be less concerned about controlling your eating, and your mood will stabilize—two conditions that are necessary to allow you to evaluate objectively the pros and cons of either continuing to work on overcoming your eating problem or going back to your present situation.

S: I don't like my life at the moment . . . I want to change.

Once Simona had agreed to start the intensive outpatient treatment, the therapist called her parents into his office to discuss this decision with them. The parents accepted the proposition enthusiastically, expressing relief at having an alternative to the current "too difficult management" of the problem that had generated an unsustainable family atmosphere. Simona and her parents agreed that she would start the intensive outpatient CBT-E the following Monday.

INTENSIVE OUTPATIENT CBT-E

Week 1

Objectives

- Starting well.
- Implementing the main treatment procedures.

Starting Well

Simona started intensive outpatient CBT-E on a Monday so as to have five weekdays in which to engage her in the treatment. The first day, the therapist who conducted the standard outpatient CBT-E welcomed Simona, went over the organization of the outpatient unit again, showed her the kitchen where the assisted eating takes place, and took her to the recreation room to introduce her to the other patients that were undergoing the intensive outpatient treatment. The therapist also repeated the key concepts described during the standard outpatient CBT-E (e.g., obtaining the maximum change early on, giving priority to treatment, playing an active role in the treatment, being punctual for sessions, developing a collaborative relationship with the therapists), and encouraged Simona to adopt these attitudes from the first assisted lunch.

On the same morning, the physician carried out a full *physical examination*, and observed the presence of bradycardia (50 beats/min), hypotension (85 mm Hg systolic), and orange discoloration of the skin of the palms and soles, but no medical contraindication to the proposed treatment.

Implementing the Main Treatment Procedures

In the morning, the dietitian met Simona in private to explain the specific strategies she would need to use in addressing assisted meals, and they went through the *treatment guidelines for weight regain and weight maintenance* (see chapter 6, textbox 6.1) and the *unit rules* (see textbox 10.3) together.

TEXTBOX 10.3. INTENSIVE OUTPATIENT CBT-E UNIT'S RULES

To obtain the maximum benefit from the treatment, you should stick to the following outpatient unit's rules. The rules have been created to help you to obtain the maximum benefit from the treatment and to guarantee the privacy of the other patients attending the outpatient unit.

- Intensive outpatient CBT-E is voluntary and should be considered as a special opportunity to overcome your eating problem. For this reason you are encouraged to put your maximum effort into the treatment and make it a priority in your life.
- You are expected to take full part in the treatment's therapeutic procedures (assisted meals, weight control, individual sessions with the dietitian and psychologist, medical examination with the physician).
- You are encouraged to present yourself to every session five minutes early to prepare the topics to discuss with your therapist.
- Alcohol or psychotropic substances are forbidden because they interfere with the treatment, preventing your mind from concentrating on the tasks necessary to overcome your eating problem. Only drugs prescribed by the team physician are allowed.
- You are requested to not speak about food, weight, or body shape with other patients, however difficult it may be. Speaking of these topics can damage your recovery and that of others because it increases the preoccupation with shape, weight, and eating control and can thereby fuel your eating problem, which is characterized by the overvaluation of shape and weight. Remember that in this program you have the responsibility to improve your behavior and not to negatively influence the behavior of other patients.
- You should avoid any discussion or comment, either before, during, or after the meal, about the food served to you—this will only increase your thoughts about eating.
- You should consider the assisted meal as a therapy session and do your best to apply the suggested techniques for lowering anxiety (i.e., eating mechanically, considering food as a medicine). You are also requested to stay in the kitchen until the end of mealtimes. After the meal you are not allowed to go to the bathroom for at least one hour.

- Once a week you will plan your diet with your dietitian on the basis of the treatment guidelines for weight regain and weight maintenance. During the week you are discouraged from asking for any changes in your diet.
- Since you decided to start the intensive outpatient CBT-E voluntarily, you are expected to do your best to interrupt all the extreme weight control behaviors (e.g., excessive exercising, vomiting) that hinder the change.
- If you have difficulties during the day you are encouraged to apply the suggested problem-solving procedures and engage in some distracting activity (i.e., read a book, listen to music, watch TV, surf the Internet, etc.).
- Leaving the outpatient unit without permission, entering the kitchen outside mealtimes, and entering the therapy offices without authorization are forbidden. If you have the urgent need to speak to a therapist you should ask the secretary.

At the end of the meeting Simona *weighed herself,* with the assistance of the dietitian. In intensive outpatient CBT-E, weight is measured collaboratively with the patient on Mondays and Fridays, in order to check any changes in weight during the week, in which the meals are consumed in the outpatient unit, and, likewise, after the weekend spent at home. As in outpatient CBT-E, patients are actively involved in interpreting their own weight changes, and learn to adopt a decentered stance, as if they were a therapist, recording their own weight on a graph designed to chart their progress, as well as in the last column of their monitoring record. The patient is also actively involved in the decision to modify his or her diet with a view to achieving a weight gain of between 0.5 to 1 kg per week.

[. . .] Selected transcripts from the first meeting with the dietitian:

D: Intensive outpatient treatment has the aim of addressing the barriers you encountered during outpatient treatment. I'd like to start straightaway—do you have any questions?

S: Yes . . . being forced to reach a BMI of between 19 and 20—isn't it possible to stop at 17?

D: You are not obliged to regain weight. However, being underweight is incompatible with overcoming your eating problem because a very low body weight can only be maintained with extreme weight control behaviors. Moreover, it is associated with starvation symptoms, and does not permit you to have a social life.

S: I know—the psychologist explained this to me in detail. But I am afraid that at a BMI of 19 I will not like myself. I started dieting when I was that weight.

D: That is a possibility, but you do not know, because at the moment you attribute excessive importance to your shape and weight, something that the treatment is designed to address.

S: Ok.

[. . .]

D: Do you mind if we go over the guidelines to weight regain?

S: Ok. I know that I should put on between half and one kilogram per week.

D: Exactly. Then, if your weight increases between half and one kilogram per week you should maintain the same eating plan. If your weight increases less than half a kilogram, you should plan to add 500 calories per day. On the other hand, if you put on more than one kilogram per week, you should plan a reduction of 250 calories per day.

S: And what happens when I reach a BMI of 19?

D: You will gradually reduce the calorie content of your diet until your weight remains stable at a BMI of between 19 and 20. In this phase, however, you will also work to address all of your residual dietary rules until you are able to maintain weight by following a healthy but flexible diet.

S: I hope that this will happen.

D: If you put all your effort into the program, there is a good chance that it will, but only you can make the change. It is important that *you* decide on the variations to make to the weekly meal plan based on your own interpretation of your own weight graph. You will become your own therapist.

S: I have another question. I have been trying to stick to a meal plan of about 2,000 calories at home, and now?

D: I suggest you maintain the same calorie content. You should do your best to follow the plan and interrupt your excessive exercising—you will be helped by the treatment.

S: Ok, I agree.

D: Do you have other questions?

S: Yes, I do. Is the meal plan precise? You know that one of the reasons I am here is because I don't trust the way my mother prepares my meals.

D: The aim is not for you to regain weight in an uncontrolled way—you should feel in control of the process of weight regain. However, you also have to work to address your excessive strictness, so the 2,000 calories are a mean of a weekly total. This means that the calorie content in a single day may vary slightly from the 2,000 calories, but your total for the week will be equivalent to 2,000 calories per day. Do you have any other questions?

S: Um . . . do I have to continue to use the monitoring record?

D: Yes, like in outpatient treatment. But during weekdays you only have to write the name of the meals you consume, for example, "lunch"; while on the weekend, as you did at home, you will have to write in advance the meals and food you will eat and monitor in real time whether or not you stick to the plan.

S: Do I have to continue to eat mechanically?

D: Yes, the same strategy you applied at home.

S: But anyway, for me the problem is not addressing the meal, but after the meal when I feel full.

D: I suggest you wear comfortable clothes and avoid checking the shape of your abdomen after eating. In addition, try to tell yourself that it is a temporary phenomenon.

S: This is what the psychologist suggested I do. But I never did it.

D: Here you have the opportunity to test the effectiveness of these strategies. In addition, you should stay in the recreation room after every meal doing something to take your mind off your feeling full. Why don't you make a list of distracting activities you might do after eating?

S: Ok . . . I will. I like to draw . . . maybe I could draw.

D: That's a very good idea. Try also to think of other activities. You may test how helpful they are here in the unit and plan to do those that are useful during the weekend.

The first *assisted eating session* took place at 12:45 in the unit refectory, together with other patients. Simona was very anxious at first, but did her best to comply with the suggestions the dietitian made.

[. . .] Selected transcripts from the first assisted meal with the dietitian:

D: Simona, welcome to your first assisted meal. I see that you have well prepared the food I gave to you on the tray. Remember that you should try to address this meal by applying the strategies we discussed this morning.

S: Ok, I'll try. But I am afraid. There is too much food here.

D: I understand your fear, but try to eat mechanically, and to consider the food as a medicine. This will help you eat with less anxiety. I am here to help you.

Simona handled the first meal, the afternoon snack, and dinner well. She finished her meals within the allotted time (forty-five minutes for midday and evening meal, fifteen minutes for snacks), she did not practice eating rituals, and did not look at what the other patients were eating. The dietitian therefore congratulated Simona for being able to accomplish such a difficult task, and accompanied her to the recreation room where she was assisted by a trainee psychologist (trained in CBT-E) to cope with the impulse to exercise to compensate for the calories ingested in the meal. As planned, Simona started sketching to take her mind of her feeling full, but had a lot of difficulty sitting still. The young psychologist encouraged her several times to sit down at her desk to draw, but met with little success. This pattern was repeated after subsequent meals, and was dealt with from week 2 onward as a primary maintenance mechanism in the *individual CBT-E sessions* with the psychologist. Simona had individual sessions on Tuesdays and Thursdays, and the first of these, like all those that followed, was structured in a similar fashion to the typical outpatient CBT-E session, i.e., in the following stages:

1. Going over the homework.
2. Setting the agenda.
3. Working through the agenda.
4. Setting homework, summarizing the session, and arranging the next appointment.

During the two sessions in the first week, Simona and her therapist went over the aims and principal procedures of intensive outpatient CBT-E, and revised her personal formulation (see figure 10.1).

[. . .] Selected transcripts from the sessions with the psychologist:

P: Simona, I suggest that we have a look at your personal formulation so we can decide together the problems to address during the course of intensive outpatient treatment.

S: I agree. Here is the formulation we drew up together in the first week of outpatient treatment.

P: Do you think that anything has changed?

S: Umm . . . not much. I've stopped checking my weight all the time, but I need to include feeling full and excessive exercising.

P: Yes, I agree. I think we should also add another mechanism that we didn't include in the initial formulation—one that increases your preoccupation with shape and weight that we discovered during the outpatient treatment.

S: Do you refer to body checking, in particular of my belly, and to the fact that I am isolated and I think about food all day?

P: Yes, we call this marginalization of other important life domains.

S: Yes, it is true—I have no interests other than controlling my weight.

P: Why we don't redraw the formulation together? Later on we can update it as your treatment progresses.

S: Ok.

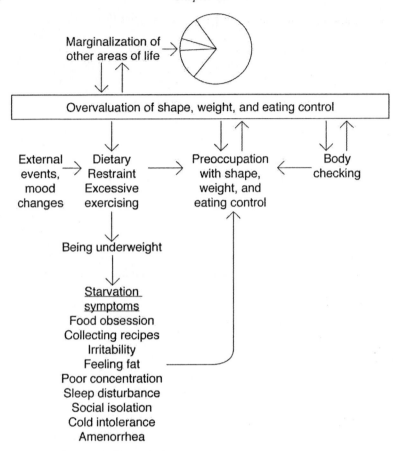

Figure 10.1.   Simona's Formulation

On Friday afternoon, the dietitian met first with Simona, and afterward her parents were called in, to plan how to they would manage her *weekend meals.*

[. . .] Selected transcripts from the session with the dietitian — weekend meal planning:

D: Simona, the aim of this meeting is for us to plan how to organize your meals during weekends.

S: Ok. I am very worried about eating with my parents.

D: If you agree, we will decide together what needs to be done and then we will ask your parents to join us so we can explain what we have planned.

S: Yes, I agree. I think this is very important.

D: Good. First of all, however, I have to congratulate you on the effort you have put into addressing your meals.

S: It isn't easy.

D: You have done very well. So that you can eat at home in the same way you eat here, we need to adopt two main procedures. The first is to give you the food to eat during weekend —as you know, this is prepackaged or frozen in single portions so your mother does not have to cook for you, a problem that represents a barrier when you eat at home.

S: This is crucial. I don't trust her—I don't think she will accept this system.

D: We'll ask her, emphasizing that this is an essential part of your treatment, as it will help you to eat with less anxiety because you know exactly what you are eating.

S: Yes, this helps me to feel in control.

D: The second thing we have to ask your parents is to avoid making any negative comments about your body or way of eating, but instead to encourage you to eat mechanically like when you eat in the unit.

S: Ok. But I think that this will be very difficult for them.

D: The last thing I suggest you to do is to write in advance, the day before, the meals and the food you plan to eat on your monitoring record. In this way it will be easy for you to monitor in real time—while you are at the table—putting a check next to the food you eat and a cross next to the food you don't eat; if you don't eat something you had planned, you should ask yourself why and make a note of your reasons. In addition, if you should eat any unplanned food, write it in brackets. On Monday, we will then be able to discuss together how things went.

S: Ok, I'll do it.

[Simona's therapist asks her parents to join the session]

D: Welcome! I have invited you to this meeting with Simona because we have to discuss how to plan the meals you will eat together during the weekend. This is a key aspect of Simona's treatment, and I must therefore stress the need for all of you to put your best efforts into putting into practice at home what we agree to do here.

M: Ok.

F: Ok.

D: Simona has made a lot of progress during the first week of this intensive treatment, and she has eaten all the meals we planned.

F: I'm glad to hear this.

D: In order to continue this progress, it is advisable that in this phase of the treatment Simona eat at home the same food she has here.

M: You explained this when you outlined the intensive treatment to us. I'm relieved from the task of cooking . . . and, to be honest, I'm glad. I'm sure that Simona will agree that in recent weeks cooking has become a nightmare for both Simona and me—she doesn't trust the way I cook and feels the need to check what I'm doing all the time.

S: You didn't weigh things and you smothered everything in sauce!

D: Using the prepackaged and frozen food supplied by the unit, you will avoid this problem; as she learned here, Simona will defrost her own food and will eat together with you.

M: Can my husband and I eat regular food?

D: Yes, of course. The only thing I must insist is that you avoid making any comments about the way Simona eats or her body.

M: And what if Simona refuses to eat?

D: You should use the strategies we use here. For example, gently remind Simona to eat mechanically and not to trust her physical sensations and thoughts. It might also be useful if you encourage Simona to write any difficulties she has in her monitoring record.

F: But we are not therapists . . . we have emotions! She is our daughter and sometimes it is difficult to keep calm.

D: I understand, but it also is very difficult for Simona to address meals and the process of weight regain.

M: I know . . . I know that she is suffering [Simona starts to cry].

D: Ok. I suggest you to try this new way of eating together. I know it will be difficult, but I think that all of you will be able to manage.

Weeks 2–10

Objectives

- Maintaining the patient's engagement.
- Addressing the primary maintenance mechanisms.
- Involving the parents.

Maintaining the Patient's Engagement

In the Tuesday session of the second week, Simona manifested her ambivalence toward the treatment. The psychologist therefore took appropriate measures to maintain her engagement, as the following transcript shows.

[. . .] *Selected transcripts from an individual CBT-E session:*

P: Simona, how was your first week in intensive outpatient treatment?

S: I ate all the food I was given . . . but I don't think I will be able to keep it up. I wasn't very convinced before . . . how can I eat all the meals and spend all day in that room without doing any exercise? Not to mention the fact that I am fatter than all the other patients. I wish I wasn't here.

P: I understand that it isn't easy for you. It isn't easy for any of the patients.

S: Maybe it is true, but the other patients are thin and have flat stomachs, even if they eat all the fatty meals provided by the unit.

P: They also have an eating problem. But they have all been here for several weeks and have got used to assisted eating. That being said, they, like you, have to cope with their eating anxiety.

S: It doesn't look like it . . . I see them sitting quietly in the recreation room.

P: They are applying CBT procedures and strategies to address their eating problems, but when their mind is focused on the control of eating, shape and weight, they also have preoccupations and negative emotions.

S: If you say so I believe you.

P: However, as in intensive outpatient treatment we will meet twice a week, we will have plenty of time to address your concerns, barriers to change, and any crises that you might have.

At the end of the session, Simona decided to persevere with the treatment. Although her ambivalence returned on occasion in the weeks that followed, it was always associated with a specific therapeutic task, in particular when asked to stop excessive exercising, but she never again expressed the desire to interrupt the treatment itself.

Addressing the Primary Maintenance Mechanisms

After revising with Simona her personal formulation, the therapist began to address the following primary maintaining mechanisms:

- Being underweight and dietary restriction.
- Feeling full.
- Excessive and compulsive exercising.
- Events and mood changes.
- Dietary rules.
- Overvaluation of shape and weight.

The first four weeks of the treatment were principally focused on tackling Simona's low body weight, feeling full, excessive and compulsive exercising, response to external events and mood changes. The treatment then gradually moved on to address her dietary restraint and overvaluation of shape and weight.

Addressing being Underweight and Dietary Restriction

This was the most important mechanism to address because it was impairing Simona's physical health and psychosocial functioning, in addition to maintaining her overvaluation of shape, weight, and eating control (see chapter 2). This mechanism was tackled by the CBT dietitian using meal planning and assisted eating procedures.

[. . .] Selected transcripts from the session with the dietitian — reviewing the weekend:

D: Simona, how did you manage your weekend meals?

S: Ok. Here are my monitoring records. I stuck to the meal plan, with the exception of Saturday, when I skipped the afternoon snack (see figure 10.2).

D: You did a great job! Can we analyze why you skipped the snack?

S: Um . . . I felt full and restless and so I went out to take a walk. When I came back, my mother told me off for exercising . . . she said that I should put more effort in trying to change . . . she doesn't understand me.

D: And then what happened?

S: I got very angry and I felt full, so I decided to skip the snack.

D: Did you skip the snack because you felt full or because your mood changed?

S: I don't know. Maybe it was for both reasons. When I am angry I feel full and the only way I can keep calm is to diet.

D: What have you learned from this experience?

S: Er . . . that my emotions and my eating problem have negatively influenced each other?

D: Yes, I think so. The first association between your eating problem and emotion was after lunch, when you felt full and restless. To cope with both of these negative feelings you went for a walk in an attempt to reduce your preoccupation with feeling full and destress.

S: Yes, you're right.

D: However, you know that exercising is not a good solution because it is a powerful maintenance mechanism that fuels your eating problem and does not permit you to manage the sensation of feeling full or negative emotions in a functional way.

S: Yes, I know.

D: The second association was when you came back home and your mother reproached you because you had been exercising. You got angry and once again the negative emotion and the feeling full interacted, and to compensate you skipped your snack. Although this helped you to become calmer and less concerned about your shape and weight, this kind of behavior can make your eating problem worse.

S: Yes, I agree . . . but what should I have done?

D: This week, I suggest you devise a proactive problem-solving strategy to help you deal with the problem, should it arise next weekend—we'll review it together during our Friday meeting. Meanwhile, I think you are doing pretty well. If you continue to put in this level of effort, you have a good chance of getting over your eating problem.

S: Thank you! I'll prepare a problem-solving strategy for Friday's session.

[. . .] Selected transcripts from the week 7 session with the dietitian—interpretation of weight:

D: Simona, please update your weight graph.

S: Ok. I weigh 44.5 kg.

D: Right. How is that compared to last week?

S: I am as heavy as I was last week.

D: And what does this mean?

S: That my weight has remained stable.

D: And in terms of energy balance?

S: It means I burned the same number of calories that I consumed.

D: All right. So do you think you should modify next week's meal plan at all?

S: Erm . . . this is the first week I haven't put on any weight . . . I don't know.

D: Let's look at the Weight Regain Guidelines—what do they suggest?

Day................ Saturday .... Date.............. March 23rd ....

Time	Food and liquids consumed	Place	*	V/L/E	Comments
9:00	1 medium cup of milk (1.8%) with 1 spoonful of sugar ✓ 5 savory biscuits ✓	Home kitchen			Everything is OK. I am always calm in the mornings
11:00	1 apple ✓	Home kitchen			I feel fine.
1:00	1 plate of pasta (80g) with meat sauce ✓ 5 slices of prosciutto ✓ 1 medium portion of raw carrots with a spoonful of olive oil ✓ 2 slices of bread ✓ 2 kiwis ✓	Home kitchen			I had the impulse to remove the fat from the ham, but I told myself to eat mechanically. I can resist this impulse
2:00				E	I feel fat and restless. I eat too much. I have to take a walk to calm myself. Walking 2:00-4:00
4:00	~~Fruit yogurt~~ ~~4 cookies~~				Mom reproached me because I exercised. She doesn't understand me. I am very angry, and I feel fat. I skip the snack
8:00	1 cup of barley and bean soup ✓ 2 scrambled eggs ✓ 1 portion of boiled potatoes ✓ 1 portion of salad with oil and vinegar ✓ 1 apple ✓	Home kitchen			I was still angry with mom. I was anxious. I eat slowly – Dad encourages me to eat at normal speed, and Mom tells me that she was not angry with me – she only wants to help me to overcome my eating problem. I feel fine.

Figure 10.2.   An Example of Simona's Weekend Monitoring Records. Adapted from figure 5.3 in *Cognitive Behavior Therapy and Eating Disorders* by Christopher G. Fairburn, 2008. Copyright Guilford Press. Reprinted with permission of The Guilford Press.

S: They say I should increase my daily calorie content by about 500 kcal and eat from Menu D (Menu D provides about 3,000 kcal per day—see chapter 8), but can't I wait another week? Maybe it was just a one-off, and next week I will put on 0.5 kg.

D: Why do you think this will happen?

S: I don't know. Last week I did not exercise more than the previous one, and I followed the meal plan.

D: In order to get a better idea, let's take a look at the trend in your weight over the last four weeks—how would you interpret your weight chart?

S: It looks like my weight regain is slowing down. At the start I put on 1 kg per week, but even the week before last it was less than that.

D: So, what do you suggest?

S: I think that I should switch to Menu D.

Throughout the treatment, Simona ate at normal speed, always finishing her meals on time, and did not practice any eating rituals or make comparisons to other patients' eating. So that she could maintain an increase in body weight between 0.5 to 1 kg per week, the calorie content of the diet was progressively increased to 3,000 kcal per day. After nine weeks of intensive outpatient CBT-E, Simona had achieved a BMI of 19.0, normal menstruation had resumed, and she started the weight maintenance phase with a diet containing around 2,500 kcal.

Addressing Feeling Full

Simona's feeling full was a powerful barrier to her increasing the amount of food necessary for her to regain weight. This was further compounded by her underweight status and undereating, and by intense and frequent tactile checking of her abdomen. The mechanism was addressed by the CBT psychologist during the individual CBT-E sessions, the CBT dietitian during assisted eating, and the assistant psychologist during the hour of distracting activities after every meal. With this assistance, Simona's feeling full decreased progressively, and she stopped reporting this negative sensation after week 9.

[. . .] Selected transcripts from individual CBT-E sessions—addressing feeling full:

P: Simona, from your monitoring record I see that yesterday you cried throughout dinner.

S: Yes, I did. The problem is that I have a constant and unsupportable feeling of fullness. I try to distract myself, but it doesn't stop . . . I feel like I am exploding . . . I find it hard to ingest the food . . . I'm going to ask the dietitian to let me skip snacks and reduce my portion size. I can't do it! [Simona starts to cry and to massage her stomach.] I have also intense pangs in my stomach.

P: If you remember, feeling full is for a large part the consequence of malnutrition and being underweight. Which strategies did you try to apply to manage this sensation?

S: I tried to distract myself. I also asked Alice [another patient] if this happens to her too, but even though she told me that she got over it after the first two weeks of the treatment, this did not help me, and in the end we started talking about the calories we eat. She eats more than me, and I became even more anxious.

P: Did you try other strategies?

S: I massaged my stomach to stop the pain but it was no use. No use . . .

P: It seems that your attempts focused your attention more on the feeling of fullness. Speaking about calories and touching your abdomen when you feel full are counterproductive—both strategies increase your concerns and amplify the sensation of being full. Speaking with other patients can be a useful strategy, but you should avoid talking about calories.

S: What else can I do when I feel full?

P: I advise you to stop touching your stomach immediately. If you find this difficult you can pick up and hold your lucky mascot teddy bear. Also, try to think that feeling full is a natural and transitory sensation after eating, and that when you improve your nutritional state, things will get better. Remember also to wear comfortable clothes—the jeans you have on are too tight—they stretch across your belly and amplify the sensation of being full.

S: Yes, you are right.

P: Finally, if you still feel full, you can listen to some music on your headphones—this can interfere with your eating problem mindset.

Addressing Excessive Exercising

Simona's overvaluation of shape and weight led her to practice excessive and compulsive exercising, which became increasingly intense and evident as the first two weeks of intensive outpatient treatment progressed. The forms of exercise observed in the unit were the following: standing up when she thought she wasn't being watched; walking backward and forward along the corridor to the bathroom without needing to go; and repeated jumping jacks, sit-ups, and bust rotations. Simona also reported that she walked alone for several hours in the countryside close to her home on the weekends. The CBT psychologist sought to address this excessive exercising in the individual CBT-E sessions, providing Simona with counteractive strategies, and the trainee psychologist helped Simona to cope with the urge to exercise during the hour of distracting activities after every meal.

Despite these interventions, it took longer than expected to get Simona to refrain from excessive exercising, mainly because at first she was unaware of doing too much exercise. Hence, at week 4, the therapist proposed that Simona wear an accelerometer for three days, so that the amount and intensity of her physical activity, the number of steps she took daily, and the time she spent asleep could be measured objectively. The accelerometer readings, together with detailed recording of her exercising on her monitoring record, gradually helped Simona become more aware of her unhealthy way of exercising. In addition, the improvement in her nutritional state was associated with a reduction in her restlessness, and by week 8 Simona no longer exhibited any form of excessive exercising.

[. . .] Selected transcripts from individual CBT-E sessions:

P: Your assistant told me that she has asked you several times to sit down during the hours after the meals when you should be practicing distracting activities. Why did she do this?

S: It's true. Today was harder than usual. Maybe the idea of the large meal I ate . . . the thought that all that food will deposit in my body . . . anyway, I was very restless . . . I was really not able to sit still.

P: Did you record these thoughts and emotions on your monitoring record?

S: No, I didn't. I don't think it'll help me. To tell the truth, I'm not really convinced that I should stay confined to a chair all the day, in particular after meals. I know many people who practice sports and are very active. Also the experts say that doing physical activity is good for you. And . . . it doesn't seem to me that I do excessive exercise.

P: You are right that the experts advise adopting an active lifestyle. However, I think that your exercise has other functions? Don't you agree?

S: Well . . . I don't know . . . I am afraid of losing control over weight . . . and it helps me to calm down.

P: I agree with your assessment. Why don't you try to stop using exercise for these functions? Then you will start to exercise to improve your health, as recommended by the experts.

S: It is difficult. I don't know how to deal with the fear of uncontrolled weight gain or my anxiety.

P: Remember that one major aim of this program is to help you to gain weight in a controlled fashion. Doing excessive exercising is stopping you putting on the weight you need, a necessary condition for you to overcome your eating problem. In addition it prevents you from reducing your fear of uncontrolled weight gain.

S: Why?

P: Because it maintains the belief that the only way of not becoming fat if you eat is to do a lot of exercise. This is not true, since most people maintain a healthy weight without exercising in the way you do.

S: Yes, I agree.

P: As homework I suggest you to record on your monitoring record in real time all the exercise that you do. It might be useful that when you have the impulse to exercise you ask yourself what is the reason behind it. If it is to deal with the anxiety, you can apply the same distracting activities we discussed for addressing your feeling full.

S: Ok, I will do my best.

[. . .]

P: We agreed that you would stop exercising for a while to see whether your prediction that you would lose control of your weight would come true or not. Have you tried to stop exercising on the weekends?

S: I thought about doing it, but I wasn't sure if it was a good idea so I decided it would be better not to try. Anyway, at home it is very difficult to resist—we have a very large garden and the area where I live has lots of footpaths in the countryside, where I love going for long walks by myself. My parents tried to stop me, but in the end I did what I had to.

P: You said you walk alone—why is that?

S: Because I have the freedom to choose the pace that I want. My friend Roberta, for example, likes to talk while she walks—this slows me down.

P: So in the past you walked in a different way with Roberta?

S: Yes, I used to enjoy chatting with her.

P: And what if Roberta wanted to go for a walk with you—would you be free to do it?

S: Well . . . maybe I would go, but I'd be thinking all the time about the how many calories I wasn't burning by walking so slowly!

P: So, can we agree that your eating problem mindset would prevent you from enjoying the countryside/her company like you did in the past?

S: I think so, yes.

[. . .]

P: I see that you often go to the restroom.

S: Yes, I often need to go.

P: I've also noted that you stay in there for a while. Why is this?

S: Well, sometimes I stay in there so I can relax.

P: I'd like you to tell me how you do this. . . .

S: I do some sit-ups and jumping jacks.

P: Did you exercise in this way before the onset of your eating problem?

S: No . . .

P: Do you relax because you are burning calories?

S: Yes, if I do these exercises my conscience is clear. But I only do a few exercises—is it a big problem?

P: Practicing these behaviors locked in the bathroom is abnormal and serves to maintain your eating problem in two ways: first because the energy you expend prevents you from regaining weight, and second because it keeps your mindset locked into the excessive control of shape and weight.

S: But it's only a way of stretching my legs. In terms of energy expenditure it doesn't count.

P: If you think it is irrelevant, why don't you try to suspend it for a couple of weeks?

S: Er . . . ok, I'll try.

P: If you have any difficulties, take out your monitoring record and record in real time the situation that triggered the exercise, and the reason why you felt the need to exercise.

[. . .]

P: Can we discuss the readings we got from your accelerometer?

S: Sure.

P: Look [shows Simona the readouts], the readings show you take an average of more than 20,000 steps and do more than five hours of moderate exercise and almost two hours of intense exercise a day.

S: Well . . . yes . . . I walk a little when I feel full and fat.

P: But in addition to that you did about two hours of intense exercise per day.

S: Yes, I did some sit-up and jumping jacks.

P: Maybe you underestimate the amount of exercise you do.

S: It looks like it—I didn't think it would be that much!

P: I suggest you record more accurately all the exercise you do in your monitoring record.

S: But sometimes I don't even know I'm doing it! Maybe I can ask my assistant here and my mother at home to let me know when I'm exercising without realizing.

P: That sounds like a good idea. And what will you do when you come to realize you are exercising?

S: I have to do something that is incompatible with movement.

P: Exactly; for example, if your mother tells you that you are lifting your legs to exercise your abdomen while you are watching TV, you could put something on your lap or cross your legs.

S: That might work.

[...]

P: Did you try to stop the excessive walking you do when you return home from the unit?

S: Yes I did. I stopped taking the long way around and I walked straight home in about ten minutes. The walk used to take me about an hour. Sometimes I have the impulse to take a detour, but then I say to myself that there are no good reasons for doing this. Now I feel much better and I have more time to do other things.

P: Very good. Would you say this walking you do is healthy?

S: Yes, I think it's normal—I used to walk like this before my problems started.

P: I agree. But to be sure that this is not a form of exercise related to the control of shape and weight, could you take the bus instead of walking one day?

S: Umm . . . I don't like to take the bus.

P: Can you agree to do it as an experiment?

S: Ok.

P: One last question—what about the feeling full that prompted you to walk after dinner?

S: That feeling has disappeared.

Addressing Events and Mood Changes

In the individual CBT-E sessions, Simona was trained to use proactive problem solving to deal with external events, and armed with strategies for modulating mood changes, as these triggered the intensification of her dietary restriction and exercising.

[. . .] *Selected transcripts from individual CBT-E session:*

P: Simona, did you apply the strategy of proactive problem solving?

S: Yes, I used it to get through Saturday afternoon without doing any exercise.

P: Which alternative activities did you plan?

S: I planned to go to the hairdresser's in the early afternoon and then to invite Roberta to see a movie at the cinema.

P: Did this work?

S: Yes, I didn't exercise, I really like my new hairstyle, and I enjoyed spending time with Roberta. The movie was very good.

P: I think you did a fantastic job. As you can see, anticipating problems and having a coping strategy ready is the best way to resolve them. I also think you made a great choice of activities to take your mind off exercise—taking care of your physical appearance can help you to feel good about yourself and improve your acceptance of your body. Also, going out to watch a movie with your friend is a functional way for you to spend your free time; it may help you to develop interests other than the control of eating, shape, and weight.

[. . .]

S: I had an argument with my father yesterday. He can't understand why I am afraid of putting on weight. I got very upset. After all the sessions he's had with you he still doesn't understand a thing!

P: How did you cope with this change of mood?

S: I went to my room and, as you suggested, I told myself that what I was feeling was just an emotion, and that I could accept it. I put on some music and then went over the situation in my mind—I realized that it is not my father's fault that he doesn't completely understand my problem; he is a man . . . and he only says these things because he wants to help me.

P: What did you learn from this situation?

S: That I can manage the change of mood without exercising and skipping meals.

P: Very good.

Addressing Dietary Rules

At first, Simona adhered rigorously to extreme and strict self-imposed dietary rules when she consumed meals outside the unit. Her principal dietary rule was to eat only foods of certain composition that had been accurately weighed. This led her to avoid any form of social eating and, as a consequence, her interpersonal relationships deteriorated progressively. For this reason, her dietitian accompanied her on two assisted meals per week outside the unit, held at suitable dining establishments, from week 8 onward. In this way, and at home, Simona was gradually exposed to mealtimes in which she had no control over content, giving her an opportunity to address dietary restraint and dietary rules with procedures gleaned from conventional outpatient CBT-E.

[. . .] Selected transcripts from assisted meals at the restaurant with the dietitian:

D: Simona, are you ready to choose what to eat? Remember that this is a treatment session designed to help you address dietary restraint and your avoidance of unweighed food of uncertain composition.

S: I am ready.

D: Try to apply the strategies we discussed yesterday.

S: Do you mean to choose a plate of pasta with tomato and cheese and a salad without checking the menu too much?

D: Yes, try also to eat focusing your attention on eating mechanically and not on the amount of food in front of you.

S: Ok, I'll do my best.

[...]

D: Simona, what did you learn from eating at a restaurant, breaking your dietary rule about not eating unweighed food of uncertain composition?

S: I realize that my fear was irrational. I did not lose control of my weight.

D: Why, in your opinion, is it important for you to eat in restaurants?

S: Erm ... maybe so I can socialize with others?

D: Yes, you are right. Do you think you could invite Roberta out for a meal next weekend?

S: Umm ... It won't be easy but I can try.

Addressing Overvaluation of Shape and Weight

While Simona was helped to regain weight she was also helped to tackle her extreme concerns about shape and weight. In her individual CBT-E sessions, she was first educated about self-evaluation in general, then helped to delineate her own self-evaluation system and to identify its implications on her quality of life. Finally, she was encouraged to devise a plan for addressing her overvaluation of shape and weight by seeking both to enhance the importance of other self-evaluation domains and to address body checking.

[...] *Selected transcripts from an individual CBT-E session — identifying overvaluation and its consequences:*

P: Simona, I suggest we analyze the main areas of your life that are important to your self-evaluation.

S: Ok.

P: Why don't we make a general list of the things that people usually use to evaluate themselves? Then you can assign the degree of importance you attribute to each one of these, and other, domains.

S: Ok. But I don't really know how to determine how important things are to my self-evaluation.

P: An easy method of doing this is to assess the degree and length of your negative reactions when things don't go well in that domain. For example, school: if you get very upset when you are given a bad mark, it is clear that this domain is very important to how you judge yourself.

S: Ah! Now I understand.

P: As well as school, let's consider interpersonal relationships, family, hobbies, personal skills, and control of eating, shape, and weight.

S: Ok . . . in the past I gave a lot of importance to my relationships with my friends and parents . . . and school, but now . . . I don't know.

P: Which of these domains affects you the most if things go badly?

S: Umm . . . certainly the shape of my body, my weight, and the control of my diet.

P: And what about the other areas?

S: Er . . . school, and my relationship with my parents . . . but much, much less.

P: Ok. Why don't you draw a pie chart like this [the psychologist shows Simona an example of a pie chart belonging to a patient with an eating problem]? The size of each slice represents the relative importance of that domain of life in your self-evaluation scheme.

[. . .]

S: [After drawing her pie chart] Here is my pie chart.

P: I see. Your pie chart includes four slices. One, representing your shape, weight, and eating control, is very large, but the others, representing your relationships with friends and family, and your school performance, are pretty small.

S: Yes. It seems stupid but that's how it is.

P: It isn't stupid, because adopting such system of self-evaluation could have some advantages. Can you tell me what they might be?

S: Er . . . I don't know . . . maybe it is an easy way of evaluating myself. It's easy for me to control my diet and feel good.

P: Yes, I agree. Using control of weight and eating to self-evaluate may initially have some advantages. It is simpler to use one domain than several domains, especially if this domain, like shape and weight, is measurable and observable.

S: Yes . . . but there are some problems.

P: What problems?

S: Umm . . . I no longer have any friends or interests.

P: We call this life-domain marginalization—you don't judge yourself on things that are generally considered important in the construction of a multifaceted, well-balanced self-evaluation system. Does this pie chart suggest to you any other problems?

S: I don't know.

P: What happens if you fail to control your diet and your weight increases?

S: It seems like the end of the world.

P: I can imagine. As you put most of your self-evaluation "eggs" in the eating, shape, and weight control "basket," you have nothing to rely on if this falls. In addition, as I remember, even when you were much lighter you were still not satisfied with the shape of your body.

S: You're right.

P: I suggest, as homework, you draw your pie chart on the back of your monitoring record every day, adjusting the number and the size of the slices as appropriate. We will see how it evolves in later sessions.

Having made Simona aware of the fact that her eating problem was marginalizing other areas of her life, the psychologist set out to provide her with strategies designed to redress the balance.

[. . .] Selected transcripts from individual CBT-E sessions—promoting the importance of other self-evaluation domains:

P: To overcome your eating problem it will be necessary for you to make the shape and weight and eating control slice smaller, leaving room for other domains. One way of achieving this is to engage in other activities that you should try to use to evaluate yourself.

S: It isn't easy.

P: Yes, I know, but it is possible. What would you like to do?

S: Umm . . . I'd like to take up drawing. I love to sketch.

P: That sounds interesting.

S: I used to be quite good. I really enjoyed drawing. When I was a child I spent hours and hours doing it.

P: And now?

S: Now I don't draw. I have no inspiration . . . I've tried doing it after the meals to distract myself—I start sketching, but I immediately have to stop because I am taken over by other thoughts. Then I get up and walk.

P: Would you like to start drawing again as you did in the past?

S: I'd love to. In the past I took part in many competitions and sometimes I even won.

P: Do you have other activities that you did in the past that you miss now?

S: Yes, I miss dancing. I used to like to dance both at the disco and at home. It would be fun to take dancing lessons, maybe with my friend Roberta . . . I also used to like making jewelry.

P: That sounds like fun—you seem to be a creative person.

S: Yes [smiling], I used to be creative . . . but now . . . people say that I am crazy. I understand what they mean—I'm obsessed by my stomach.

P: I am sorry about the comments you receive. However, now that you are getting over your eating problem, you could also take up the things that you like to do again.

S: I'd like to start, but I'm afraid of losing my control over eating.

P: Remember that the aim of the treatment is not for you to lose the control of your eating, but for you to reduce the excessive dependence you have on eating control and to promote a self-evaluation based on several life domains. Usually, it is an excessive control over eating that triggers the loss of control and can lead to binge eating.

S: Ok, I want to try. Maybe I could buy some drawing pencils . . . and some beads to make bracelets.

P: I think that would be a good idea. Please write all the steps you take in these two areas in the last column of your monitoring record.

S: And what about the dance course?

P: I suggest you wait until you normalize your weight. You still do some residual excessive exercising, and adding further physical activity might interfere with your recovery. When you stop excessive exercising, joining a dance school with your friend will be a very good opportunity for you to keep in shape, develop a new interest, and make friends.

S: Ok.

It emerged that Simona felt compelled to perform a great deal of body checking—scrutinizing her own figure and, in particular, comparing it with that of other patients'. As this represented a significant reinforcement mechanism of her overvaluation of shape and weight, it was dealt with by the psychologist as follows.

[. . .] Selected transcripts from individual CBT-E sessions—addressing comparison body checking:

P: How do you find life together with the other patients here in the outpatient unit?

S: It is one of the most difficult things in the treatment. I spend most of my time comparing myself with them . . . with one girl in particular.

P: How does this comparison make you feel?

S: I feel terrible—the other girls here are really skinny and above all they have flat stomachs . . . I look at their stomachs and then I look at mine and [starts to cry] . . . my stomach is disgusting.

P: I understand how you feel. Shall we address this topic to see what mechanisms lead you to this conclusion?

S: Ok.

P: Who are the patients you compare your body to?

S: All of them, but particularly Giulia. She has the flattest belly out of all of us. That's why I like her.

P: Can we review how you assess the shape of Giulia's abdomen?

S: I look at her stomach several times a day. She is a beautiful girl.

P: Do you look at Giulia's body in the same way you check your own?

S: Um . . . I don't know. What do you mean?

P: I mean, do you spend the same amount of time checking Giulia's abdomen as you do your own?

S: I don't understand.

P: I mean, have you ever pinched Giulia's abdomen to see how much fat is there? And are you seeing Giulia's abdomen from the same angle you see your own?

S: [Smiling] No, of course I don't touch Giulia's stomach! I only take a quick glance because I don't want her to notice . . . and I don't look at her stomach from above.

P: I think that the way you compare yourself with Giulia is problematic. You check your own stomach thoroughly for long periods of time and you touch it continuously. In contrast, you only have occasional glimpses of Giulia's stomach from a different perspective, and you don't touch it. This type of checking makes it easy for you to find defects in your own body and not in Giulia's.

S: Hmm . . . maybe you're right.

P: Another question—which of Giulia's features make you see her as a beautiful girl?

S: She's really thin and she has a flat belly.

P: So, if I understand, you like Giulia only because of her weight and the shape of her stomach. It is interesting that these are the features that worry you most about yourself. Don't you take into consideration any other of Giulia's attributes?

S: For example?

P: What about her personality, her way of interacting with others, and other features not related her body? Don't forget that Giulia has an eating problem too, and that she, like you, is here to normalize her body weight because she is, frankly, very underweight.

S: I only check her stomach, and I don't judge her on any other features.

P: Why don't you try, just as an experiment, to see if you can observe people in a different way?

S: Can you make an example?

P: First, you might change who you check. For example, instead of concentrating on Giulia, try to check the body of every third person you meet. Second, you could check other people's bodies the way you might check your own. Third, try looking at the other features of the people you encounter, such as their hairstyle or clothes. And do not forget to report all this on your monitoring record.

S: Ok [smiling].

[. . .]

P: Can we go over your homework? How did you go on with this new way of looking at and comparing yourself to other people?

S: Fine. Here are my monitoring records . . . I tried to look Giulia's body in a different way, and noticed that her eyes, for example, are less expressive than mine. The color of my eyes is also less common. Many people say nice things about the color of my eyes.

P: Did you notice anything else?

S: She isn't as good as me at putting on makeup. This something I do very well. She is not very good at making the most of her looks. I also prefer my hairstyle and color to hers.

P: Good. I see that you have made a more balanced evaluation of Giulia's body, not only her stomach. Next time you see her, try to assess her other attributes, not only physical, for example, her personality and the way she interacts with other people.

S: Ok.

P: Did you also look at any other people's bodies?

S: Yes, I went in town and I tried to look, as you suggested, at the body of every third person.

P: And how did you find the experience?

S: I thought it was an easier assignment. I realized that I tend to look only at skinny women with a flat stomach.

P: What conclusions can you draw from this?

S: That I compare my body only with those of a certain type of woman: those that are skinny and have a flat stomach. In reality, I came across many other girls who didn't have these features, but by ignoring them I tend to judge myself as the fattest and least attractive of all the girls. A similar thing happens when I read fashion magazines.

P: I understand, and I therefore suggest that you stop reading fashion magazines. It is very dangerous and unrealistic for you to compare yourself with these images. To start with, the women in these magazines are very atypical and their photos have usually been altered.

S: I know this. But often I forget . . . the models seem born with those bodies! I have to remember to use a more critical eye.

Involving the Parents

On the Friday of the second week, the dietitian held a family session to review the difficulties encountered during weekend meals. The use of pre-packaged and frozen food resolved most of the problems they had encountered during the outpatient CBT-E, and both parents were doing their best to follow the psychologist's advice to refrain from making negative remarks about Simona's body shape or style of eating. Nevertheless, further parental sessions designed to improve the management of family meals were arranged for weeks 4 and 6. A later family session, held in week 8, was dedicated to deciding how best to introduce and organize regular meals at home. The result of this discussion was that Simona and her mother agreed to discuss what food they would eat the day before, and to follow the indications of the dietary exchange system of Menu D (about 3,000 kcal per day—see chapter 8). Simona also agreed that her mother, as in most families, was the person in charge of food shopping, preparation, and serving, and to let her do this unhindered.

[. . .] Selected transcripts from the family session (week 8) with the dietitian:

D: Simona has agreed that this weekend she will start to eat regular food at home. The aim of this session is therefore to discuss how best to organize these meals. What do you think?

F: I think that it's a good idea.

M: Yes, but I hope that Simona is ready to go on to eating regular food.

S: Don't you believe I am ready?

M: I am a little worried, because we had a lot of problems with regular food before the intensive treatment.

S: I have been eating regular food twice a week outside the unit in restaurants, pizzerias and fast-food joints, and I haven't had any problems.

D: Have you noticed any improvement in Simona's way of eating?

M: Yes, I have. Now the atmosphere is more relaxed, and the family meals are similar to those we had before Simona started having problems.

F: Yes, it is true. Now Simona eats at a normal speed, and we can freely discuss various things. The only difference is that she has been eating frozen food.

D: Simona, do you feel ready to eat regular food with your parents?

S: Yes, I do.

D: Good. Well, as you know, Simona is currently following Menu D in order to achieve a weight gain of between 0.5 and 1 kg per week.

M: Yes, Simona explained this to me, and that to gain 1 kg per week she has to eat about 1,000 kcal a day more than those she would normally consume.

D: Very good. The menu plan is based on the exchange system. As you see, lunch, for example, comprises a portion of pasta, a portion of meat, a portion of vegetables, half a portion of bread, and a portion of fruit. Each one of these portions can be one of a large number of options within the same food group. For example, the portion of chicken can be replaced by a portion of fish, ham, or cheese, etc.

M: Yes, I understand.

D: Simona and I have agreed that you will plan her meals in advance with her, for example, the day before. Do you also agree?

M: Yes, but I can't prepare different food for all the family.

D: You are right. However, the exchange system should allow you to plan nutritious meals for all the family. Simona has also agreed that her choice should not influence too much what the rest of the family eats. Isn't that right, Simona?

S: Yes, you're right.

D: We have also agreed that, as in most families, you, her mother, are the person responsible for food shopping, preparation, and serving.

M: If Simona agrees, it will be a pleasure for me to do this.

D: Will you try to do your best to follow the dietary plan?

M: Of course, but what about the portions of the food?

D: At first you should weigh the portions, but you should gradually introduce portions that haven't been weighed, as in most families.

M: But does Simona agree?

S: Yes, I agree. Here I've learned that it is not necessary to weigh food precisely to control my weight.

M: Ok, good. If Simona is ready then I'm ready.

F: I also think this is a good idea. It seems that things are gradually getting back to normal.

D: Good, that's settled then. I suggest that all of you do your best to address meal planning and family meals. We will fix another family session in two weeks to review how you have been getting on.

Weeks 10–12

Objective

- Step down the treatment from intensive outpatient to standard CBT-E.

*Stepping Down the Treatment from Intensive Outpatient
to Standard CBT-E*

In the last two weeks of intensive outpatient CBT-E, Simona ate only her Monday meals at the unit, and had only one session a week with the psychologist and one session a week with the dietitian. The aim was to gradually transform the intensive outpatient CBT-E into standard outpatient CBT-E. By week 11, Simona had reached a BMI of 19.7 (29th percentile), and had started to address the residual dietary restraint and rules by the same procedures adopted in outpatient CBT-E, as well as to maintain her weight following a flexible healthy diet based on national dietary guidelines. Simona agreed to see the psychologist only once a week during the outpatient treatment, but asked for the possibility to contact the dietitian in case of necessity.

OUTPATIENT CBT-E (FOLLOWING INTENSIVE OUTPATIENT CBT-E)

In Simona's case, the outpatient CBT-E program following the intensive phase of outpatient treatment lasted twelve weeks. The main focus was to tackle Simona's residual dietary restraint and overvaluation of shape and weight, and to address the events and associated mood changes that could influence her eating.

[. . .] Selected transcripts—addressing residual dietary rules:

P: Well, I see that you did the homework, classifying the food you avoid into four groups. Are you ready to address these residual dietary rules?

S: The foods in the fourth group terrify me.

P: Don't worry. We will start with the food in the first group.

S: I hope so, otherwise I'm leaving [smiling]!

P: Ok, next week I suggest you choose some foods from the first group and try to eat them.

S: Should I decide when to eat them?

P: Yes, it is useful to plan breaking a dietary rule. I suggest also that you plan what to do after you introduce the avoided food.

S: Sure, I should avoid doing sit-ups [smiling]. I think I will play on the computer or draw.

P: Both very good ideas.

S: Ok, tomorrow I will try to introduce a slice of chocolate cake.

After seven weeks of outpatient CBT-E, Simona reported long periods characterized by the absence of preoccupations about her shape, weight, and eating, and her mindset appeared compatible with the situation she faced. The next step was to help her to control her eating problem mindset.

[. . .] Selected transcripts—learning to control the eating problem mindset:

P: You told me that you haven't been thinking about your shape and weight much recently.

S: That's right—for example yesterday I took a walk with Roberta and I didn't think about burning calories. The same thing happened last week at the dance lesson. I concentrated only on the movements of my body, and I enjoyed chatting with the other students.

P: Very good. This is the right moment for you to learn to control your eating problem mindset.

S: Can you explain this concept better?

P: Of course! Think of your mind as a DVD container. In general, you use a specific DVD for specific situations. For example, when you are out having fun with Roberta, you are using the "friend" DVD—it allows you to do what you need to do in that situation. Likewise, with your parents you activate the "daughter" DVD, and so on. However, you also have the "eating problem" DVD. This made it very difficult for you to use the appropriate DVD for a particular situation. When you started treatment this DVD was always operating, and so, when you were with Roberta, your mind was thinking about food and the shape of your stomach rather than what she was saying, and the same thing happened at school.

S: Yes, it's true.

P: However, the treatment has enabled you to interrupt the main mechanisms feeding the eating problem DVD, for example, being underweight, extreme and strict dietary rules, excessive exercising, body checking, and marginalization of other areas of life. This has produced a gradual reduction of your preoccupation about your control over eating, shape, and weight, and now you can use the right DVD to deal with the situation at hand. For example, last week when you were dancing, you easily activated the "dance class" DVD.

S: Yes, I understand.

P: However, although the "eating problem" DVD no longer interferes with your daily life, there is still a danger that some events might reactivate it.

S: For example?

P: Try to think of some possibilities.

S: Er . . . maybe if my weight goes up or I eat too much.

P: Yes, and it is common in cases of interpersonal difficulties or changes in mood.

S: Yes, it happens more frequently when I am upset or in a bad mood.

P: In these cases, you should be ready to decenter yourself rapidly from the eating problem DVD. In other words, you should recognize immediately the start of the eating problem DVD and turn it off without any hesitation, usually by doing the opposite of what the eating problem DVD wants you to do.

S: For example, if I have the impulse to skip a meal, I should eat.

P: Yes, precisely.

S: Ok. I get it.

[. . .]

S: It is difficult for me not to think about my figure and weight when I watch television—it only shows beautiful, skinny women with flat stomachs.

T: Yes, you are right. The media proposes that ideal of beauty and today thinness has been idealized by our society. For example, as you certainly know, that in the 1950s and 1960s the actresses and models had a completely different body shape—think of Sophia Loren or Marilyn Monroe. Beauty ideals also vary from place to place—for example, in Arabic countries, curvaceous women are admired.

S: This means that there is no such thing as an objective beauty norm.

P: Exactly! Plus, wherever we live, only very few people will fit the subjective cultural beauty norm because the shape of our body is strongly influenced by genetics. In our present day society, thinness is considered the ideal, in addition to being a sign of success and control. This idea, together with intense media pressure, makes women especially want to diet, to live up to these expectations, no matter what their genetic makeup.

S: This happened to me. If had been born in an Arabic country, I would probably have had fewer problems in accepting the shape of my stomach. I spent so much time comparing the shape of my stomach to those of other people, Giulia for example, that I lost sight of the fact that every women has her distinctive shape.

P: I agree.

S: I have to admit that the criticism about the shape of my belly I received from my classmates offended me and led me to conclude that I am a worthless person.

P: I understand that it was not nice to be bullied. However, it is impossible to ignore the social pressure to be thin. Luckily, in most cases bias related to the body shape may influence our initial opinion of a person, but it plays no part in the maintenance of a good and lasting relationship.

S: Yes, I agree.

P: One last thing—do you have any ideas on how to address any criticism about your body shape?

S: Well, my friend hasn't made any more comments about my body. However, if it happens I will try to say to myself that they are prejudiced, and that there is nothing wrong with my body.

P: Very good. I also suggest you to hang out with people who do not give too much importance to your thinness, and who, instead, appreciate your other assets.

The last three session were fixed for every two weeks and followed the same procedures and strategies described in Stage Four of chapter 9 (i.e., addressing concerns about the end of the treatment, phasing out treatment procedures, ensuring that progress is maintained, minimizing the risk of relapse in the longterm, and fixing the post-treatment review sessions).

Table 10.1 shows Simona's clinical state during the course of treatment, and at twenty- and forty-week follow-up.

Table 10.1. Simona's clinical status before and after treatment and at twenty- and forty-week follow-up

	Before	After four weeks of outpatient CBT-E	End of intensive outpatient CBT-E	End of outpatient CBT-E	Twenty-week follow-up	Forty-week follow-up
Weight (kg)	37.5	37.0	48.5	49.0	48.5	49.5
BMI (kg/m^2)	15.2	15.0	19.7	19.9	19.7	20.1
EDE-Q						
Global	5.2	4.6	2.2	0.5	0.6	0.5
Dietary restraint	5.0	4.2	1.8	0.2	0.3	0.2
Eating concern	4.4	3.6	1.2	0.4	0.5	0.3
Weight concern	5.4	4.6	2.4	0.6	0.6	0.6
Shape concern	6.0	6.0	3.6	1.0	1.0	0.8
Objective bulimic episodes[a]	0	0	0	0	0	0
Subjective bulimic episodes[a]	0	0	0	0	0	0
Self-induced vomiting[a]	0	0	0	0	0	0
Laxative misuse[a]	0	0	0	0	0	0
Diuretic misuse[a]	0	0	0	0	0	0
Driven exercise[a]	70	70	10	0	0	0
CIA	40	40	25	10	8	8

Notes: EDE-Q = Eating Disorder Examination Questionnaire; CIA = Clinical Impairment Assessment

[a]Number episodes over the past twenty-eight days

Chapter Eleven

Case Study C: Inpatient CBT-E

The case presented here illustrates the typical procedures and strategies applied in inpatient CBT-E, and shows how it can be used to help a patient with a long-standing eating disorder that has failed to respond to several outpatient treatments. Many details of the case have been modified to conceal the patient's identity and selected transcripts have been adapted for brevity.

CASE DESCRIPTION

Francesca, a thirty-three-year-old woman, was referred to our unit by her family doctor, who was concerned about the deterioration in her physical and psychosocial well-being. The CBT physician assessed the patient in two evaluation sessions, following the procedures and strategies described in chapter 4, and eventually opted for inpatient CBT-E.

At the first evaluation interview, Francesca reported she had been overweight during her childhood and early adolescence; in particular she remembers weighing 70 kg at the age of fourteen. At that time, however, she was not particularly concerned about her weight or shape, despite the fact that she was often teased and criticized about her figure by friends and family members. Indeed, her mother, who worked as a dressmaker, was particularly critical of Francesca's body shape, and, since she made her clothes, had the occasion to monitor its changes.

In fact, it was after an interchange with her mother that Francesca remembers deciding to start dieting for the first time. In this episode, still very vivid in her memory, she was walking with her mother and paused to admire a skirt in a shop window, which prompted her mother to reproach her as follows: "Don't even look at clothes like that—how can you expect to wear that with all your flab!" The day after this event, Francesca began to eliminate several "bad" foods (cookies, chocolate, pasta, and bread) from her diet and stopped all eating between meals. She also began to reduce her portion sizes and to skip meals when she was alone at home or when no one was checking up on her. In about six months she had lost 20 kg, arriving at a body weight of 50 kg, and she describes this period as the best in her life. She felt in control and special, and she received lots of positive feedback about her new body shape from both her mother and her friends.

In the following three months she lost another 8 kg, reaching a body weight of about 42 kg, and her periods ceased. Her mother's praise was gradually replaced by a renewal of severe criticism, this time for the abnormal eating behavior and excessive weight loss. Both her mother and her (obese, diabetic) father began to force her to eat when she sat down for family meals. Francesca reacted to this pressure by self-inducing vomiting after every meal consumed with her parents (usually the evening meal), and hiding food when she could, to throw away when no one was watching. In addition, she began to walk for several hours every day to increase her energy expenditure.

She maintained these behaviors and low weight until the age of eighteen years, when she met a boy, who later became her husband. Without undergoing any therapy, she began to eat regularly at this point, interrupting the self-induced vomiting and decreasing the amount of daily walking to no more than one hour a day, and, although she maintained residual dietary rules (i.e., avoiding sweets, limiting the amount of carbohydrates and fats), she reached a body weight of 52 kg and her periods returned. However, she continued to harbor a moderate fear of putting on weight, and lurking concerns about shape and weight, which were expressed through frequent weight checking (at least once a day) and checking the shape of her stomach, legs, and bottom in the mirror.

After nine years of engagement, she had an unplanned pregnancy. She married, and went to live in a little apartment with her husband. She successfully carried the child to term while maintaining her residual dietary rules, putting on an adequate amount of weight during her pregnancy (about 10 kg). At birth, the weight of her son was 2.9 kg. She did not breastfeed him, and about four weeks after childbirth she started to suffer from sadness, fatigue, changes in sleeping patterns, reduced libido, crying episodes, anxiety, and irritability (typical symptoms of post-partum depression). Her fear of gaining weight also dramatically escalated at this time, triggering recurrent thoughts such as: "I will get fat, like most married women," "I feel caged in this little apartment—I can't exercise as I would like." Perhaps inevitably this fear of weight gain brought on a relapse in the old extreme weight control behaviors such as vomiting after meals or skipping them altogether, as well as excessive and compulsive exercising.

This control of weight, shape, and eating consequently reactivated the positive feeling of self-control and mastery she felt in the first period of weight loss when she was fourteen years old, and within a few months, she had lost a large amount of weight, arriving at a body weight of 35 kg. Her husband and parents pressured her to begin a course of a psychodynamic psychotherapy, which she continued for four years. The focus of this therapy was the insecure attachment with her mother, who had given birth to Francesca at fifteen years of age and seemed to have had an ambivalent affect toward her child. Francesca went on to develop strong feelings of anger and hostility toward her mother, and blamed her for being the cause of her eating problem: "My mother never wanted me and still does not accept me as a daughter—that's why I'm sick with anorexia." Psychotherapy failed to change this mindset and produced no significant improvement in Francesca's eating problem, and her body weight remained stable at around 33 kg. At the age of thirty-one years, at the suggestion of her therapist, Francesca left her job at the tobacconist's that she managed with the help of her mother. Despite this, however, the family relations became increasingly tense and cold.

In the two years previous to my seeing her, after having dropped out of psychodynamic psychotherapy, Francesca reported frequent bouts of depression and one suicide attempt, in which she attempted to overdose on the benzodiazepines prescribed by her family physician. Over this period she received psychiatric treatment with antidepressants, atypical neuroleptics, and mood stabilizers, as well as two successive psychotherapy treatments, one of which was based on broad-CBT, to address both clinical depression and an eating disorder. These treatments, however, failed to produce any improvement in her eating disorder psychopathology.

Coinciding with a progressive deterioration in her family life, the severity of her eating disorder worsened (she reached a body weight of around 31 kg); at this time her husband spent long periods working away from home, and when he was at home vehemently criticized Francesca's eating behaviors. In addition, Francesca's son was being cared for in the afternoons after school by her mother.

Textbox 11.1 shows a summary of Francesca's case and textbox 11.2 shows the abbreviations used in the transcripts.

TEXTBOX 11.1. CASE C SUMMARY

Personal information and home life

- Age: Thirty-three years
- Occupation: Unemployed

- Marital status: Married
- Home life: Residing with her forty-year-old husband, a sales rep, and her twelve-year-old son
- Social class: Middle

Eating problem onset

- Age: Fourteen years
- Weight at the onset of the eating problem: 70 kg
- Behavioral precursor: Dieting
- Stated reasons for dieting: Losing weight and improving figure

The twelve months before the onset

- Events that may have triggered the control of eating, shape, and weight: Criticism and teasing about her weight by friends and mother

The six months after the onset

- She felt in control and special, and received positive comments about her new body shape

Since then

- After six months: Onset of self-induced vomiting after the meals consumed with parents, excessive exercising associated with dietary restriction; maintenance of these behaviors and a body weight of 45 kg until the age of eighteen
- Eighteen to twenty-seven years of age: After her engagement, interruption of self-induced vomiting and maintenance of residual excessive exercising and dietary restraint associated with moderate concerns about shape and weight; maintenance of body weight around 52 kg and return of regular periods
- Twenty-seven to thirty-one years of age: Unplanned pregnancy and marriage; post-partum depression associated with intensification of concerns about shape and weight, and the adoption of extreme weight control behaviors; maintenance of body weight around 33–35 kg until the age of thirty-one; psychodynamic psychotherapy for four years without any improvement

- Thirty-one to thirty-three years of age: Gave up work; increased severity of clinical depression with one suicide attempt, and deterioration of family relationships; no response to psychiatric treatments with drugs and two psychotherapies, one based on broad-CBT; maintenance of a body weight around 31–33 kg and habitual extreme weight control behaviors

Current state of the eating problem (last four weeks and last three months for DSM diagnosis)

- Current weight: 31 kg
- Current height: 155 cm
- BMI: 12.9
- Frequency of menstruation: 0 in the last three months
- Weight changes: Lost 1 kg
- Dietary restraint: Present
- Self-induced vomiting: Twenty-eight episodes per week (120 in the last three months) after every evening meal
- Objective binge eating, subjective binge eating, excessive exercising: Absent
- Smoking: Twenty cigarettes a day
- Substance or alcohol misuse: Both absent
- Weight checking: Once a day in the morning
- Shape checking and avoidance: Present
- Preoccupation with shape, weight, and eating control: Present
- Feeling fat and feeling full: Present
- Physical health, psychosocial functioning, and work: Impaired
- DSM-IV diagnosis: Anorexia nervosa (307.1)

Personal and family medical history

- Past and current medical and psychiatric comorbidity: Viral pneumonia at the age of thirty-two years. Borderline personality disorder diagnosis at the age of thirty-one
- Current medications: Fluoxetine 40 mg daily; Sodium valproate 500 mg daily
- Family medical and psychiatric history: Father obese and diabetic. A female cousin on the father's side with probable eating disorder

Physical Examination

- Bradycardia (heart rate 45 beats/min). Hypotension (80 mm Hg systolic). Cyanotic and cold hands and feet. Dry skin; lanugo hair on forearms. Orange discoloration of the skin of the palms and soles. Erosion of inner surface of front teeth (perimylolysis). Weak proximal muscles.

TEXTBOX 11.2. ABBREVIATIONS IN SELECTED TRANSCRIPTS

F = Francesca; AC = Assessing Clinician; D = Dietitian; N = Nurse; P = Psychologist; Ph = Physician; G = Gianni (the husband); C = Chicca (another patient in the unit); A=Arianna (another patient in the unit).

ASSESSING AND PREPARING FOR INPATIENT CBT-E

First Evaluation Interview

Objectives

- Assessing the patient's attitude toward the interview.
- Assessing the nature and the severity of the eating problem.
- Preparing the patient for inpatient treatment.

Assessing the Patient's Attitude toward the Interview

This was tackled in the first part of the interview, and, in particular, the assessing clinician set out to determine whether Francesca came to the consultation on her own accord or with reluctance.

[. . .] Selected transcripts:

AC: Did you come to this evaluation interview through your own choice?

F: I was a little pressured by my family doctor.

AC: Why did you agree to come here?

F: Well, I too wish to address my eating problem.

Assessing the Nature and Severity of the Eating Problem

The focus of the interview then shifted to assessing the development, nature, and severity of Francesca's present psychopathology:

[. . .] Selected transcripts:

> AC: Well. Do you agree that the main purpose of this evaluation interview is to exchange information about your eating problem and the treatments available? If you agree, we will analyze together the onset of your problem and the consequent course, and then we may go on to discuss the main treatment options that could help you to address your eating problem.

> F: Yes, I agree.

> AC: Well, let's start with the beginning of your eating problem. How old were you?

> F: I was fourteen. I was overweight and started a diet to lose weight.

> AC: What was your weight?

> F: I was very heavy. I weighed 70 kg.

> AC: Do you remember any important event that might have made you want to diet?

> F: Oh yes! I was looking at a skirt in a shop window, and my mom said: "Don't even look at clothes like that—how can you expect to wear that with all your flab!"

> [. . .]

> AC: Do you remember how you felt in the first months of dieting?

> F: It was fantastic. I was euphoric. I lost 20 kg in a few months, and I felt light and in control for the first time in my life. I received compliments about my new figure from many friends and my mom.

> AC: Do you still feel this way?

> F: Rarely, only when my scales show me I've lost weight, but it disappears in a second. Plus, now all my relatives criticize my eating behavior and weight.

AC: I am sorry about that.

[...]

AC: Well Francesca, now that I know a little bit about you, I would like to ask you a difficult question, and I want you to think very carefully before you answer. Do you think that the control of eating, shape, and weight is a healthy choice or a problem?

F: Um, it is not easy to say. For many years, I was sure that watching my weight and dieting was the best choice I had made in life, but now, I guess it has become a major problem.

AC: What are the clues that led you to conclude that it has become a problem?

F: Well, I have no life.

AC: Do you mean that your eating problem has damaged your life?

F: Yes.

AC: Which life area in particular do you think has been damaged by your eating problem?

F: I have no friends, my marriage is in crisis, and I do not work.

AC: Do you think that your eating problem has also influenced your psychological functioning?

F: Yes, of course. I used to be a sunny person—now I am really depressed.

AC: And what about your physical condition?

F: You can see what I look like. . . .

AC: I realize that you really do see the control of eating and weight as a problem. However, it is not clear to me why you do not try to change. I understand that this is difficult to explain but I think it is crucial that we analyze this issue.

F: I don't know . . . or rather, I know that I have to change and put on weight, but in practice, when food is in front of me, I find myself unable to eat . . . I am too afraid to eat, and of losing control of my weight . . . I also feel better when I am able not to eat.

AC: And when you do eat, for example your evening meal . . .

F: I feel full, and I have the uncontrollable urge to be sick. I can't stop myself.

AC: So . . . I understand that you see the eating problem as a very important problem, but you don't feel able to change because you are too afraid, because eating makes you feel uncomfortably full, and not eating makes you feel good, more in control.

F: Yes, that's it.

The first evaluation session was then wound up after recording Francesca's weight (she weighed herself and told the assessing clinician the reading on the scale) and height, followed by a physical examination (see chapter 4).

Preparing for Inpatient Treatment

To prepare Francesca for the inpatient treatment, the assessing clinician followed the following steps:

- *Educating her about her eating problem*: this was performed through drawing up a provisional formulation of Francesca's eating problem to include the main maintenance mechanisms reported by her in the first part of the evaluation session. In particular, the assessing clinician explained the effect of being underweight and the symptoms of starvation, the effect of self-induced vomiting, and informed her about the overvaluation of shape, weight, and eating control and the self-perpetuating nature of the eating problem (see chapter 2).
- *Providing detailed information about the treatment*: the assessing clinician explained the inpatient CBT-E treatment in detail and gave Francesca an information pamphlet, after which they visited the unit together.
- *Setting homework*: at the end of the first evaluation session the assessing clinician asked Francesca to do three items of homework prior to the following evaluation session: (i) to consider the pros and cons of doing inpatient CBT-E; (ii) to read the information pamphlet on inpatient CBT-E; and (iii) to create a list of questions about the inpatient treatment to discuss with the therapist.

[. . .] Selected transcripts:

AC: Francesca, have you already done any research on eating problems?

F: Um . . . I've read a few books written by patients. . . .

AC: Would you be interested in having some information about some of the main mechanisms behind your eating problem? This will help you to better understand the targets of the treatment.

F: Yes, ok.

[. . .]

AC: Francesca, looking at this diagram (her provisional personal formulation), in your opinion what should be the target of a treatment to overcome your eating problem?

F: Um . . . I don't know . . . maybe being underweight?

AC: Yes. You are right. As you can see, being underweight and the associated starvation symptoms, for example, a slow metabolism and the continued preoccupation with food, intensify your need to control your eating. In addition, the symptoms of starvation are associated with changes in mood and personality, and a tendency to avoid social interaction—all problems that need to be addressed if we are to overcome your eating problem. But do you think that this can be done by normalizing your body weight alone?

F: No, absolutely not.

AC: Look at the formulation. Why do you maintain a strict diet and vomit after small meals?

F: Because I am afraid of gaining weight and losing my control over eating.

AC: Yes, you are right. That's the reason why the final aim of the therapy is to reduce the importance you attribute to shape, weight, and eating control. In other words, to overcome your eating problem it is necessary that you gradually develop a self-evaluation system based on other domains, not only your shape, weight, and eating control.

F: Um . . . I'm not sure I understand. . . .

AC: Take a look at these pie charts. Every slice of the pie chart represents the relative importance that a person gives to a particular life domain when one decides his or her own worth. As you can see in this first chart [shows Francesca a healthy chart], this person judges him- or herself on lots of different things—doing well at school, having good friends, etc.— not only on what he or she looks like or weighs. This pie chart, on the other hand, shows a self-evaluation system typical of a person with an eating problem. What do you notice?

F: The slice of shape and weight is predominant.

AC: And (indicating the other slices)?

F: There aren't many other slices and they are all very small.

AC: You are right! Look again at this first pie chart (that of the person without the eating problem)—why is it different?

F: There are more slices.

AC: Yes, and none is predominant. As you can see, this person gives some importance to the control of shape and weight (indicating the corresponding slice), but this is not excessive, and, in addition, there are many other domains of self-evaluation.

F: That's clear.

AC: Would you say that your pie chart would be more like the first or more like the second?

F: If I'm honest, the second.

AC: Ok, to put it simply, the aim of the treatment is to change your pie chart, developing one that is more like the first.

F: Ah . . . now I understand!

AC: However, if you take another look at this diagram, which we call your formulation, you will see that to reach this goal, it will be necessary to gradually interrupt all your extreme weight-control behaviors, including dietary restriction and self-induced vomiting, and also normalize your body weight, as you said before, because all of these features are obstacles to the development of a self-evaluation system less dependent on shape, weight, and eating control.

F: I agree, but it won't be easy to change after so many years. I have already failed at many outpatient treatments and I am not hopeful about my chances of success.

AC: I understand your difficulties. It was for this reason that your family doctor referred you here, and this is why I think we should talk together about the pros and cons of getting you into a specialist inpatient unit to overcome your eating problem.

F: But I am a chronic case!

AC: I prefer to use the term long-standing eating problem, rather than the term chronic case. Chronic means that there are no possibilities of recovery—in my clinical practice I have seen many patients who, like you, have a long-standing eating problem, but go on to recover completely.

F: That makes me feel a little more hopeful.

AC: Good, because there is hope!

F: My family doctor explained something to me about your kind of treatment, but I would like to have more information.

AC: Right, let's go over what the treatment involves.

F: Ok.

AC: First, hospital admission is voluntary, and is reserved for patients who want to change but need a little more help than outpatient treatments can give.

F: Like me . . .

AC: Exactly. But you should know that since you have an eating problem that has lasted for many years, you are going to need to put all your effort into the treatment if it is going to be successful. To overcome your eating problem you will need to work hard and make your treatment your number one priority, but I assure you it will be worth it. The more you put in, the more you will get out.

F: I agree.

AC: You should also see the treatment as positive opportunity to make a fresh start, a chance to build a new life where you are no longer conditioned by your eating problem. Like any change there are risks, but the benefits you can achieve are enormous—we aim to get you thinking more freely, without being continuously oppressed by thoughts about what you're eating, how you look, and what you weigh. Think how it will feel to be happier, less irritated, more flexible, and have a broader perspective on things, to improve your physical well-being and family life.

F: I understand.

AC: Although you will need to come stay in the unit at first, you won't be locked in—as long as your medical conditions are stable you are perfectly free to go out and about. Likewise, your friends and relatives can visit you anytime other than mealtimes and scheduled sessions. You are responsible for your own behavior, and therefore your own progress.

F: I like this aspect of the treatment. I would not like to feel as if I were in a cage.

AC: The treatment is an intensive adaptation of outpatient cognitive behavioral therapy, one of most effective treatments for eating problems. It is primarily focused on what is maintaining, or fueling, your eating problem (indicating the personal formulation). The main procedures used in the unit are assisted eating, until you reach a BMI equal to or greater than 18.5; individual sessions with the psychologist, twice a week in the first four weeks, and then once a week; group sessions three times a week; a review meeting with all the therapists once a week; and two sessions of light physical exercise a week.

F: Is the program the same for all patients?

AC: No. The treatment is individualized to address the specific mechanisms maintaining your eating problem. You and your therapists will need to become experts on your particular eating problem and what is fuelling it, and will work together as a team to tackle it. Together, you will decide on specific tasks—or "next steps"—that you will agree to carry out between sessions. The tasks are extremely important and will need to be given absolute priority. It is what you do between sessions that will largely determine the benefits you will gain from the treatment. The more active your role in the treatment, the greater your chances are of overcoming your eating problem.

F: How many therapists will I have?

AC: You will be assigned five main therapists, who are all fully trained in cognitive behavior therapy: a dietitian, a psychologist, a physician, a psychiatrist, and a nurse; each of them has a specific role in the treatment. If any of these people are absent due to sickness, etc., they will be substituted by other therapists so that your treatment is not interrupted.

F: And what about the target weight?

AC: As we discussed before, the main goal of the treatment is to obtain a psychological change and, in particular, a self-evaluation less influenced by shape weight, and eating control. To achieve this goal you will be helped to reach and maintain a body weight at the lower end of a normal weight range, a BMI between 19.0 and 20.0, and you will follow flexible dietary guidelines, as part of your addressing the overvaluation of shape, weight, and eating control.

F: In term of body weight, what is my target?

AC: Between 45 and 48 kg.

F: It is too high—I can't imagine weighing that much!

AC: I understand how you feel. However, as we discussed before, if you wish to overcome your eating problem, you should gradually normalize your weight. The treatment will teach you many strategies for reducing your preoccupations with weight, and you will be actively involved in checking and interpreting your weight and in planning the diet to reach and then to maintain the target weight.

F: But, what if I am unhappy at that weight?

AC: First I suggest you decide to see what feels like to be a normal, albeit low, weight and to stop the control of shape, weight, and eating running your life—a kind of experiment, if you will. Then, if you feel dissatisfied with the outcome you can always go back to how you were.

F: Um . . . and how long does the treatment last?

AC: The treatment usually lasts twenty weeks, thirteen of which you will spend in the inpatient clinic and seven as a day patient, but you should know that the day treatment period may be prolonged to address some specific issues. Do you have any other questions?

F: Um . . . how many patients recover from their eating problem with this treatment?

AC: Our data indicates that about 90 percent of patients complete the inpatient treatment, and almost 60 percent of completers have a satisfactory outcome at one-year follow-up. If you give priority to the treatment, you have a good prospect of being in the group with a positive outcome.

[. . .]

AC: For the next evaluation session I suggest you think about the pros and cons of starting the inpatient treatment and writing these down on a list. Try not to focus only on the short term—try to include the long-term effects as well. Think about what your eating problem is doing to your health, psychological functioning, relationships and work performance, and, conversely, whether there is anything positive that your eating problem gives you that you are afraid to lose. I'm sure you will also have many questions regarding the treatment, so I suggest you make a list of those too. Do you agree to do this homework?

F: Yes, I'll do it.

Second Evaluation Interview (three days after the first)

Objectives

- Weighing up the wisdom of treatment and reinforcing interest in change.
- Obtaining Consent to Inpatient Treatment.

Weighing Up the Wisdom of Treatment and Reinforcing Interest in Change

Along with Francesca, the assessing clinician went over the pros and cons of starting the treatment while reinforcing interest in change and addressing any questions she had. During this discussion, the assessing clinician helped Francesca to focus on her life aspirations and not just on the present, reinforcing every reason for change. He then helped her to analyze the disadvantages of change, and to reach the conclusion that the positive aspects of her eating problems (feeling in control and avoiding difficulties in life) were transitory and unfailingly associated with a severe impairment in her quality of life. Time was also spent reassuring Francesca that the adoption of the CBT-E strategies for weight regain and maintenance would help her to maintain long-term weight control in the lower normal weight range (i.e., a BMI between 19.0 and 20.0). Finally, he addressed all Francesca's questions about the treatment and asked her whether she would agree to sign up.

[. . .] Selected transcripts:

F: Can I stop treatment whenever I want?

AC: Yes, you can interrupt the treatment whenever you wish. However, leaving the treatment prematurely is rarely, if ever, a good idea. Most patients who leave the treatment prematurely still have their eating problem one year after discharge. If you decide to undertake the inpatient treatment, it is better for you to *find solutions* to the difficulties associated with the change and not seek ways to avoid them.

F: Do I have to eat all the food they give me?

AC: Yes, but you will be assisted by a dietitian during the first, most difficult, phase of the treatment, and you will learn many strategies to help you tackle your fear and concerns about eating. Every week you will decide, following the *Unit Weight Regain Guidelines*, the energy intake you will need to achieve an increase in weight between 1 to 1.5 kg per week. If you don't put on as much as you expect, you will modify your diet plan accordingly. The idea is that you will be in control during the difficult phase of weight regain, although our staff will be on hand to help you. When you will reach a BMI between 19.0 and 20.0, you will no longer be assisted during eating, and you will learn to maintain your weight by following flexible dietary guidelines.

F: What happens if I fail to recover from my eating problem?

AC: About 90 percent of patients complete the treatment, and most of them substantially improve their eating problem. However, at the end of inpatient treatment it is rare that patients are fully recovered from their eating disorder—most have residual issues, particularly concerns about shape and weight, which will then be addressed in outpatient treatment. Thus, the aim of inpatient treatment is not to recover completely from the eating problem, but to reach a condition that will permit you to obtain a successful outcome from the outpatient treatment.

F: I know that many patients improve with the inpatient treatment but then relapse when they return home.

AC: You are right, Francesca! This is why this inpatient treatment has been developed to include specific strategies that will reduce the likelihood of you relapsing after discharge. First, it is focused on modifying the mechanisms behind your eating problem, and you will learn personalized relapse-prevention skills before you go home. Second, you will be free to go outside, so you will still be exposed to the types of environmental stimuli that tend to maintain your problem. Third, during day-hospital prior to discharge, you will work with your therapists to identify likely triggers of your eating problem that do not operate in the hospital setting. Finally, if you agree, toward the end of treatment your relatives will be involved in creating a positive, stress-free home environment in preparation for your return.

F: The eating problem is the only thing I have, it is a big part of my life. I'm worried about who I will become without it.

AC: I understand your concerns. Your eating problem has gone on for so many years that it has become a part of you. However, as you agreed, the eating problem has impaired your life. Without the eating problem, you will improve your physical health, fitness, mood, interpersonal functioning, and self-esteem, and you will no longer be controlled by your overvaluation of shape and weight. Also, think how exciting and interesting it will be to discover your true personality and who you are without the eating problem!

Obtaining Consent to Inpatient Treatment

Francesca, although ambivalent about the prospect of change, decided that she would sign up for the inpatient CBT-E program and her admission was scheduled for the following Monday morning.

INPATIENT CBT-E

Stage One (Week 1)

Objectives

- Starting well.
- Implementing the main treatment procedures.

Starting Well

The first day of treatment is crucial. Francesca was admitted on Monday so as to have five weekdays in which to engage her in the treatment. At admission, the nurse welcomed Francesca, assigned her a room, explained the organization of the unit, and went over the weekly therapeutic plan displayed on the unit's notice board. The nurse also met with Francesca's husband to explain practical aspects of unit organization (e.g., visiting times, appropriate times to call for information about Francesca's treatment, and the ban on taking any food or beverage into the unit). Francesca then had a session with the dietitian, who explained the specific strategies for addressing assisted meals and illustrated the treatment guidelines for weight regain and weight maintenance. In this meeting, the dietitian repeated the key concepts described by the assessing clinician during the evaluation interviews (e.g., obtaining the maximum change early on, giving priority to treatment, playing an active role in the treatment, being punctual for sessions, developing a collaborative relationship with the therapists), and suggested that Francesca try to adopt these attitudes starting from the first assisted lunch. On the same morning of admission, the physician recorded medical histories, carried out a full physical examination, and prescribed laboratory and other tests. The following morning the physician also measured Francesca's resting metabolic rate with the indirect calorimetry.

[. . .] Selected transcripts from the session with the dietitian:

D: Francesca, I know that you discussed with Doctor X (the assessing clinician) the weight goals and general procedures used by our treatment to help you start eating properly and restore a healthy weight.

F: Yes, but not in detail.

D: Good. Now is the perfect occasion to explain you the *Weight Regain Guidelines* of the treatment.

F: Ok.

D: First. Do you know how to calculate your BMI?

F: Yes. It's my weight in kilograms divided by the square of my height in meters.

D: That's right. Do you know your current BMI?

F: It is about 12.

D: When is a BMI considered underweight?

F: I am not sure, but I think under 18.5.

D: Yes, that's right. So you are underweight.

F: Yes, according to the BMI definition. But sometimes I feel fat.

D: Right, but is it clear to you why we have to address your low weight to overcome your eating problem?

F: Er . . . yes and no.

D: Ok, there are three main reasons. First, many of your current behaviors and experiences, such as food obsessions, low mood, irritability, lack of interest in socializing, loss of sex drive, and the fact that you no longer get your period, are caused by your low body weight. These are called starvation symptoms, and I think you can agree that they are neither healthy nor pleasant. Second, all these negative effects of low weight will disappear when you reach a healthy weight. Third, as you saw in your formulation, your low weight is actually serving to maintain your eating problem.

F: Why is it a maintaining factor?

D: Because it is associated with starvation symptoms, because you need to take extreme weight control measures to maintain it, and, last but not least, it does not allow you to have a normal, healthy social life.

F: I understand *why* I need to put on some kilograms, but . . . I'm terrified of doing it and losing control of my eating and weight.

D: I know, and this was the main reason you decided to come here, so that we can help you deal with these fears. We are going to teach you some strategies to help you put on weight with less anxiety and without that feeling of losing control. To start with, let's review together the treatment's *Weight Regain Guidelines*.

F: Ok.

D: The guidelines have been developed to help you keep active control in the process of weight regain and weight maintenance. You know that since you are underweight, your target is a BMI between 19 and 20, as this range of BMI can usually be maintained without dietary restriction, it is not associated with symptoms of being underweight, and permits a social life; knowing that this is your target, it is you that has to take control of reaching it.

F: How do I do that?

D: You should aim for a gain of 1 to 1.5 kg per week—you should be able to do this if you stick to this diet plan. Since you are severely underweight, if you eat too much at once, your body will not be able to handle the change and you may develop a condition called refeeding syndrome; for this reason your initial diet will contain no more than 1,000 calories per day. You will increase this to 1,250 after three days, and add another 250 calories after the following three days. After this initial period, it is you who will have to interpret your weekly weight change, which you will record on a personalized weight graph, and decide on the modifications to your diet on the basis of these guidelines.

F: I don't understand—you are saying that I can choose what I eat?

D: Yes, the point is that you know your target and you are in charge of getting there. We have drawn up these guidelines to help you. As it says here, if your weight increases between 1 to 1.5 kg per week you are on the right track and should maintain the same calorie content as the previous week. If, however, your weight increases by less than 1 kg per week, you will know that you will have to increase your daily calorie intake by 500 kcals. If, on the other hand, your weight increases *more* than 1.5 kg per week, you should decrease the calorie content of your diet by 250 kcals per day.

F: What happens when I get to a BMI of 19.0?

D: You will gradually reduce the calorie content of your diet until you find a level where you maintain a BMI of between 19.0 and 20.0.

F: Are you sure that I will not go over a BMI of 20.0?

D: Yes, absolutely! Following this plan you will realize that to regain weight at an average rate of 1 kg per week you will need to consume, on average, an extra 1,000 kcal of energy each day over and above what you are currently consuming, assuming your weight is stable.

F: But, what will I be eating?

D: The diet is flexible but you will follow the nutritional dietary guidelines for a healthy diet. This means that you will be eating a wide range of foods, and that you will not have to stick to a rigid calorie target per day, rather a weekly mean. To help you get used to this new way of eating, the nurses will serve you your food in the first week.

F: But I am afraid to eat. I know I won't be able to eat pasta and other carbs without panicking.

D: Don't worry. My colleagues and I will be there to help. What I want you to bear in mind, however, is that for you at the moment food is like medicine; you should try to eat mechanically, ignoring any sensations of hunger or fullness or preoccupations about food and eating. Think of a meal as a pill you have to take four times a day at the right dose in order to get better—you may not enjoy the process but you should soon reap the rewards. Also remember that a calorie is a calorie, whatever form it takes.

F: What do you mean "a calorie is a calorie"?

D: I mean that a calorie from fat is identical to a calorie from proteins and carbohydrates, so you shouldn't feel a particular aversion to specific food groups.

F: Um . . . and how long should I eat in this mechanical way?

D: You should continue this type of eating until you can eat a healthy diet on your own without fear of losing control.

F: And . . . what if I have the impulse to vomit after eating?

D: To deal with the urge to vomit, you will not have access to the bathroom for 1 hour after eating; instead you will stay in the recreation room where you can read, listen to music, use the computer, chat to the staff or other patients, watch television, and generally do anything you need to do to distract yourself. Try to consider the impulse to be sick as a transitory phenomenon that you can tolerate.

Implementing the Main Treatment Procedures

The first procedure to implement is *assisted eating*. The CBT-E-trained dietitian oversees this process, typically over the first six weeks, or until a patient reaches a BMI greater than or equal to 18.5, using cognitive behavioral procedures to help patients eat. In this phase patients eat three meals and a snack each day (breakfast, lunch, midafternoon snack, and evening meal) in the dining room, together with their fellow patients.

[. . .] Selected transcripts from the first assisted meal with the dietitian:

D: Francesca, welcome to your first assisted meal. I understand that it is difficult for you to tackle this meal, but try to apply the strategies we discussed. Try to eat mechanically, and to consider the food as a medicine. This will help you eat with less anxiety.

F: Ok, I will try.

D: I will be here to help you to address any difficulties you may experience.

During this first meal, Francesca was extremely slow to eat, and cut the food into very small pieces. The dietitian therefore gave her several suggestions designed to help her tackle the meal with less preoccupation and anxiety.

[...]

F: There is too much food here; it's too much. . . .

D: Try to eat mechanically. Tell yourself that this is not food, but a medicine with a dosage right for your needs. Its color or taste is not important: it is exactly the right amount.

[...]

D: Try to make forkfuls the same size you would give to a friend with a broken arm.

[...]

D: Try not to focus on the pain associated with eating, but on the fact that eating will help you to recover.

With extreme difficulty, Francesca managed to complete her first meal. At the end of the meal, the dietitian therefore praised her efforts and her ability to successfully address one of the most difficult tasks in the treatment. She also went on to emphasize that getting off to a good start meant that she was on track for a successful treatment outcome. Afterward, the dietitian accompanied Francesca to the recreation room. In the afternoon, Francesca participated in a psychoeducational group session and was then similarly assisted while she ate her afternoon snack and evening meal.

The next technique to implement was *weight monitoring*. During Stage One, this is carried out once a week with the assistance of the nurse. The patient is encouraged to weigh him- or herself using the unit's private scales, featuring subdivisions of 0.5 kg. Indeed, smaller subdivisions (e.g., 0.1 kg) are viewed as unhelpful in eating disorder patients, who would tend to focus on even the slightest variation in their weight. Accordingly, Francesca recorded her own weight on a graph designed to chart her progress, as well as in the last column of her monitoring record. Francesca was also encouraged to write her interpretation of weight change on the monitoring record, adopting a decentered stance, as if she were a therapist.

[. . .] Selected transcripts from the weigh-in session with the nurse:

F: Yesterday I ate too much . . . I don't want to weigh myself. It makes me feel anxious and it will make it more difficult for me to eat.

N: I understand, but weight avoidance is common in people with eating disorders and tends to maintain concerns about weight. Knowing your weight is fundamental to overcoming your eating problem. Gradually you will be become less and less anxious about your weight; you will become an expert in interpreting your weight changes, and this will help you to decide how to adjust your diet appropriately to regain and then to maintain your weight. Let's try. I know that it is difficult for you, but I am here to help.

F: Ok.

After successfully weighing and monitoring, Francesca was encouraged to *evaluate her progress*, by filling out the Eating Problem Checklist (see appendix).

[. . .] Selected transcripts of the nurse explaining the use of Eating Problem Checklist:

N: Francesca, this is your Eating Problem Checklist; it is a list of behaviors and concerns typically experienced by people with eating problems. You should report how often you have experienced any of these things over the last seven days.

F: Ok, I understand. But why do I have to do this?

N: So I can insert the data into the computer, which will help us make a table showing your treatment course and progress. This will not only help you see how you are progressing, but you will also discuss your scores together with your therapists in the weekly review meeting.

Once a week, a *weekly review meeting* is held. This is scheduled on the same morning as the weighing and monitoring session, and is attended by the patient and all the patient's therapists (i.e., physician, psychologist, dietitian, and nurse). At this round table, the various aspects of the treatment and their relationship to one another are discussed. The weekly review meeting is a fundamental procedure to adopt in the inpatient unit since it permits all team members to have a complete picture of the patient's eating disorder and to avoid the delivery of mixed messages. The patient's personal formulation, the weight graph, and the progress table based on the Eating Problem Check-list scores are placed on the table so that everyone can see them. The review meeting starts by setting the agenda of the topics to address together with the patient, who is then asked to give an interpretation of his or her weight chart.

[. . .] Selected transcripts from the first weekly review meeting:

Ph: Francesca, can we discuss your weight graph?

F: Ok.

Ph: In this program you should become an expert in interpreting your weight. This will help you to feel in control during the entire process of the treatment.

F: I know, the nurse explained this procedure to me.

Ph: Is the weight graph clear to you?

F: Yes, it is quite clear. The vertical axis shows my weight in kilograms, and the horizontal axis the weeks of treatment.

Ph: Perfect. Do you remember your weekly weight-gain target?

F: Yes, it is between one and one and a half kilograms per week but . . . if I eat like I did yesterday, I will surely put on more than this.

Ph: Have you been given information about the energy surplus you need to regain one kilogram per week?

F: I discussed this with the dietitian, but I'd prefer to go over it again.

Ph: No problem. To achieve an increase of one kilogram per week, you need a surplus of 1,000 calories per day. The mean daily calorie content of your diet for this week is about 1,200, a low energy content to prevent the development of refeeding syndrome.

F: Yes, the dietitian explained this problem to me.

Ph: This morning the indirect calorimetry test showed that you have a resting energy expenditure of 800 calories, i.e., you burn 800 calories a day, even at rest. Supposing that you use just 200 calories in your normal activities during the day—this means that you have a positive energy balance of about 200 calories per day. What does this tell you?

F: Um . . . that I will probably put on less than half a kilogram per week.

Ph: Exactly, probably less than half a kilogram. However, since you are very dehydrated, it is possible that in the first two or three weeks you will put on a little more weight from water—this is a natural phenomenon called rehydration.

F: Yes, I understand.

[. . .]

Ph: In the next weekly review meeting we will be able to see how much weight you have put on, and you will then interpret this and decide how to modify your diet to maintain a weight regain within your one- to one-and-a-half-kilogram weekly target.

F: I know, the dietitian explained this.

Ph: Good. I suggest that as well as on your graph, you write your weight and your interpretation of it in the last column of your monitoring sheet. But we will discuss this in detail during the individual CBT-E sessions.

F: Ok.

In the following weekly review meetings, the therapists and Francesca, after her weight change interpretation and the according adjustment to her diet plan, evaluated the state of her personal formulation and her Eating Problem Checklist scores. The barriers and difficulties encountered in the previous week were also discussed, as well as the target maintenance mechanisms to be addressed in the next seven days, and any practical problems associated with the treatment (e.g., permission for exams, organization of weekends at home). At these meetings any possible coexisting medical and psychiatric problems are also assessed and treated.

Twice weekly in the first four weeks and then once a week, *individual CBT-E sessions* are scheduled. These are conducted by a psychologist trained in CBT-E and each lasts fifty minutes. In Francesca's case, the first session was fixed for the Tuesday, the day after admission, and included the following components:

- *Engaging the patient in treatment and change.* Even if Francesca decided voluntarily to be admitted, she was very ambivalent about the change, and the process of admission, including addressing eating, increased her reluctance. As with outpatient CBT-E, it is essential that the therapist is empathetic to the patient's ambivalence and addresses this issue accordingly.
- *Explaining what the treatment involves.* Much of the information provided during the pre-admission evaluation was gone over, and the importance of "starting well" and "ending well" (i.e., completing the treatment) were both emphasized.
- *Assessing the nature and severity of the psychopathology.* This was the focus of the first individual CBT-E session. The aim was to evaluate Francesca's present state and the maintenance mechanisms behind it so as to construct the personalized formulation. As the procedure is similar to that used for outpatient CBT-E, it is not described here.
- *Creating the patient's formulation of the processes maintaining the eating problem.* The personal formulation was constructed in collaboration with Francesca, who helped to identify the maintenance mechanisms to address in the treatment. Using the formulation, the therapist explained how these mechanisms work (see chapter 2), and then the discussion centered on Francesca's core eating disorder psychopathology (i.e., the overvaluation of shape, weight, and eating control), and her main maintenance mechanisms (e.g., strict dieting, being underweight and starvation syndrome, binge eating, and self-induced vomiting, body checking and avoidance, feeling fat, marginalization of other areas of life).
- *Setting up real-time self-monitoring.* The psychologist then explained to Francesca the rationale behind self-monitoring, and gave practical suggestions on how to use the monitoring records. As the procedure is similar to those used for outpatient CBT-E, I will not describe it here. The only difference in this case was that during assisted eating Francesca was encouraged to write only the name of the meal and not every item of food she consumed.
- *Setting homework.* At the end of session 1, the psychologist asked Francesca to complete two homework assignments for the next session, namely beginning real-time meal monitoring and reviewing her provisional formulation.
- *Summarizing the session and arranging the next appointment.* The session ended by collaboratively summarizing its content, reiterating the homework, and reminding Francesca of the next appointment.

[. . .] Selected transcripts from the first individual CBT-E session with the psychologist:

P: Francesca, how has being in the unit affected your motivation to change?

F: It is very hard, especially the eating. Yesterday evening I was thinking about going home, but then I decided to persevere. I want to overcome my eating problem.

P: I know that it is not easy, but I am glad to know that you are motivated to change. Do you have any concerns?

F: Do you really think I will be able to complete the treatment and get better? I have had my eating problem for so many years.

P: Based on the data we have on our inpatient treatment, the duration of the eating problem does not influence the outcome. In addition, I cannot see why you should not benefit from the treatment. I suggest that you don't waste time thinking about this issue. It would be better for you to throw yourself into treatment and give it priority—the more you put in, the more probability you have of overcoming your eating problem.

F: But . . . the eating problem is my life.

P: I understand that you see yourself as defined by your eating problem, making it difficult to let go of, but we have also seen how it seems to have a negative impact on all other aspects of your life. Without it you will be far stronger and happier than you assume.

[. . .]

P: Francesca, may we review what the individual sessions will involve? You have already discussed this with the assessing clinician, but I think it would be better if we go over certain points.

F: Ok.

P: You know that the treatment is based on CBT-E, one of the most effective treatments for eating disorders.

F: I read the patients' information pamphlet.

P: The goal of the treatment is to obtain a psychological change, and in particular a self-evaluation less influenced by shape, weight, and eating control. To achieve this goal you will try to reach and maintain a body weight at the lower range of normal weight using flexible dietary guidelines, and addressing the overvaluation of shape, weight, and eating control.

F: Rationally I agree with these goals, but the target weight is too high. I really do not know if I will be able to reach and to tolerate a BMI of 19. It frightens me just to think about it.

P: Yes, I understand your fears. But do you really think that it is possible to overcome an eating problem maintaining an unhealthily low body weight?

F: No. I know that I will have to address the weight regain. I discussed this issue with the dietitian too.

P: Right then, let's focus on the content of the treatment. You know that the things we will talk about in our sessions will be highly individualized to address the specific mechanisms maintaining your eating problem. We will both need to become experts on your eating problem and on what is keeping it going.

F: I like this approach. It was one of the reasons I decided to come to this unit.

P: Your attitude toward the treatment is crucial for its success. I encourage you to see the treatment as an opportunity to make a fresh start.

F: The assessing clinician stressed this concept to me.

P: Good. In other words, this treatment should be seen as an opportunity to build a new life without being conditioned by your eating problem. For this reason I suggest you really try to get off to a good start—the improvements you obtain in the first weeks are crucial to your success.

[...]

P: Regarding the frequency of our sessions, we will see each other twice a week in the first four weeks, and then once a week. If for any reason I am absent, a substitute therapist will lead the session.

F: That is unusual. It never happened in my previous treatments.

P: In this treatment it is crucial not to have any breaks, to develop a momentum toward change. It is also essential to conclude the entire treatment, like it is to take an entire course of antibiotics, for example, because an early interruption will not allow you to obtain the necessary changes to overcome your eating problem. If you put your maximum effort into the treatment you will have a concrete possibility of successfully addressing your eating problem.

[...]

P: Each session will start by us reviewing the previous week, and we will then go on to set an agenda for the next session.

F: Ok.

P: Do you have any questions or concerns?

[...]

P: Francesca, can we discuss the main problems that we should address with the treatment?

F: Yes, of course.

P: Do you know what the core psychological problem of your eating problem is?

F: The assessing clinician told me that it is the excessive importance I give to the control of shape and weight.

P: Yes, you are right. We call this the overvaluation of shape and weight. In other words you tend to judge yourself predominantly on your figure and what you weigh.

F: Yes, it is the most important aspect of my life.

P: Indeed, but most of the clinical features of your eating problem derive directly or indirectly from this core psychological problem.

F: Can you explain this concept better?

P: For example, your overvaluation of shape and weight (the psychologist writes "overvaluation of shape and weight" on a blank sheet of paper) explains your extreme weight control behaviors such as the strict diet and self-inducing vomiting after your evening meal (the psychologist draws an arrow from the overvaluation of shape and weight and writes at the end of the arrow "strict diet and self-induced vomiting"). These behaviors produced a persistent negative energy balance and, as a consequence, your severely low body weight. Undereating and low body weight in humans are associated with distinctive symptoms, called starvation symptoms (the psychologist draws an arrow from "strict diet and self-induced vomiting" and writes at the end of the arrow "low body weight and starvation symptoms").

F: Can you give me more information about these starvation symptoms?

P: Starvation symptoms occur in humans when they are underweight and aren't getting enough to eat. They include both physical and psychosocial symptoms, for example, typical physical symptoms are your periods stopping, reduction of basal energy expenditure (the energy you burn to live), feeling cold, prolonged digestion, brittle bones, extreme weakness, low blood pressure and slowed heart rate; the most common psychological symptoms are food obsessions, eating rituals like eating slowly or cutting food into small pieces, mood swings, depression, irritability, social withdrawal, low sex drive, and changes in personality, making you more rigid, indecisive, and prone to procrastination.

F: You describe me exactly. I have all these symptoms.

P: I can imagine, and this means that these symptoms are not the expression of your personality, but rather the consequence of your being underweight.

F: Do you mean that my depression, lack of interest in my life and other people could be the consequence of my being underweight?

P: Yes. This means that if you want to eliminate these symptoms it will be necessary for you to stop undereating and increase your body weight to at least low normal levels.

F: Er . . .

P: Let me put it another way: imagine you are a starving animal; does Mother Nature want you to spend your time grooming, playing, or looking for a mate?

F: No, she wants me to look for food!

P: Exactly, and she reduces your metabolic rate so that you can do it. This is also true of people, after all, we are animals too: if you aren't getting enough food, you have inbuilt mechanisms that make you think about food all the time.

F: I see, so I think about food all the time because my body is making me do it to improve my chances of survival.

P: That's right, it's a vicious circle, and the only way you can break it is to get to a healthy body weight. Only then will Mother Nature give you the space to concentrate on other aspects of a healthy life.

F: Yes, that's clear. But why do I try to avoid food rather than eat it?

P: This is because you overvalue your shape and weight. The fact that you give too much importance to these factors influences your interpretation of starvation symptoms, and these symptoms lose their original function.

F: I don't understand.

P: For example, you may equate the feeling you get when you are hungry as a fear of losing control. In this scenario, a reduction of energy expenditure may be interpreted as the need to intensify control and restriction of food intake, and you may see the perfectly natural obsession with food as a threat to your control over eating. Likewise, if you aren't getting enough food, you won't be interested in other people and your sex drive will become non-existent, but your social withdrawal is likely to fuel your use of shape and weight as principal means of judging yourself (the psychologist draws a line from the starvation symptoms to the overvaluation of shape and weight).

F: I see. This is what has happened to me.

P: So Francesca, if you look at this diagram, what do you think are the first problems that you should address with the treatment?

F: The most important thing has to be to reduce the overvaluation of shape and weight but . . . if I look at the diagram, maybe I should address the strict diet and vomiting first so I can increase my weight to eliminate the starvation symptoms.

P: You are right. This is the reason why in the first stage of this treatment you should principally focus on weight regain. However, this is not enough; you are also going to need to deal with your overvaluation of shape and weight.

[. . .]

P: Francesca, for the next session, if you agree, I suggest you do two homework assignments. The first is starting real-time recording from the next meal onward—you will need to write down everything you eat, and any thoughts or feelings you had. The second is to review each day the personal formulation we drew together in the session. I suggest you re-draw your formulation and read this table reporting the main starvation symptoms (chapter 2, see textbox 2.1) include the symptoms from the table that you are experiencing in your formulation. Do you think you will be able to do this homework?

F: Yes, I will try.

P: Thank you. Remember, what you do outside the sessions is crucial to overcoming your eating problem.

The second session was fixed three days after the first. The top priority in session 2 was still engaging Francesca in the treatment. Accordingly, the psychologist did her best to cultivate Francesca's enthusiasm, hope, and determination, and at the same time to address her concerns, mistrust, and pessimism. The session, and all those that followed, was structured in a similar fashion to the typical outpatient CBT-E session as follows:

- Reviewing the homework.
- Setting the agenda
- Working through the agenda.
- Setting homework, summarizing the session, and arranging the next appointment.

[. . .] *Selected transcripts from the second CBT-E session with the psychologist:*

P: Francesca, can we go over your homework?

F: Of course.

P: Was it difficult to for you to self-monitor?

F: Yes, especially when I was very anxious about eating.

P: How do you think you did?

F: Well, I might have done better; I didn't record all the emotions and the thoughts I had.

[. . .]

P: Did you also monitor in real time during the assisted eating?

F: Only once. I kept cutting the food into small pieces, and the dietitian suggested that I write that down and how I was feeling.

P: Was it useful?

F: Yes, I realized that I was fixated on the amount of calories in the food, and not on how to address the meal. This helped me to finish eating in a reasonable time.

P: You did a great job. Congratulations! This is the way to overcome your eating problem.

[. . .]

P: Francesca, did you review your personal formulation?

F: Yes I did (putting the personal formulation on the table—see figure 11.1).

P: Did you include the starvation symptoms you are experiencing?

F: Yes, and I realize that many of my problems are caused by my being underweight.

P: Good. You will see as your diet improves, many of these symptoms will disappear. When this happens, you should remember to congratulate yourself and remove these symptoms from the formulation. Remember that the formulation is provisional and needs to be modified during the course of the treatment, and that it highlights only what needs to be targeted in treatment.

[. . .]

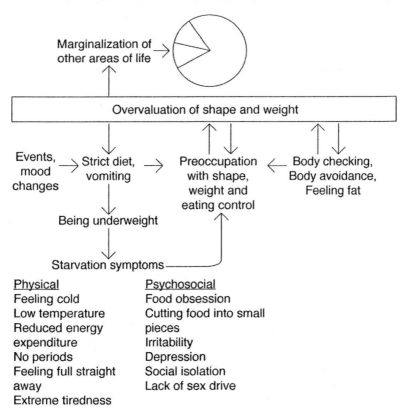

Figure 11.1. Francesca's Formulation

P: Did you manage to stop doing some of the things you wrote on the formulation?

F: Yes, I didn't vomit, even if I had a strong urge to do so after eating. But staying in the recreation room with the other patients for an hour after meals helped me to distract myself . . . but the urge is still very strong . . . I don't know how long I will be able to go on without vomiting.

P: You have made an excellent start. I really understand your difficulties, but if you draw on the same commitment that you have shown this first week, your urge to vomit and worries about food will gradually decrease.

[. . .]

P: How do you feel about having started the inpatient treatment? Do you have any worries or concerns about treatment that you would like to discuss?

F: I am afraid of putting on weight, and I feel full all day, but I am determined to go on.

P: Excellent. Do you have any questions about the Weight Regain Guidelines, your weight chart or monitoring record, or how to interpret your weight change?

F: No, it is all clear.

Two types of *group treatment sessions* were started in the first week of treatment: psychoeducational (twice a week), and CBT-E (once a week). These group sessions, as described in chapter 7, are used to supplement the individual meetings. Psychoeducational group sessions generally last sixty minutes each, and exploit visual teaching materials such as slides; they are organized similarly to school lessons, but are very interactive, and conducted by educators and physicians from the unit. This format allows the time dedicated to education in individual sessions to be reduced, as well the extensive use of audiovisual aids, and offers more opportunities for a patient to compare his or her experiences with those of others. CBT-E groups are open, last ninety minutes, and are conducted by a psychologist familiar with CBT-E and trained in conducting group sessions. The number of participants in each group ranges from four to six.

Before she joined the group Francesca was seen by the psychologist on a one-to-one basis to inform her about the aims, organization, and rules of the group sessions. In the first week of the treatment and for the remainder of Stages One and Two, the CBT-E group was focused on training Francesca, along with her fellow patients, on the use of proactive problem solving and modulating mood in a functional way. During the group discussion, Francesca was encouraged and helped to resolve her problems by "older" group members. In the first group, for example, Francesca was helped by Chicca, a patient in her fifth week of treatment, to address the problem of feeling full.

[. . .] Selected transcripts from the first CBT-E group session:

F: I feel really full after eating. I don't know if I can stand this feeling. I feel fat.

C: Francesca, I had the same problem the first three weeks, but now I feel fine. For me, wearing clothes that are loose across the stomach, not touching my stomach and telling myself it is a transitory state helped a lot.

F: Chicca, did your full feeling really disappear?

C: Yes, now I feel fine.

P: Feeling full is common when you start to eat regularly after a prolonged period of undereating. This happens because the undereating makes your stomach retain food longer. The good news is that eating normally and weight restoration will speed this up so it will go away. In this difficult phase, as suggested by Chicca, you should try to think that it is a transitory sensation, and not make it worse by checking your stomach or wearing tight clothes. It is also important that you try not to equate feeling full with "I am fat."

F: Ok, I understand.

Physical activity sessions also form part of the treatment program. However, Francesca's participation was contraindicated at this early stage due to her severely low weight associated with a moderate physical risk.

As regards *medical assessment and management*, at admission, Francesca presented a condition of severe malnutrition. She looked emaciated, her skin and mucosae were very dry, her palms and soles exhibited an orange discoloration, her extremities were acrocyanotic, and her front teeth perimolytic. Tests showed she also had bradycardia (44 beats per minute), hypotension (80/50 mm/hg), moderate hypokalemia (2.7 meq/L) and moderate leukopenia (2600/uL), in addition to increased levels of serum alanine aminotransferase (80 U/L) and cholesterol (270 mg/dL). The DXA showed the presence of osteoporosis (T-score -3.1) and a body fat percentage of 2.5, while indirect calorimetry showed a low resting energy expenditure (857 kcal/day).

Hypokalemia was treated with hydration and a saline solution with 40 mEq KCl per liter over three to four hour volume once a day for four days, and then with oral potassium chloride supplements for another week. To prevent the onset of refeeding syndrome, the refeed was begun with a low calorie diet (approximately 1000 kcal/day) and then the calorie intake was gradually increased. During the first ten days of feeding, oral thiamin, vitamin B complex, balanced multivitamin/trace element supplement, and phosphate and magnesium supplements were also prescribed. To manage the osteoporosis, the diet was supplemented with calcium and vitamin D throughout treatment.

Francesca's *psychosocial assessment* at admission showed severe eating disorder psychopathology (Eating Disorder Examination—EDE.16.0 global score: 4.2; mean community norms <1.74) (Fairburn, Cooper, & O'Connor, 2008), severe clinical impairment (Clinical Impairment Assessment Questionnaire—CIA: 42, normal values < 16) (Bohn et al., 2008), and severe general psychopathology (Brief Symptom Inventory—BSI Global Severity Index 1.8; normal values < 1) (Derogatis, 1993).

Having completed the first week as described above, Francesca was reasonably engaged in the treatment, she had addressed assisted eating quite well—although she was very slow to consume meals, she did not vomit after eating, and understood and accepted the initial personal formulation and weekly weighing, and adopted a real-time monitoring. Accordingly her therapy progressed to the next substage.

Stage One (Weeks 2–4)

Objectives

- Maintaining the patient's engagement.
- Addressing the most powerful maintenance mechanisms.

Maintaining Patient Engagement

On week two Francesca developed visible edema on the legs, and her body weight increased by 2 kg. During the weekly review meeting she appeared very anxious and asked to be discharged immediately.

[. . .] Selected transcripts from the second weekly review meeting:

F: I've put on two kilograms, over half a kilogram over the target weight gain. I feel bloated and fat. I want go home, this treatment is not for me. It's too hard.

Ph: I understand your feelings, Francesca. Can we analyze the possible reasons for this weight regain?

F: I eat too much . . . I eat like a pig.

Ph: Are there any other possible reasons?

F: I don't know . . . my legs are swollen.

Ph: Let me see.

[. . .]

Ph: Yes, you have a pitting edema on your legs. As you see if I apply pressure with my finger here (pretibial area), I cause an indentation that persists for some time. It seems to me that you have also difficulty in putting on shoes.

F: Yes.

Ph: So, do you think that your weight gain is due to fat or water?

F: I don't know . . . maybe water.

Ph. Yes, this is the main reason. The edema—or swelling—is the consequence of refeeding, and the interruption of vomiting. It will go away within two to three weeks and won't do you any harm; the increase in your body weight is due to fluid retention. To help you manage this condition I suggest you keep your legs raised; we will put you on a low-salt diet (less than 3 g per day), and I will also prescribe you spironolactone (25–50 mg per day) for two weeks, a drug that will help you get rid of excess water.

F: Ok. And what about the diet?

Ph: You should decide on the basis of the dietary guidelines that you discussed with the dietitian.

F: Well, I gained two kilograms . . . so I should reduce my intake by about 250 calories . . . [smiling].

Ph: In theory, you are correct, but . . .

F: You said that the weight gain was principally water . . . so I don't know.

Ph: I suggest, if you agree, that you maintain the same diet (1,500 calories) for another week.

F: I agree.

[. . .]

Ph: Francesca, for tomorrow's individual session can you write down the pros and cons of continuing the treatment?

F: Yes, ok.

Francesca decided to persevere with the treatment. The pedal edema cleared up within a week, and this was associated with a normalization of potassium levels.

Addressing the Most Powerful Maintenance Mechanisms

In the following weeks of Stage One, the treatment was focused on addressing the following main mechanisms maintaining Francesca's eating problem:

- *Low body weight and dietary restriction.* This was the top priority because Francesca was severely underweight and her physical condition was potentially harmful. In addition, the psychosocial consequences of starvation were identified as powerful maintainers of her eating problem. She handled assisted eating with some difficulty, but managed to finish most of her meals, and gained about 1 kg per week during this period.
- *Self-induced vomiting.* Francesca had several episodes of vomiting one hour after meals in week two, when she was suffering from pedal edema. However, after the physician explained to her that the dehydration caused by vomiting might worsen the edema, she stopped this behavior.
- *Feeling bloated and feeling full.* The bloating feeling was addressed with education and medical management (see above), while the feeling full was tackled in both individual and group CBT-E sessions.
- *Events and mood changes.* The rapid increase in body weight, the swift interruption of vomiting, and her missing home and family were associated with negative emotion that were addressed by the nurse in the unit, as well as in the individual and group CBT-E sessions.

[. . .] Selected transcripts from the individual CBT-E sessions (weeks 2–4):

P: Francesca, can we review your personal formulation?

F: Yes (putting the formulation on the table).

P: Do have something to add or to remove?

F: Well, I reduced vomiting and dieting . . . I also no longer have some starvation symptoms, such as extreme tiredness, cutting food into small pieces, and social isolation. My mood has improved, but I am still a little sad and irritable.

P: That will pass. Through your self-monitoring, have you discovered any other potential mechanisms maintaining your eating problem?

F: Um . . . maybe my sensation of feeling full?

P: Why do you think that feeling full may be maintaining your eating problem?

F: Because, for me feeling full means that I eat too much, and this increases my preoccupation with eating and weight. If I were not here, I would restrict my diet or vomit to deal with this sensation.

P: I'm glad you have been making an effort not to do those things. I agree with you, feeling full may be a potent maintenance mechanism that we will have to deal with. Why don't you write it on your formulation?

[. . .]

P: Francesca, can we have a look at your monitoring record?

F: Yes, but I only recorded for four days. When I am upset about feeling full and fat I am not in the right frame of mind to record.

P: I understand your feelings and difficulties. However, as we discussed last week, self-monitoring is an essential procedure for overcoming your eating problem. With accurate self-monitoring you will gradually become an expert in your eating problem. Do you remember the main functions of recording?

F: Er . . . does it enable me to identify the things that maintain my eating problem?

P: Yes, and there is another important function: it helps you to change, because becoming aware of what you are doing, thinking, and feeling in the precise moment at which an event is taking place facilitates the interruption of some of this behavior, for example, the urge to vomit.

F: Ok, but why should I record if I cannot choose the food I eat during assisted eating?

P: Good question. It is true that in this part of the treatment you are not choosing your own food, but the monitoring record is not merely a food diary. During assisted eating you should simply write the name of the meal you consume in the unit, and describe the thoughts and feelings you experience, and any behavior associated with your eating problem that you notice. You should also record your weekly weight and the interpretation of your weight change, a key strategy for overcoming your eating problem.

F: Ok.

P: Another question. Do you self-monitor in real time?

F: Not always.

P: Try to use the procedure in this way. For example, when you have an urge to vomit, write in the last column your thoughts and feelings in that precise moment, and then write what you can do to overcome the urge.

F: Sometime I do this in my mind, but it doesn't always work.

P: Well, next week try to stick to recording in real time, and then we will review together if this method has been successful.

F: Ok.

[. . .]

P: Looking at your monitoring record it is clear that you have dramatically reduced the episodes of vomiting after meals.

F: Yes, when I was at home I vomited every day. This week I have only vomited three times.

P: Well done! However, we should try to address this residual vomiting because it might hinder the change.

F: Yes, I agree.

P: Francesca, what is the function of your vomiting?

F: I use it to manage the experience of feeling full, and also to have a flat stomach.

P: Do you know that purging has several negative consequences?

F: Yes, I can imagine.

P: It causes dehydration, electrolyte disturbances, irritation of the esophagus, heart problems, and wears down the inner surface of the front teeth.

F: Yes, I know.

P: It is also highly harmful from a psychological perspective because it requires secrecy and subterfuge and is often associated with feelings of shame and guilt.

F: Yes, I feel guilty and ashamed of this behavior.

P: Last but not least, it hampers treatment and weight restoration.

F: I know, but I want to have a flat stomach when I lie down.

P: But you know that vomiting does not completely empty the stomach, and does not eliminate fat from the stomach.

[. . .]

P: Can we review your strategy for addressing the urge to vomit?

F: Yes. I have to record it in real time.

P: Well, and I also suggested that you adopt the strategy of "things to say and do." Did you write the things to say and do on a memo card?

F: Yes. Here is my memo. As "things to say," I wrote that the urge to vomit is a temporary phenomenon, and that I must not succumb. For "things to do" I wrote: listening to music, chatting with other patients, and avoiding bathrooms.

P: Well. When you have the urge to vomit, read the memo card immediately and try to put into practice what you wrote.

F: Ok, I will try to do what you suggest.

P: Well, in the next session we will see how you've been getting on.

[. . .] *Selected transcripts from assisted eating (weeks 2–4):*

F: I don't want to eat. I've put on another kilogram (Francesca refuses to eat after a 1 kg increase in her weight).

D: Try to remember where we are. We are in an eating disorder unit and together we are putting into practice a treatment that involves weight regain according to the guidelines that you are familiar with. Your weight gain is in the weight regain range you decided and you will not lose control of your weight. Try to think of this change as an experiment. If you are not satisfied with the results later, you will be free to return to your emaciated state.

F: But I've gained one kilogram. This is too much food.

D: Do not believe your worries about food and eating. Distance your behavior from these thoughts. . . . In time you will realize that these preoccupations are not real and will gradually disappear.

[. . .]

F: I do not want to eat (Francesca repeatedly mixes up her food).

D: Try not to focus on the pain associated with eating, but on the fact that eating will help you to recover.

F: But it is too much.

D: Try to adopt the mental state of an athlete before a high jump. He concentrates on the technique to use and not on the fear of failing or on how high the bar may be. You can do it, but you have to apply the right technique: Try to eat mechanically.

Francesca eventually, albeit reluctantly, completed her meal.

Stage Two (Weeks 5–6)

Objectives

- Conducting a joint review of progress.
- Identifying emerging barriers to change.
- Reviewing the personal formulation.
- Deciding whether to use the broad or focused form of inpatient CBT-E.
- Designing Stage Three.

The psychologist took charge of achieving these objectives during the individual CBT-E sessions, which at this point were held once a week, but the conclusions reached in these sessions were discussed with all team members at the weekly review meeting. At the same time, the treatment continued with the same procedures introduced in Stage One. Once again, Francesca was asked to fill out an EDE-Q (Fairburn & Beglin, 2008), CIA (Bohn et al.,

2008) and the measure of her general psychiatric features, so that together with her therapists she could objectively assess the nature and extent of change.

Conducting a Joint Review of Progress

The rationale behind conducting a progress review at this stage stems from the clinical observation that the magnitude of changes in the first weeks of treatment seems to influence the treatment outcome, and in order to prevent poor outcome it is therefore crucial to adjust the treatment when the progress is limited.

[. . .] Selected transcripts of individual CBT-E sessions:

P: Francesca, after four weeks of treatment I think it is time to review your progress. How much progress do you feel you have made?

F: I don't know . . . I gained four and a half kilograms . . . that's all.

P: Don't you think that you see your progress unduly negatively?

F: Maybe, but I am still underweight and obsessed by food and weight.

P: In order to put things in perspective, let's review together the aims of this first part of the treatment.

F: Ok.

P: The aims of this part of the treatment were: increasing your engagement in the treatment, improving your knowledge about the main processes maintaining your eating problem, measuring and interpreting your weight once a week, using self-monitoring in real time, interrupting the extreme weight control behaviors, such as self-induced vomiting, and starting the process of weight restoration. Which of these goals did you achieve?

F: Almost all.

P: Yes, I agree. I think you did a great job.

Identifying Barriers to Change

The second task in Stage Two is for any barriers to change to be identified. Two main sources of barriers were picked up on: the eating problem itself and other general factors.

[. . .] Selected transcripts from individual CBT-E sessions:

P: Let's analyze the principal barriers to you overcoming your eating problem.

F: Ok.

P: I would like to focus on one potential barrier that I have observed in our sessions: your fear of change.

F: Yes, it is one of my biggest obstacles.

P: What are you afraid of?

F: I don't know . . . maybe losing control . . . and . . . I don't know, in the past I felt special when I was able to control eating, but now I feel miserable; but the control of eating and weight is still very important.

P: I think you have hit the nail on the head: it seems that the issue of control is at the psychological heart of your eating problem. However, we should consider two facts. The first is whether you really have good control with your eating problem or . . .

F: No. I'm overcontrolling. . . . It is excessive.

P: Yes, I agree with you. Excessive eating and weight control damages important areas of your life, such as your physical health, your psychological functioning, interpersonal relationships, work . . . this means that although you may be controlling your eating, you will be losing control of other important areas of your life. The second fact to consider is, as you have experienced in these four weeks, that the treatment was designed to help you to feel in control and to reach a healthy control of your eating and weight.

F: Yes, I appreciated this. The strategy of learning how to interpret my weight change and deciding on my dietary changes for the next week helped me to reduce my anxiety about losing control. Also, predicting my weight change associated with the dietary changes I plan is another strategy that helps me feel more in control. However, I am still afraid of losing control over eating and weight.

P: I understand your fear, and I appreciate your efforts to address your eating problem. I suggest that you take it day by day, working to overcome your eating problem by applying the strategies suggested by the program. Focusing on what will happen in the future does not help you change.

F: I agree—it is the strategy that I applied in these first four weeks.

[...]

P: And . . . what about the feeling of fullness?

F: I feel much better—in the last week this sensation was very weak.

P: Why do you think this happened?

F: I don't know. However, I think it helped to wear comfortable clothes, to think that feeling full is transitory, and to remind myself that feeling full is not the same as being fat.

Reviewing the Personal Formulation

The personal formulation was revised in light of what Francesca had changed during Stage One and what emerged during progress review at the beginning of Stage Two. Francesca was able to remove some maintenance mechanisms from her formulation (e.g., some starvation symptoms, binge eating).

Deciding Whether to Use the Broad or Focused Version of CBT-E

In general, the more severe the eating problem, the more the focus should be on addressing the specific features of the eating disorder (e.g., undereating and being underweight), because these tend to be the prime culprits of eating problem maintenance. For this reason, not to mention the fact that Francesca had also undertaken broad-type CBT without success, the psychologist, upon agreement with Francesca, decided that the focused form of CBT-E would be more appropriate for her needs.

Designing Stage Three

The problems to address in Stage Three depend on the maintenance mechanisms operating in the patient. In Francesca's case, the main mechanisms to address were: completing weight restoration, the overvaluation of shape and weight, dietary rules, and events and mood changes influencing eating.

[. . .] Selected transcripts from individual CBT-E sessions:

P: Francesca, the last thing we have to do in this stage is to decide what we are going to do in Stage Three.

F: Ok.

P: Do you have any ideas about the problems you need to address to overcome your eating problem? Why don't we take a look at your personal formulation?

F: Well . . . I still need to put on weight . . . and reduce my concerns about eating and weight . . . I also need to deal better with my mood changes, especially those that influence my motivation to change and keep eating.

P: I agree with you. In addition, if you agree, I think we should put one more thing on your list—so that you will be able to keep the weight on once you have reached your target, I think we should take a look at your rigid and extreme dietary rules.

F: Yes, it will be a very difficult task but I think it's a good idea.

P: So, in summary, during Stage Three we have to address the following problems: completing weight restoration, addressing residual dietary rules once you achieve your target weight, addressing the overvaluation of shape and weight, and dealing with events and emotions influencing your motivation and eating. Do you agree?

F: Yes, I agree.

Stage Three (Weeks 7–17)

Objectives

- Completing the process of weight regain.
- Addressing the overvaluation of shape and weight.
- Addressing the residual dietary rules.
- Continuing to address events and associated mood changes influencing eating.
- Involving significant others.
- Learning to control the eating disorder mindset.

In Stage Three the main mechanisms maintaining Francesca's eating problem were addressed by continuing to use the procedures and strategies introduced in Stage One. However, in this stage, two new core procedures were introduced, namely non-assisted eating and the involvement of significant others, while other core procedures, for example, weight monitoring and the individual CBT-E sessions, were modified. Indeed, at week 14, Francesca moved from inpatient to day treatment, and was gradually exposed to the external environment she would encounter after discharge. During the final few weeks of treatment, Francesca spent weekends and weekdays at home, while still having the support of the team. These changes were made with the aim of gradually transforming the inpatient treatment into a form and a style that was similar to outpatient CBT-E, the treatment that Francesca would continue after discharge.

Completing the Process of Weight Regain

Francesca, after the initial difficulties of Stage One, had become fully engaged in the treatment and had reached a BMI of 19.0 (46 kg) at week 17. She had stopped using her eating rituals and normalized her speed of eating. In addition, her interpretation of changes in her weight improved, and she made sensible suggestions that would enable her to maintain a weight regain between 1 to 1.5 kg per week.

[. . .] Selected transcripts from week 13 weekly review meeting:

> Ph: Francesca can you interpret your change in weight on the weight chart?
>
> F: I am in the target weight regain range, but this week I put on half a kilogram.
>
> Ph: How do the Weight Regain Guidelines suggest you change your diet at this point?
>
> F: I wish to maintain this diet without any change . . . but . . .
>
> Ph: But . . .
>
> F: But . . . I think it would be better, as suggested by the guidelines, to increase by 500 calories per day.
>
> Ph: Well, I think that is a good idea. How do you feel?
>
> F: Pretty good—I feel in control.

Addressing the Overvaluation of Shape and Weight

With the interruption of dietary restriction and vomiting, and with better management of event and mood changes influencing eating, Francesca noticed a marked reduction of eating worries and dietary restraint. However, the consequent increase in her body weight and the associated rapid changes in shape intensified her concerns about shape and weight. For this reason, the main focus of Stage Three was to address the overvaluation of shape and weight in individual CBT-E sessions and the overvaluation of shape and weight in group sessions.

Francesca was first educated about self-evaluation, then helped to identify her self-evaluation schematic and its implication, developing an extended personal formulation, and finally to devise a plan for addressing her overvaluation of shape and weight. This goal was pursued by both seeking to enhance the importance of other domains in Francesca's self-evaluation system and addressing her shape checking and avoidance, and feeling fat.

[. . .] Selected transcripts from individual CBT-E sessions:

P: Francesca, I would like to analyze with you the main domains of your life that have an impact on your self-evaluation. Their importance can be determined by the degree and duration of negative reactions when things are not going well in that domain.

F: Er . . . Some examples?

P: For example, you may consider work, interpersonal relationships, family, hobbies, personal skills, and of course the control of eating, shape, and weight. You should assign the degree of importance you attribute to every one of these or to other domains, and then draw a pie chart like this (the psychologist shows an example of a pie chart of a patient with eating problem), the size of each slice representing the relative importance of that domain of life in your self-evaluation schematic.

F: So, if I understand correctly . . . the size of the slices should be determined by the degree of my negative reaction when things go bad in that domain?

P: Yes, and also by the duration of the negative reaction.

F: [After drawing her pie chart] here is my pie chart.

P: It is clear that the predominant slice is that representing your shape and weight, and you have included only one other little slice . . . family.

F: Yes. With my eating problem I lost my job and all my other interests.

P: Francesca, let's look at the implications of having a pie chart like this. One, as you said, is the marginalization of other important areas of life, such as work and interpersonal relationships, which in general help people to achieve a satisfying self-evaluation. Do you see other problems in this pie chart?

F: Well. If I fail to control the eating, shape, and weight, my self-esteem collapses.

P: Yes, we can say that it is extremely risky for a person to judge one's self-worth predominantly in only one domain. But tell me, Francesca, did you ever reach a point where your control of shape and weight made you feel good about yourself?

F: Only for brief periods . . . I am really never satisfied with my level of control.

P: This means that in this domain it is quite difficult to reach lasting success. I think that this depends on the fact that a perfect figure is an impossible goal.

F: I agree. That was my experience.

[. . .]

P: Well. From now on you should draw your pie chart on the back of your monitoring record every day, and we will review its evolution in the following sessions.

[. . .]

P: The aim is not to eliminate the slice of shape and weight but to make it smaller, leaving room for other domains. One way of achieving this is trying to develop other aspects of your life.

F: Yes, I understand, but I have no life.

P: Can we review those interests that you used to have but were interrupted after developing your eating problem?

F: I was young . . . I don't know.

P: Can you think of any activities that you would like to do but have never done?

F: I would love to dance, especially Latin American; that is my dream.

P: There is a dance school close to the hospital. You could go and get some information about their courses. I'll give you the address. Are there other activities that you can start?

F: Um . . . I would like to take artistic photos.

P: Well, why don't you try to find out where you can learn how to improve your photography skills?

F: Yes, I will do. I also want to go back to work when I get back home.

P: I think that is a good idea. For now, however, I suggest you focus on dance and photography. Every day you should record any steps you take in these two areas in the last column of your monitoring record.

[. . .]

P: Francesca, we talked about the importance of body checking in increasing body dissatisfaction. Since body checking is often automatic and you may be not aware of doing it, I suggest that over the next two days, whenever you check your body you record it in real time in the last column of your monitoring record; this will help you to work out how often you do it.

F: Ok, I will.

[. . .]

P: Can we review your body checking monitoring record? How was the experience?

F: It was a little stressful. I realized that I check my body very frequently.

P: What are the functions of your body checking?

F: Sometimes I check my body to understand what my stomach, bottom, and legs look like . . . I have put on a lot of weight, you know. . . .

P: I understand, but maybe you are not aware that scrutinizing parts of the body tends to magnify apparent defects. In other words, the more you check that part of the body, the more you find defects—does that make sense?

F: Yes, I think you are right. I noticed this.

P: Are there any other functions of body checking?

F: I'm also checking whether I'm getting fat.

P: Are you sure that this is an accurate method of estimating changes in your figure?

F: I don't know, but it gives me a sense of control.

P: You should know that body checking is not a reliable way of assessing changes in body shape because humans have a poor photographic memory of their body. For example, we cannot accurately compare the perceived image of our shape in the morning with that of the afternoon.

F: Yes, I agree. I often think I see differences in my body shape at different times during the same day.

P: How often do you check your body?

F: Very frequently. When I wake up the first thing I do is to pinch the rolls of fat on my stomach and legs, and I touch my hipbones. Then I go to the mirror in the bathroom and . . . I look at my stomach, legs, and bottom from different angles. I touch these parts of the body several times during the day, especially after the meals . . . I also check my body on all reflective surfaces . . . I want to be sure that my body is not changing.

P: Francesca, do you really think that the shape of your body may change so rapidly and in absence of a change in body weight?

F: No, but I am afraid. However, I noticed that my stomach does get bigger after eating.

P: Don't you think that the fluctuations in abdomen shape are natural and that they are not indicative of weight gain, nor are they perceptible to others?

F: Are you sure?

P: I'm sure—it is a transitory phenomenon due to the presence of food in the stomach, not to an increase in body fat.

F: Ok.

P: Do you also check a part of your body that you like?

F: No. I only look at my legs, stomach, and bottom.

P: Do you feel better about yourself if you check only these specific parts of your body?

F: Sometimes I feel reassured about not being fat, but other times I feel fat and . . . in any case I am always concerned about my body shape.

[. . .]

P: Do you compare the shape of your body with those of other people?

F: Yes. In particular with the patients that are thinner than me or with some very thin women.

P: Which part of the women's body do you check?

F: Stomach, legs, and bottom.

P: And what are your conclusions?

F: Women are thinner than me.

P: Are you sure? Have you never tried to look at other parts of their body or to stop selecting very emaciated women?

F: No.

P: The type of comparison you use has two problems. The first is that you select atypical women—we call this selective attention. The second is that you conclude that women are thinner than you—we call this generalization.

F: I understand.

P: So, in summary, we can say that the body checking has three main negative consequences. First, it maintains body dissatisfaction because involves the repeated scrutiny of parts of the body you find unattractive. It also highlights defects because you find what you are looking for, and because you concentrate on certain parts of the body. In addition, selecting atypical women and looking only at specific parts of their bodies fuels the belief that you are bigger than other women.

[...]

P: Francesca, we should decide which body checking behaviors to stop and which to adjust—do you have any thoughts?

F: No.

P: The body checking habits to stop are those that increase body dissatisfaction. For example, feeling bones and pinching parts of your stomach and legs to assess their fatness. The body checking behaviors to adjust are those that may be useful for functional verification of weight and appearance.

F: I don't understand.

P: For example, weight checking and mirror checking are two typical examples of body checking to adjust. You have already adjusted the frequency of weight checking.

F: Yes, from once a day to once a week.

P: And what did you learn from this change in frequency?

F: At first, I was very anxious. Now I am less worried about my weight, and I feel that I can keep control of my weight even with less frequent checking.

P: Good. I think you realize that the aim of the treatment is not to eliminate control, but to maintain a healthy control of your weight without increasing the concerns about it.

F: Yes, I do.

P: I suggest you adopt the same approach for mirror checking. What would be a useful way to use a mirror?

F: Well. To check my hair and clothes before going out, or to apply or remove makeup.

P: Yes. It is also important to avoid focusing on body parts that you dislike, such as your stomach, bottom, and legs. Another suggestion is for you to look at neutral body areas, such as hands, feet, knees, and hair, and to look at your background environment—this may help you to give you a sense of scale.

F: I will try.

P: Francesca, how many mirrors do you have at home?

F: Lots, at least six or seven.

P: I also suggest you reduce the number of mirrors in your house. One for the face and one full-length are sufficient.

F: I will have to speak to my husband, but I don't think that it will be a problem for him. He doesn't really care about his appearance.

P: Good. Do you agree that for the next session you should try to be aware of your mirror use in real time and question yourself what are you looking for when you look in the mirror?

After this session, Francesca addressed shape comparison through real-time awareness of any inherent bias, and broadened the focus of her attention (e.g., to include the person's hair and shoes and other characteristics such as the person's behavior, sense of humor). She was also encouraged to stop buying fashion magazines and watching fashion TV channels. The interruption of dysfunctional body checking also led to the remission of feeling fat, and Francesca understood that this sensation had been the mislabeling of adverse events, the body dissatisfaction caused by scrutinizing her body.

[. . .] *Selected transcripts from the overvaluation of shape and weight group sessions:*

P: Would you like to tell me about your trip to the swimming pool with Arianna (another patient) last Sunday? What did you learn from the experience?

F: I was very anxious and ashamed to expose my body.

A: I too was very scared.

F: However, we supported each other, and we applied the proactive problem-solving solutions that we had planned beforehand.

P: What solutions were these?

F: To focus our attention on the people and not our bodies, avoiding any form of body checking.

A: We also planned to maintain a neutral approach toward our bodies without making any negative comments.

P: Great! And what was the outcome?

F: We enjoyed swimming and spending time together.

A: I was very relaxed after the swim.

P: Did you make any form of body comparison?

F: I had a quick look at the flat stomach of a swimming pool attendant. She was very pretty. But . . . as you suggested, I then looked in detail at her body, and I realized that she had some cellulite on her legs, and her arms were too big. I also looked at other women.

P: And what did you learn?

F: Women have different body shapes.

Addressing Residual Dietary Rules

At week 15, Francesca had reached a BMI of 19.0, had started to eat without assistance and to practice weight maintenance addressing residual dietary rules. In this phase, she chose food from the unit menu, and had free access to bathrooms after eating. The menu included options for three main courses, accompanied by different types of vegetables, pasta or rice, and fruit. To mimic a real-world situation (e.g., a university refectory), Francesca got her planned food from a self-service station in the unit's kitchen. From week 14, in the day treatment phase, she gradually began to consume meals outside the unit, further to her eating all meals outside the unit in the last two weeks of the treatment. In this phase Francesca was encouraged to take several risks in typical situations triggering dietary restraint. Examples included making portions without weighing the food, eating socially (e.g., with others at the restaurant, fast-food places, pizzerias, or bars) and introducing previously avoided foods. When she ate outside the unit and spent weekends at home, she was helped to manage her eating (e.g., shopping and cooking food), to pay attention to the environmental triggers of dietary rules, and to address these triggers. In this phase, Francesca also started to weigh herself without the assistance of the nurse, first in the unit and then at home using her own scales.

[. . .] Selected transcripts from the weekly review meetings:

D: Francesca, the time to practice eating without assistance has arrived.

F: I have been waiting for this moment for several weeks.

D: You should plan in advance the food you will eat, choosing from the unit menu, and you will have free access to bathroom after eating.

F: Yes, I know. I've seen the other patients doing this.

D: You should also include all the food and liquids you consume in real time on your monitoring sheet.

F: Ok.

D: A major aim of this stage is to learn to maintain your body weight following healthy but flexible dietary guidelines. To reach this goal we have to identify your residual rigid dietary rules and then break them, and evaluate the real consequences of doing this.

F: I understand.

D: The main dietary rules we have to tackle are: when to eat, for example, skipping meals or delaying eating; what to eat; how much to eat; food avoidance, which means eating food you have previously avoided; and food checking, for example, weighing food and calorie counting; and making comparisons with the eating behavior of others.

[. . .] Selected transcripts from dietary restraint group sessions:

D: Can we review your monitoring record for the last seven days?

F: Ok.

D: Did you break any dietary rules?

F: Yes, I did not weigh my portions and I ate pasta with tuna. I also introduced chocolate cake for an afternoon snack, and I ate potato and bread in the same meal (Francesca shows the dietitian her monitoring record—see figure 11.2).

D: Great! What did you learn from the experience?

F: Well, I was pretty scared of making all these changes, but now I feel less afraid. . . . My weight did not change . . . and I enjoyed chatting with Giovanna at the bar.

D: So, what conclusion can you reach?

F: Well . . . maybe I can maintain my weight without rigid rules.

[. . .]

D: Francesca. Which dietary rules do you plan to break next week?

F: Going for a ham and cheese pizza with my family. I haven't eaten pizza for several years.

D: What is the worst thing that can happen if you eat a pizza?

F: Um . . . putting on weight?

D: We've already talked about this. How many calories do you need to put on one kilogram of fat?

F: About 7,000.

D: And how many calories might a ham and cheese pizza have?

F: About 1,000.

D: So . . . what are the most probable consequences of eating a pizza?

F: Er . . . not gaining weight.

D: Are there any advantages of eating a pizza?

F: Yes, I can eat with my husband and son.

D: Can you write on the back of your monitoring record the most probable consequences and advantages of breaking this rule?

F: Ok.

D: Then you should write in the last column of monitoring record the real consequences you experienced, and the advantages of being free from such a rule.

Day.......... Tuesday ....   Date.......... June 15th ....

Time	Food and liquids consumed	Place	*	V/L/E	Comments
7:45		Home			Body weight: 46.5 kg. My weight is fluctuating in the maintenance range. I take a shower
8:00	Milk, coffee with sugar, 6 cookies, 1 orange juice	Kitchen			I feel fine.
12:00	Pasta with tuna 5 slice of ham 1 cup of salad dressed with 1 tablespoon of olive oil and balsamic vinegar ½ slice of bread 1 medium banana	Dining room hospital			I put the tuna in the pasta. I was anxious of mixing protein with pasta. I talk with Chicca. I feel fine, only a little full, but it will pass
16:00	A slice of chocolate cake NEW 1 cappuccino with sugar	Bar with Giovanna			I am anxious. However, the introduction of an ice cream did not changed my body weight last week. I enjoyed talking with Giovanna. I touched my stomach after eating the cake, but I stopped myself immediately
19:00	chicken with potato NEW 1 slice of bread 1 cup of salad with 1 table spoon of olive oil and balsamic vinegar 1 medium apple	Dining room hospital			I feel fine.
22:00	One chocolate bar		*		I had not planned the chocolate bar, but I do not feel guilty. I am working well on my food control rigidity

Figure 11.2. A Typical Day from Francesca's Monitoring Record during Non-Assisted Eating. Adapted from figure 5.3 in *Cognitive Behavior Therapy and Eating Disorders* by Christopher G. Fairburn, 2008. Copyright Guilford Press. Reprinted with permission of The Guilford Press.

Continuing to Address Events and Associated Mood Changes Influencing Eating

Typical events triggering Francesca's changes in mood and eating behavior during Stage Three were arguments with her husband. To address these events, Francesca made considerable use of proactive problem solving and strategies for modulating mood changes, such as accepting the change of emotion and listening to music.

[. . .] Selected transcripts from individual CBT-E sessions:

> P: Francesca, I would like to know whether you applied the strategy of "Things to say and do," the same strategy you used to address the urge to purge, to cope with the changes in mood that influence your eating behavior?
>
> F: Yes, yesterday after a discussion with Gianni (her husband). I was very angry with him because he does not understand how difficult it is for me to deal with my eating problem. For him is just a question of willpower.
>
> P: Did you use proactive problem solving to prevent this?
>
> F: Yes, but the solution I had planned, not giving much importance to his comment and changing the subject of the discussion, didn't work. I was very angry.
>
> P: And what did you do to avoid the changes in eating?
>
> F: I told him that I had to go, then I took out my memo card with the "things to say and do," and I said to myself that I was able to tolerate this change of mood, that it is a transient state . . . then I listened to some music on my headphones.
>
> P: Did it work?
>
> F: Yes, after about half an hour I was calm and I sat down to dinner without restricting what I ate or vomiting.
>
> P: Great!

Involving Significant Others

As the above transcript shows, Francesca's husband Gianni could potentially play a very influential role in her recovery, and accordingly she agreed to involve him. He attended three sessions with his wife, each lasting about forty-five minutes, which took place immediately after Francesca's routine individual CBT-E sessions. The first session was arranged just before Francesca was scheduled to consume her first meal outside the unit with her husband. The second session was fixed after the first of two weekends Francesca spent at home, and focused on reviewing the difficulties observed and any changes that needed to be made at home. The third, one week before discharge, was set up to plan how to help Francesca on her return home. These meetings involved: (i) an explanation of the treatment, Francesca's progress, and which barriers to change needed addressing; (ii) listening to Francesca's husband's point of view, answering his questions, and addressing his issues; (iii) discussing how the husband could be of practical help to Francesca.

[. . .] *Selected transcripts of significant other participation sessions:*

P: Do you mind if we discuss the help you can give to Francesca?

G: It is difficult for me. When I make a comment about her behavior she becomes very hostile.

F: You are always very critical with me.

G: I criticize because I want to help you.

P: Did your criticism help your wife to address her eating problem?

G: No.

F: No . . . no . . . I feel guilty or angry . . . and when I was home I skipped meals or vomited afterward.

P: Criticism does not generally help the person suffering from an eating problem. On the contrary, it often produces the opposite effect, because the change in mood generated by it tends to trigger a change of eating. Gianni, do you really think that your wife's eating problem is a question of willpower?

G: No . . . no . . . I know that it is a severe psychological problem. It is not her fault . . . but it is difficult to live with a person with such a problem.

P: I understand. Why don't you try to adopt the same attitude you would have, say, if your wife were suffering from a physical complaint, for example, a neurological disease that meant she can't walk. Would you criticize your wife for not being able to walk?

G: No, of course . . . I understand . . . for her the problem is eating.

P: Yes, it is. Francesca is very afraid to eat and to lose the control of her shape and weight. Francesca, what can your husband do to help you?

F: I don't know. If he stopped criticizing me and accepted me as a person I would be happy.

G: Francesca, I will try.

Learning to Control the Eating Disorder Mindset

Toward the end of Stage Three, Francesca experienced prolonged periods free from her preoccupation with shape and weight. This phenomenon became evident when she eroded the main maintenance mechanisms of her eating problem. It was at this point that Francesca was informed about the concept of an eating disorder mindset and taught how to control it.

[. . .] Selected transcripts from individual CBT-E sessions:

P: Francesca, we have reached a very important phase of treatment. You told me that you have spent prolonged periods without thinking about food, shape, and weight.

F: Yes! It is a new experience. I am surprised.

P: It is a very positive experience that occurs when the treatment goes well.

F: I'm glad.

P: To understand this experience, we should discuss the concept of mindsets. Our mind can be likened to a box of DVDs. It may contain, for example, the "friend" DVD, the "mother" DVD, the "wife" DVD, and the "sports" DVD, etc. Each of these DVDs represents a specific and characteristic mindset that you "play" in specific situations. For example, you play the "work" DVD at work, and the "friends" DVD when you are out with friends; these mindsets process information quite differently and appropriately for the situation.

F: I understand.

P: Some people have the "eating problem" DVD. This DVD, unlike the others, tends to be locked into place and plays on a continuous loop, whatever the circumstances. So, whatever the situation, you remain concerned about shape, weight, and eating control, and adopt specific behaviors, such as body checking and dieting. In the early phases of the eating problem, it's possible with some effort to eject the "eating problem" DVD and force the appropriate DVD into place—for example, the "work" DVD at work. However, as your eating problem progresses, it becomes more and more difficult to eject this DVD, which remains jammed in the player, preventing you from playing any other, whatever the circumstance.

F: Yes. That was my experience. When I was with my son, I thought about my stomach and what to eat.

P: Exactly! However, with the application of the treatment procedures you disrupted most of the maintenance mechanisms of your eating problems, making it easier for you to play the appropriate DVD. Now you experience progressively longer periods in which the "eating problem" DVD is not playing.

F: It is clear.

P: Now that you know how to eject the DVD, it is time you learn how to decenter from your eating problem so that you can recognize events that may trigger its activation.

F: Can you explain this concept better?

P: Triggers are situations that may activate your concerns about eating, shape, and weight. Looking at your monitoring records, can you identify some common triggers of your eating problem?

F: Yes. One is when my weight goes up. Other triggers are when I feel full or I check my body . . . also when I have discussions with my husband or feel sad.

P: Very well. So your triggers are related to eating, shape, or weight-related events, to interpersonal events, and to negative mood states.

F: Yes. In these situations, it is automatic for me to think about my body and eating, and I feel an urge to diet or to vomit.

P: Using the DVD concept, we can say that in these situations your eating problem DVD inserts itself in response to these triggers. Luckily, we know that it easy to turn off the eating problem DVD in the first phases of its activation, but this becomes progressively more difficult with the passing of time, because the main eating disorder maintenance mechanisms start to kick in.

F: You mean, that I should pay attention to the early signs of my eating problem, and then to avoid adopting behaviors dictated by my concerns about eating and weight?

P: Yes, exactly. When you see the first scenes of your eating problem DVD playing, you should take pains to do the opposite, for example, eating when you feel the urge to fast and not skipping meals.

F: I understand. I have already applied this strategy. It works

P: Good. Next week you will spend several days at home, and I expect that you will encounter several occasions where your eating problem DVD starts playing. I suggest you practice identifying these triggers, and decentering from the DVD—count to ten if it helps. It would also be a good idea for you to write a list of the triggers you meet at home in the last column of your monitoring records.

Stage Four (Weeks 18–20)

Objectives

- Addressing concerns about ending treatment.
- Evaluating the progress achieved during treatment.
- Preparing the post-inpatient plan.

Addressing Concerns about Ending Treatment

Francesca was very concerned about returning home because she was aware that she would have to address several triggers of her eating problem not encountered thus far during the treatment. She was also aware of the need to address some difficulties that she had previously avoided by means of her eating problem (e.g., her relationship with her husband, and work) without the intensive support of the inpatient team. Her principal fear was that she would not be able to cope with all these difficulties and would therefore relapse.

[. . .] *Selected transcripts from individual CBT-E sessions:*

P: Francesca, how do you feel about your treatment ending?

F: Mixed feelings. On the one hand I am happy to go back home. Gianni has been very supportive and kind to me over the last few weeks, and also my son was very happy to see that I am well. However, on the other hand I am worried because I will have to face many life difficulties and I am afraid of relapsing.

P: I understand your fear. It is true that at home you will be exposed to various difficulties that may increase the risk of relapse in your eating problem. However, you are aware of these difficulties and you have developed skills to cope with them effectively.

F: That's true. The last weekend I spent home I didn't have any setbacks.

P: Good, but it is fundamental that you continue to address your eating problem with an outpatient treatment conceptually similar to the approach you have experienced here. This will help you both to address your residual eating problems and to cope with the problems you will face at home.

F: Last week I saw the therapist you recommended to me. I liked her. She also uses the same CBT approach. I am also lucky that her office is close to my house.

P: That therapist is fully trained in CBT-E and in treating patients after discharge from our unit.

F: Good.

P: The first few months are going to be crucial, but if you consider the outpatient treatment as a priority you will have more chance of overcoming your eating problem. As with the inpatient treatment, outpatient treatment will not be easy but it will be worth it. Remember, the more you put in, the more you will get out.

Evaluating the Progress Achieved during Treatment

Francesca's progress was assessed using three strategies: (i) informally, by asking her what had changed; (ii) formally, using the EDE interview to measure eating disorder features and the CIA to measure secondary psychosocial impairment; and (iii) globally, reviewing whether changes had also been maintained during the weekends and weekdays spent at home. At this stage Francesca was also instructed to use the monitoring record in real time during the weekend to monitor all behaviors that might be triggered by the home environment (e.g., dietary restraint, body checking and avoidance, feeling fat).

[. . .] Selected transcripts from individual CBT-E sessions:

P: Francesca, can we review the progress you have made with the treatment?

F: Well . . . I normalized my weight . . . and eating. I also stopped vomiting after meals.

P: Nothing else?

F: Um . . . I feel better in general. My mood is stable and I am less concerned about weight. . . . My weight now is stable (showing her weight graph to the therapist—see figure 11.3), and I feel in control.

P: Are you more aware of the mechanisms maintaining your eating problem?

F: Yes. I am an expert now (smiling).

P: Which residual problems do you think you still need to address to overcome your eating problem?

F: Well. I am still too rigid about my diet . . . and I am still concerned about the shape of my stomach, legs, and bottom.

P: Nothing else?

F: Yes, I am still vulnerable when I encounter negative events and my mood changes.

P: Can we redraw your formulation, including only the residual problems you have now?

F: Ok.

Preparing the Post-Inpatient Plan

The post-inpatient plan (see textbox 11.3) was developed jointly with Francesca and involved the detailed evaluation of four aspects: (i) her life after the inpatient CBT-E (e.g., living situation, work, relationships with others); (ii) outpatient treatment after inpatient CBT-E; (iii) problems to focus on after discharge; (iv) minimizing the risk of setbacks.

TEXTBOX 11.3. FRANCESCA'S POST-INPATIENT PLAN

This document is important. It will help me to minimize problems after discharge from the unit and reduce the risk of setbacks. I will read it at regular intervals.

My life after discharge

- Work: I will look for a job as a shop assistant
- Residence: I will go to live with my husband and son. With my husband I will work to improve our relationship. I will try to create a home environment that will not encourage dieting and concerns about shape and weight
- Interpersonal relationships: I will commit myself every day to developing new interpersonal relationships
- Interests to marginalize my eating problem: I will enroll in a dance course

My outpatient therapy

- Where: I will do the therapy in my hometown
- Date of the first appointment: I have already fixed my first appointment for the first Monday after discharge at 5 p.m.
- With whom: I will do the outpatient therapy with a psychotherapist who follows the CBT-E approach

Problems that I have to focus on after discharge

- Dietary restraint and restriction:

  1. I will try to adopt the dietary guidelines I learned at Villa Garda in a flexible way
  2. I will eat every four hours. I will not avoid certain foods for fear of gaining weight and I will not binge eat
  3. I will make portions of food without weighing it, and I will try to serve myself portions of normal size
  4. I will eat with other people (e.g., with my husband and son, at a restaurant)

- Excessive exercising:

  1. I will avoid excessive exercising, but I will practice dance to maintain a healthy fitness level

- Weight maintenance:

  1. I will check my weight once a week on Mondays
  2. I will try to maintain my weight in the goal range (from 45 kg to 48 kg)
  3. If my weight falls below the goal range, I will add 500 extra calories every day
  4. If my weight falls below 45 kg (BMI < 18.5) on two consecutive readings I will contact my outpatient therapist

- Concerns about shape and weight:

  1. I will avoid unhelpful body shape checking (frequent mirror use, pinching/prodding, comparing self with others)
  2. I will not avoid looking at my body
  3. I will use mirrors carefully (only before going out and to check that my appearance is in order)
  4. If I feel fat, I will try to identify the triggers and I will label them (especially body checking)
  5. I will avoid weighing myself outside the set weekly time, and I will not interpret single readings alone, but in conjunction with the three previous readings
  6. I will try to maintain other life interests (work, dance)

  How I will minimize the risk of setbacks

- Procedures that I will continue to adopt:

  1. I will continue to use the monitoring record, the weight graph, and the Eating Problems Questionnaire

- Realistic expectations:

  1. I will be ready to face difficulties in response to some events or problems. My eating problem will be always my Achilles heel— however, I have learned effective strategies for dealing with it

- Strategies to minimize the risk of setbacks:

  1. I will maintain a pattern of regular eating. I will avoid dieting, especially rigid and extreme diets and ones that exclude a lot of foods
  2. I will maintain my weight within the goal range
  3. I will maintain and develop other life interests
  4. I will be aware of engaging in unhelpful body checking and body avoidance
  5. I will use proactive problem solving to tackle life's problems

- Circumstances that might increase the risk of setbacks:

  1. Life changes and difficulties. Weight loss or weight gain. Low mood

- Dealing with triggers and setbacks:

  1. I will identify triggers. I will deal with triggers using proactive problem solving
  2. I will label a setback as a lapse and not a relapse. I will nip setbacks in the bud by following the treatment guidelines
  3. As a general guideline, I will do the opposite of what my eating problem DVD makes me want to do
  4. I will try to involve myself in other aspects of life to marginalize the eating problem DVD

Figure 11.3 shows Francesca's weight graph during the course of inpatient CBT-E.

Follow-Up

Francesca had several setbacks after discharge (vomiting and some dietary restriction in the first two months after discharge when her BMI was 20.0), but at both six- and twelve-month follow-up she had a "good BMI outcome" (defined as a BMI of 18.5 or more) and a "full response" (defined as a BMI of 18.5 or more and minimal accompanying eating disorder psychopathology—i.e., having a global EDE score below 1 standard deviation above the community mean of 1.74) (see table 11.1). The impact of the eating problem on her life was minimal, as evidenced by the low scores of the CIA, and she also showed a marked improvement in general psychopathology, measured

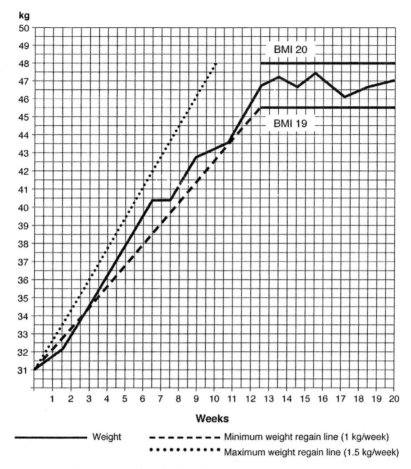

Figure 11.3.   Francesca's Weight Graph

by BSI. She completed the post-inpatient CBT-E after six months, and at twelve-month follow-up she was working as a shop assistant in a shoe store, and she was still living with her husband and son.

Table 11.1. Francesca's clinical state before inpatient CBT-E, after inpatient CBT-E, and at twenty- and forty-week follow-ups

	Before treatment	After treatment	Twenty-week follow-up	Forty-week follow-up
Body weight (kg)	31	46	47.5	48
Body mass index (kg/m^2)	12.9	19.1	19.8	20
EDE				
Global	3.7	1.7	1.7	1.6
Dietary restraint	4.2	0.8	1.4	1.4
Eating concern	3.4	1.2	1.4	1.4
Weight concern	3.6	2.0	1.6	1.6
Shape concern	3.6	2.9	2.3	2.2
Objective bulimic episodes[a]	0	0	0	0
Self-induced vomiting, number[a]	28	5	3	0
Laxative misuse[a]	0	0	0	0
Diuretic misuse[a]	0	0	0	0
Driven exercise[a]	0	0	0	0
CIA	42	15	14	10

Notes: EDE = Eating Disorder Examination (version 16.0D); CIA = Clinical Impairment Assessment
[a]Number of episodes over the past twenty-eight days

Conclusion

CBT for eating disorders has made considerable advances over the last ten years. Major steps forward have doubtless been the development of a transdiagnostic theory and treatment, the adoption of an individualized approach focused on patients' psychopathology rather than their DSM diagnosis, and the applicability of CBT-E to the whole range of care settings, from outpatient to intensive care contexts, according to a stepped-care approach. In particular, the very nature of multistep CBT-E makes the treatment ideal for implementing in specialized eating disorder units, where patients with different DSM diagnoses and clinical severity often seek treatment.

Indeed, available data shows that CBT-E is as effective for not-underweight eating disorder NOS patients as it is for those with bulimia nervosa, with a good outcome reported in two-thirds of patients who completed treatment. Furthermore, emerging data indicate that the treatment is also promising in adult and adolescent patients with anorexia nervosa in both outpatient and inpatient settings, like in the three clinical cases described in this book. Nevertheless, there is still a long road ahead, and many challenges still remain to be faced.

First among these challenges is the issue of dissemination—very few therapists use CBT-E in outpatient settings, and the CBT-E units across the world applying intensive outpatient and/or inpatient CBT-E can be counted on the fingers of two hands. It is clear that the traditional methods of promoting evidence-based psychotherapy, such as the scientific papers, one- or two-day workshops, and treatment manuals are not enough to enable the clinician to acquire the necessary skills to apply CBT-E at different levels of care. Although this book, which illustrates in detail how to treat clinical cases in the real world and how the CBT-E team works at intensive levels of care, may be useful, it can only go so far. Indeed, in order to equip the clinician with the tools needed to implement this effective, evidence-based treatment, new forms of training are required.

This was the ethos behind the First Certificate of Professional Training in Eating Disorders, established in Italy to offer intensive training in multistep CBT-E. The course lasts one year, is based on an interactive didactic approach, and includes observation of simulated CBT-E sessions at different levels of care, as well as role-playing, to help therapists to acquire the knowledge and skills necessary for them to practice multistep CBT-E. Since the course is attended by professionals from different backgrounds (e.g., physicians, psychiatrists, psychologists, dietitians, and nurses), several role-playing sessions are also dedicated to the practice and administration of CBT-E by a multidisciplinary team, as is recommended at intensive levels of care. To date more than five hundred professionals have thus been trained in multistep CBT-E, and several CBT-E teams have consequently been set up in Italy.

Unfortunately, the trainer can only be sure that the trainee has absorbed the necessary know-how and skills when these are observed in action. This brings me to the second challenge regarding implementation of multistep CBT-E, namely helping therapists to practice the treatment correctly. In particular, the two mistakes that I most commonly observe during clinical supervision are introducing strategies and procedures from other psychotherapeutic practices and deviating from the protocol to assist patients with severe eating problems and comorbidity problems, or if their progress is slow or difficult.

CBT-E practitioners need to be aware that available data indicate that using CBT-E in combination with conceptually different treatments does not improve the outcome and may in fact increase the risk of confusing the patient and undermining recovery. The clinical experience of therapists using CBT-E also suggests that the greater the severity of the eating disorder, the more the focus should be on addressing the problems related to the underlying psychopathology (e.g., undereating and being underweight), since these are usually the prime culprits maintaining the eating problem itself. Thus, when faced with patients whose progress is slow or absent, it is better to persevere with CBT-E while trying to understand and address the reasons for lack of progress. That being said, if barriers to change seem insurmountable, rather than prolonging CBT-E or using other psychotherapeutic approaches, it would better to intensify treatment—which is where the stepped-care approach comes into play (e.g., patient care can be stepped up from intensive outpatient CBT-E to inpatient CBT-E).

Good implementation of the treatment in intensive CBT-E settings, where several therapists from different backgrounds may be called upon to administer it, is particularly complex. However, it is my experience that several strategies can prove useful in helping to improve the team adherence to the CBT-E line. First of all, it is essential that therapists are carefully selected, choosing not merely those who are available, but those who are highly motivated to work as part of a CBT-E team. Second, it is fundamental to plan an intensive training period of about six to twelve months for new team members; therapists in training should be encouraged to study the CBT-E manuals (Dalle Grave, 2012; Fairburn, 2008a) in detail, listen to recorded sessions held by senior colleagues, and participate in the weekly team meetings. Moreover, when they start to see patients, they should be encouraged to review the treatment manual section on the relevant phase of treatment before every session, and to apply the protocol correctly. It is also recommended that weekly peer supervision meetings are organized to provide a setting in which all team members can discuss their clinical work freely. Furthermore, as in the CBT-E trials conducted to date, the psychologist responsible for individual sessions should be substituted by another CBT-E-trained therapist during his or her absence to ensure continuity and coherence of care. In such a case, a recording of the last individual CBT-E session should be available to the replacement, making it advisable to record all patient sessions. Finally, the team director should periodically monitor each therapist's fidelity to the treatment protocol, and should promptly nip in the bud any deviation from standard CBT-E procedures. In most cases, it is sufficient to speak openly with the non-compliant therapist to get him or her back onto the right track. However, if the therapist persists in deviating from the treatment protocol, he or she should be asked to step down from the team.

The third major challenge clinicians face is to understand how and when to simplify or intensify the treatment. It is clear that some patients may recover with simpler, shorter forms of CBT-E, such as guided self-help, while others will need a prolonged intensive treatment, such as inpatient CBT-E. Unfortunately, at this stage we do not yet have reliable clinical predictors of treatment outcomes at different levels of care. Likewise, we have yet to discover the inactive and active elements of the treatment program, that is, those that might be eliminated or given more weight, and the decision to intensify the treatment is still necessarily based on clinical judgment rather than empirical data.

Something that the empirical data does make clear, however, brings me to the final, but by no means least challenging, hurdle to be overcome by proponents of CBT-E, namely that the treatment still needs to be improved. Indeed, despite its encouraging success rates, some patients do not recover even with the most intensive form of CBT-E, inpatient treatment. Hence, further research is needed to analyze the reasons behind these failures and to generate innovative procedures and strategies for increasing the CBT-E effectiveness at all levels of care. It is my dearest wish that these challenges will be overcome, if not in my time then by the next generation of researchers and clinicians, who I hope will in some small way have been inspired by the contents of this book.

Appendix

Instructions: This questionnaire has been designed to monitor the state of your eating problem. You should compile the questionnaire once a week immediately after checking your weight. The following questions are concerned with the last seven days only.

THE EATING PROBLEM CHECKLIST 2.0

How many times in the past seven days ...	No. of episodes
Have you eaten an unusually large amount of food with a sense of having lost control (objective bulimic episode)?	
Have you eaten a not large amount of food episode with a sense of having lost control (subjective bulimic episode)?	
Have you made yourself sick (vomiting) as a means of controlling your shape and weight?	
Have you taken laxatives as a means of controlling your shape and weight?	
Have you taken diuretics as a means of controlling your shape and weight?	
Have you exercised in a "compulsive" way as a means of controlling your weight, shape, or amount of fat, or burning calories?	

	No. of days
Have you skipped a meal as a means of controlling your shape and weight?	
Have you reduced food portions as a means of controlling your shape and weight?	
Have you avoided some foods as a means of controlling your shape and weight?	
Have you checked your weight?	
Have you done food checking (e.g., calorie counting, checking the food's calories, making comparisons with the eating behavior of other people)?	
Have you done shape checking (e.g., measuring circumferences of the body, pinching parts of the body to assess "fatness," looking at parts of the body in the mirror; making comparisons with other people)?	
Have you done shape avoidance (e.g., avoiding particular clothes, avoiding looking at your body in the mirror)?	
Have you felt fat?	
Have you had preoccupations with your eating?	
Have you had preoccupations with your shape?	
Have you had preoccupations with your weight?	
Events and emotions influenced your eating?	
Has your eating problem marginalized your life?	

References

Agras, W. S., Crow, S., Mitchell, J. E., Halmi, K. A., & Bryson, S. (2009). A 4-year prospective study of eating disorder NOS compared with full eating disorder syndromes. *International Journal of Eating Disorders, 42*, 565–570.

Agras, W. S., Walsh, T., Fairburn, C. G., Wilson, G. T., & Kraemer, H. C. (2000). A multicenter comparison of cognitive-behavioral therapy and interpersonal psychotherapy for bulimia nervosa. *Archives of General Psychiatry, 57*, 459–466.

Allison, K. C., Lundgren, J. D., O'Reardon, J. P., Geliebter, A., Gluck, M. E., Vinai, P., et al. (2010). Proposed diagnostic criteria for night eating syndrome. *International Journal of Eating Disorders, 43*, 241–247.

American Diabetes Association, A. D. A. (2003). *Exchange lists for meal planning.* Chicago: American Dietetic Association and American Diabetes Association.

American Psychiatric Association. (2000). *Diagnostic and statistical manual of mental disorders, 4th ed. (text revision).* Washington, DC: American Psychiatric Association.

Ardovini, C., Caputo, G., Todisco, P., & Dalle Grave, R. (1999). Binge eating and restraint model: Psychometric analysis in binge eating disorder and normal weight bulimia. *European Eating Disorders Review, 7*, 293–299.

Aronoff, N. J., Geliebter, A., & Zammit, G. (2001). Gender and body mass index as related to the night-eating syndrome in obese outpatients. *Journal of the American Dietetic Association, 101*, 102–104.

Attia, E., & Roberto, C. A. (2009). Should amenorrhea be a diagnostic criterion for anorexia nervosa? *International Journal of Eating Disorders, 42*, 581–589.

Barry, D. T., Grilo, C. M., & Masheb, R. M. (2002). Gender differences in patients with binge eating disorder. *International Journal of Eating Disorders, 31*, 63–70.

Beck, J. S. (1995). *Cognitive therapy: Basics and beyond.* New York: Guilford Press.

Ben-Tovim, D. I., Walker, K., Gilchrist, P., Freeman, R., Kalucy, R., & Esterman, A. (2001). Outcome in patients with eating disorders: A 5-year study. *Lancet, 357*, 1254–1257.

Bohn, K., Doll, H. A., Cooper, Z., O'Connor, M., Palmer, R. L., & Fairburn, C. G. (2008). The measurement of impairment due to eating disorder psychopathology. *Behaviour Research and Therapy, 46*, 1105–1110.

Bohn, K., & Fairburn, C. G. (2008). Clinical Impairment Assessment Questionnaire (CIA 3.0). In C. G. Fairburn (Ed.), *Cognitive behavior therapy and eating disorders* (pp. 315–317). New York: Guilford Press.

Brownley, K. A., Berkman, N. D., Sedway, J. A., Lohr, K. N., & Bulik, C. M. (2007). Binge eating disorder treatment: A systematic review of randomized controlled trials. *International Journal of Eating Disorders, 40*, 337–348.

Bulik, C. M., & Reichborn-Kjennerud, T. (2003). Medical morbidity in binge eating disorder. *International Journal of Eating Disorders, 34 Suppl*, S39–46.

Bulik, C. M., Sullivan, P. F., Fear, J., & Pickering, A. (1997). Predictors of the development of bulimia nervosa in women with anorexia nervosa. *Journal of Nervous and Mental Disease, 185*, 704–707.

Byrne, S. M., Fursland, A., Allen, K. L., & Watson, H. (2011). The effectiveness of enhanced cognitive behavioural therapy for eating disorders: An open trial. *Behaviour Research and Therapy, 49*, 219–226.

Carter, J. C., McFarlane, T. L., Bewell, C., Olmsted, M. P., Woodside, D. B., Kaplan, A. S., & Crosby, R. D. (2009). Maintenance treatment for anorexia nervosa: A comparison of cognitive behavior therapy and treatment as usual. *International Journal of Eating Disorders, 42*, 202–207.

Carter, J. C., Stewart, D. A., & Fairburn, C. G. (2001). Eating Disorder Examination Questionnaire: Norms for young adolescent girls. *Behaviour Research and Therapy, 39*, 625–632.

Cooper, Z., & Stewart, A. (2008). CBT-E and the younger patient. In C. G. Fairburn (Ed.), *Cognitive behavior therapy and eating disorders* (pp. 221–230). New York: Guilford Press.

Crisp, A. (1997). Anorexia nervosa as flight from growth: Assessment and treatment based on the model. In D. Garner & P. Garfinkel (Eds.), *Handbook of treatment for eating disorders* (pp. 248–277). New York: Guilford Press.

Crow, S. J., Peterson, C. B., Swanson, S. A., Raymond, N. C., Specker, S., Eckert, E. D., & Mitchell, J. E. (2009). Increased mortality in bulimia nervosa and other eating disorders. *American Journal of Psychiatry, 166*, 1342–1346.

Dalle Grave, R. (2005). A multi-step cognitive behaviour therapy for eating disorders. *European Eating Disorders Review, 13*, 373–382.

Dalle Grave, R. (2009). Features and management of compulsive exercising in eating disorders. *The Physician and Sportsmedicine, 37*, 20–28.

Dalle Grave, R. (2011a). Eating disorders: Progress and challenges. *European Journal of Internal Medicine, 22*, 153–160.

Dalle Grave, R. (2011b). Intensive cognitive behavioural treatment for eating disorders. *European Psychiatric Review, 4*, 59–64.

Dalle Grave, R. (2012). *Intensive cognitive behavior therapy for eating disorders*. Hauppauge, NY: Nova.

Dalle Grave, R., Calugi, S., Doll, H. A., & Fairburn, C. G. (2012). Enhanced CBT for adolescents with anorexia nervosa: An alternative to family therapy? *Behavior Research and Therapy*. http://dx.doi.org/10.1016/j.brat.2012.09.008.

Dalle Grave, R., Bohn, K., Hawker, D., & Fairburn, C. G. (2008). Inpatient, day patient, and two forms of outpatient CBT-E. In C. G. Fairburn (Ed.), *Cognitive behavior therapy and eating disorders* (pp. 231–244). New York: Guilford Press.

Dalle Grave, R., & Calugi, S. (2007). Eating disorder not otherwise specified in an inpatient unit: The impact of altering the DSM-IV criteria for anorexia and bulimia nervosa. *European Eating Disorders Review, 15*, 340–349.

Dalle Grave, R., Calugi, S., Centis, E., El Ghoch, M., & Marchesini, G. (2011). Cognitive-behavioral strategies to increase the adherence to exercise in the management of obesity. *Journal of Obesity, 2011*, 348.

Dalle Grave, R., Calugi, S., Corica, F., Di Domizio, S., & Marchesini, G. (2009). Psychological variables associated with weight loss in obese patients seeking treatment at medical centers. *Journal of the American Dietetic Association, 109*, 2010–2016.

Dalle Grave, R., Calugi, S., & Marchesini, G. (2008a). Is amenorrhea a clinically useful criterion for the diagnosis of anorexia nervosa? *Behaviour Research and Therapy, 46*, 1290–1294.

Dalle Grave, R., Calugi, S., & Marchesini, G. (2008b). Compulsive exercise to control shape or weight in eating disorders: Prevalence, associated features and treatment outcome. *Comprehensive Psychiatry, 49*, 346–352.

Dalle Grave, R., Calugi, S., & Marchesini, G. (2008c). Underweight eating disorder without over-evaluation of shape and weight: Atypical anorexia nervosa? *International Journal of Eating Disorders, 41*, 705–712.

Dalle Grave, R., Calugi, S., & Marchesini, G. (2009). Self-induced vomiting in eating disorders: Associated features and treatment outcome. *Behaviour Research and Therapy, 47,* 680–684.

Dalle Grave, R., Calugi, S., Petroni, M. L., Di Domizio, S., & Marchesini, G. (2010). Weight management, psychological distress and binge eating in obesity: A reappraisal of the problem. *Appetite, 54,* 269–273.

Dalle Grave, R., Di Pauli, D., Sartirana, M., Calugi, S., & Shafran, R. (2007). The interpretation of symptoms of starvation/severe dietary restraint in eating disorder patients. *Eating and Weight Disorders, 12,* 108–113.

Dalle Grave, R., Pasqualoni, E., & Calugi, S. (2008). Intensive outpatient cognitive behaviour therapy for eating disorder. *Psychological Topics, 17,* 313–327.

Dalle Grave, R., Pasqualoni, E., & Marchesini, G. (2011). Symptoms of starvation in eating disorder patients. In V. R. Preedy (Ed.), *Handbook of behavior, food and nutrition.* New York: Springer Science+Business Media.

Dalle Grave, R., Ricca, V., & Todesco, T. (2001). The stepped-care approach in anorexia nervosa and bulimia nervosa: Progress and problems. *Eating and Weight Disorders, 6,* 81–89.

Davey, G. C. L. (1994). Pathological worrying as exacerbated problem solving. In G. C. L. Davey & F. Tallis (Eds.), *Worrying: Perspectives on theory, assessment and treatment.* Chichester: Wiley.

Derogatis, L. R. (1993). *BSI Brief Symptom Inventory: Administration, scoring, and procedures manual* (4th Ed.). Minneapolis, MN: National Computer Systems.

Diabetes Prevention Program Research Group. (2002). Reduction in the incidence of type 2 diabetes with lifestyle intervention or metformin. *The New England Journal of Medicine, 346,* 393–403.

Dingemans, A. E., Bruna, M. J., & van Furth, E. F. (2002). Binge eating disorder: A review. *International Journal of Obesity, 26,* 299–307.

Eddy, K. T., Celio Doyle, A., Hoste, R. R., Herzog, D. B., & le Grange, D. (2008). Eating disorder not otherwise specified in adolescents. *Journal of the American Academy of Child and Adolescent Psychiatry, 47,* 156–164.

Fairburn, C. G. (1995). *Overcoming binge eating.* New York: Guilford Press.

Fairburn, C. G. (1997). Interpersonal psychotherapy for bulimia nervosa. In D. M. Garner & P. E. Garfinkel (Eds.), *Handbook of treatment for eating disorders* (pp. 278–294). New York: Guilford Press.

Fairburn, C. G. (2005). Evidence-based treatment of anorexia nervosa. *International Journal of Eating Disorders, 37 Suppl,* S26–30; discussion S41–22.

Fairburn, C. G. (2008a). *Cognitive behavior therapy and eating disorders.* New York: Guilford Press.

Fairburn, C. G. (2008b). Eating disorders: The transdiagnostic view and the cognitive behavioral theory. In C. G. Fairburn (Ed.), *Cognitive behavior therapy and eating disorders* (pp. 7–22). New York: Guilford Press.

Fairburn, C. G. (2008c). Enhanced CBT (CBT-E) for anorexia nervosa: Findings from Oxford, Leicester and Verona. Paper presented at the 14th EDRS Annual Meeting, Montreal.

Fairburn, C. G., Cooper, Z., Palmer, R. L., Doll, A. H., O'Connor, M. E., & Dalle Grave, R. (2012). A UK-Italy study of enhanced cognitive behaviour therapy for anorexia nervosa. *Behaviour Research and Therapy.* 10.1016/j.brat.2012.09.010.

Fairburn, C. G., Agras, W. S., Walsh, B. T., Wilson, G. T., & Stice, E. (2004). Prediction of outcome in bulimia nervosa by early change in treatment. *American Journal of Psychiatry, 161,* 2322–2324.

Fairburn, C. G., & Beglin, S. J. (2008). Eating Disorder Examination Questionnaire (EDE-Q 6.0). In C. G. Fairburn (Ed.), *Cognitive behavior therapy and eating disorders* (pp. 309–313). New York: Guilford Press.

Fairburn, C. G., & Bohn, K. (2005). Eating disorder NOS (EDNOS): An example of the troublesome "not otherwise specified" (NOS) category in DSM-IV. *Behaviour Research and Therapy, 43,* 691–701.

Fairburn, C. G., Cooper, Z., Doll, H. A., Norman, P., & O'Connor, M. (2000). The natural course of bulimia nervosa and binge eating disorder in young women. *Archives of General Psychiatry, 57*, 659–665.

Fairburn, C. G., Cooper, Z., Doll, H. A., O'Connor, M. E., Bohn, K., Hawker, D. M., et al. (2009). Transdiagnostic cognitive-behavioral therapy for patients with eating disorders: A two-site trial with 60-week follow-up. *American Journal of Psychiatry, 166*, 311–319.

Fairburn, C. G., Cooper, Z., & O'Connor, M. (2008). Eating Disorder Examination (Edition 16.0D). In C. G. Fairburn (Ed.), *Cognitive behavior therapy and eating disorders* (pp. 265–308). New York: Guilford Press.

Fairburn, C. G., Cooper, Z., & Shafran, R. (2003). Cognitive behaviour therapy for eating disorders: A "transdiagnostic" theory and treatment. *Behaviour Research and Therapy, 41*, 509–528.

Fairburn, C. G., Cooper, Z., & Shafran, R. (2008). Enhanced cognitive behavior therapy for eating disorders ("CBT-E"): An overview. In C. G. Fairburn (Ed.), *Cognitive behavior therapy and eating disorders* (pp. 23–34). New York: Guilford Press.

Fairburn, C. G., Cooper, Z., Shafran, R., Bohn, K., & Hawker, D. (2008). Clinical perfectionism, core low self-esteem and interpersonal problems. In C. G. Fairburn (Ed.), *Cognitive behavior therapy and eating disorders* (pp. 197–220). New York: Guilford Press.

Fairburn, C. G., Cooper, Z., Shafran, R., Bohn, K., Hawker, D. M., Murphy, R., & Straebler, S. (2008). Enhanced cognitive behavior therapy for eating disorders: The core protocol. In C. G. Fairburn (Ed.), *Cognitive behavior therapy and eating disorders* (pp. 45–193). New York: Guilford Press.

Fairburn, C. G., Cooper, Z., & Waller, D. (2008). "Complex cases" and comorbidity. In C. G. Fairburn (Ed.), *Cognitive behavior therapy and eating disorders* (pp. 245–258). New York: Guilford Press.

Fairburn, C. G., & Harrison, P. J. (2003). Eating disorders. *Lancet, 361*, 407–416.

Fairburn, C. G., Jones, R., Peveler, R. C., Hope, R. A., & O'Connor, M. (1993). Psychotherapy and bulimia nervosa. Longer-term effects of interpersonal psychotherapy, behavior therapy, and cognitive behavior therapy. *Archives of General Psychiatry, 50*, 419–428.

Fairburn, C. G., Marcus, M. D., & Wilson, G. T. (1993). Cognitive-behavioral therapy for binge eating and bulimia nervosa: A comprehensive treatment manual. In C. G. Fairburn & G. T. Wilson (Eds.), *Binge eating: Nature, assessment and treatment* (pp. 361–404). New York: Guilford Press.

Fairburn, C. G., Shafran, R., & Cooper, Z. (1999). A cognitive behavioural theory of anorexia nervosa. *Behaviour Research and Therapy, 37*, 1–13.

Fairburn, C. G., & Wilson, G. T. (1993). Binge eating: Definition and classification. In C. G. Fairburn & G. T. Wilson (Eds.), *Binge Eating: Nature, Assessment and Treatment* (pp. 3–14). New York: Guilford Press.

Gadalla, T., & Piran, N. (2007). Co-occurrence of eating disorders and alcohol use disorders in women: A meta analysis. *Archives of Women's Mental Health, 10*, 133–140.

Garner, D., Vitousek, K., & Pike, K. (1997). Cognitive-behavioral therapy for anorexia nervosa. In D. M. Garner & P. E. Garfinkel (Eds.), *Handbook of treatment for eating disorders* (pp. 94–144). New York: Guilford Press.

Garner, D. M. (1997). Psychoeducational principles in the treatment of eating disorders. In D. M. Garner & P. E. Garfinkel (Eds.), *Handbook of treatment for eating disorders* (pp. 145–177). New York: Guilford Press.

Gowers, S. G., & Shore, A. (1999). The stigma of eating disorders. *International Journal of Clinical Practice, 53*, 386–388.

Greenberger, D., & Padesky, P. A. (1995). *Mind over mood*. New York: Guilford Press.

Halmi, K. A. (2009). Salient components of a comprehensive service for eating disorders. *World Psychiatry, 8*, 150–155.

Harvey, A., Watkins, E., Mansell, W., & Shafran, R. (2004). *Cognitive behavioural processes across psychological disorders*. Oxford: Oxford University Press.

Herzog, D. B., Dorer, D. J., Keel, P. K., Selwyn, S. E., Ekeblad, E. R., Flores, A. T., et al. (1999). Recovery and relapse in anorexia and bulimia nervosa: A 7.5-year follow-up study. *Journal of the American Academy of Child and Adolescent Psychiatry, 38*, 829–837.

Hoek, H. W. (2006). Incidence, prevalence and mortality of anorexia nervosa and other eating disorders. *Current Opinion in Psychiatry, 19*, 389–394.

Hudson, J. I., Hiripi, E., Pope, H. G., Jr., & Kessler, R. C. (2007). The prevalence and correlates of eating disorders in the National Comorbidity Survey Replication. *Biological Psychiatry, 61*, 348–358.

Isager, T., Brinch, M., Kreiner, S., & Tolstrup, K. (1985). Death and relapse in anorexia nervosa: Survival analysis of 151 cases. *Journal of Psychiatric Research, 19*, 515–521.

Kaplan, A. S., Walsh, B. T., Olmsted, M., Attia, E., Carter, J. C., Devlin, M. J., et al. (2009). The slippery slope: Prediction of successful weight maintenance in anorexia nervosa. *Psychological Medicine, 39*, 1037–1045.

Katzman, D. K. (2005). Medical complications in adolescents with anorexia nervosa: A review of the literature. *International Journal of Eating Disorders, 37 Suppl*, S52–59; discussion S87–59.

Kaye, W. H., Nagata, T., Weltzin, T. E., Hsu, L. K., Sokol, M. S., McConaha, C., et al. (2001). Double-blind placebo-controlled administration of fluoxetine in restricting and restricting-purging-type anorexia nervosa. *Biological Psychiatry, 49*, 644–652.

Kaye, W. H., Weltzin, T. E., Hsu, I., K., McConaha, C. W., & Bolton, B. (1993). Amount of calories retained after binge eating and vomiting. *American Journal of Psychiatry, 150*, 969–971.

Keel, P. K. (2007). Purging disorder: Subthreshold variant or full-threshold eating disorder? *International Journal of Eating Disorders, 40 Suppl*, S89–94.

Keel, P. K., & Brown, T. A. (2010). Update on course and outcome in eating disorders. *International Journal of Eating Disorders, 43*, 195–204.

Keys, A., Brozek, J., Henschel, A., Mickelsen, O., & Taylor, H. L. (1950). *The biology of human starvation* (Vol. 2). Minneapolis: University of Minnesota Press.

Klerman, G. L., Weissman, M. M., Rounsaville, B. J., & Chevron, E. S. (1984). *Interpersonal psychotherapy of depression*. New York: Basic Books.

Lai, K. Y., de Bruyn, R., Lask, B., Bryant-Waugh, R., & Hankins, M. (1994). Use of pelvic ultrasound to monitor ovarian and uterine maturity in childhood onset anorexia nervosa. *Archives of Disease in Childhood, 71*, 228–231.

Lock, J., Le Grange, D., Agras, W. S., & Dare, C. (2001). *Treatment manual for anorexia nervosa: A family-based approach*. New York: Guilford Press.

Lock, J., Le Grange, D., Agras, W. S., Moye, A., Bryson, S. W., & Jo, B. (2010). Randomized clinical trial comparing family-based treatment with adolescent-focused individual therapy for adolescents with anorexia nervosa. *Archives of General Psychiatry, 67*, 1025–1032.

McElroy, S. L., Kotwal, R., & Keck, P. E., Jr. (2006). Comorbidity of eating disorders with bipolar disorder and treatment implications. *Bipolar Disorders, 8*, 686–695.

McIntosh, V. V., Bulik, C. M., McKenzie, J. M., Luty, S. E., & Jordan, J. (2000). Interpersonal psychotherapy for anorexia nervosa. *International Journal of Eating Disorders, 27*, 125–139.

Mehler, P. S., & Andersen, A. E. (2010). *Eating disorders: A guide to medical care and complications* (2nd ed.). Baltimore: Johns Hopkins University.

Miller, K. K., Grinspoon, S., Gleysteen, S., Grieco, K. A., Ciampa, J., Breu, J., et al. (2004). Preservation of neuroendocrine control of reproductive function despite severe undernutrition. *The Journal of Clinical Endocrinology & Metabolism, 89*, 4434–4438.

Miller, W. R., & Rollnick, S. (2002). *Motivational interviewing* (2nd ed.). New York: Guilford Press.

Milos, G., Spindler, A., Schnyder, U., & Fairburn, C. G. (2005). Instability of eating disorder diagnoses: Prospective study. *British Journal of Psychiatry, 187*, 573–578.

Mitchell, J. E., Halmi, K., Wilson, G. T., Agras, W. S., Kraemer, H., & Crow, S. (2002). A randomized secondary treatment study of women with bulimia nervosa who fail to respond to CBT. *International Journal of Eating Disorders, 32*, 271–281.

National Institute for Clinical Excellence. (2004). Eating disorders: Core interventions in the treatment and management of anorexia nervosa, bulimia nervosa and related eating disorders. Clinical Guideline 9: National Collaborating Centre for Mental Health.

National Institute of Mental Health. (2011). Antidepressant medications for children and adolescents: Information for parents and caregivers, from www.nimh.nih.gov.

National Institutes of Health. (1998). Clinical guidelines on the identification, evaluation, and treatment of overweight and obesity in adults: The evidence report. National Institutes of Health. *Obesity Research, 6 Suppl 2,* 51S–209S.

Nicholls, D., & Bryant-Waugh, R. (2009). Eating disorders of infancy and childhood: Definition, symptomatology, epidemiology, and comorbidity. *Child & Adolescent Psychiatric Clinics of North America, 18,* 17–30.

Pike, K. M. (1998). Long-term course of anorexia nervosa: Response, relapse, remission, and recovery. *Clinical Psychology Review, 18,* 447–475.

Pike, M. K., Walsh, B. T., Vitousek, K., Wilson, G. T., & Bauer, J. (2003). Cognitive behavior therapy in the posthospitalization treatment of anorexia nervosa. *American Journal of Psychiatry, 160,* 2046–2049.

Rand, C. S. W., Macgregor, A. M. C., & Stunkard, A. J. (1997). The night eating syndrome in the general population and among postoperative obesity surgery patients. *International Journal of Eating Disorders, 22,* 65–69.

Ricca, V., Mannucci, E., Mezzani, B., Di Bernardo, M., Zucchi, T., Paionni, A., et al. (2001). Psychopathological and clinical features of outpatients with an eating disorder not otherwise specified. *Eating and Weight Disorders, 6,* 157–165.

Rodriguez, N. R., DiMarco, N. M., & Langley, S. (2009). Position of the American Dietetic Association, Dietitians of Canada, and the American College of Sports Medicine: Nutrition and athletic performance. *Journal of the American Dietetic Association, 109,* 509–527.

Rosen, J. C. (1997). Cognitive-behavioural body image therapy. In D. M. Garner & P. E. Garfinkel (Eds.), *Handbook of treatment for eating disorders* (pp. 188–201). New York: Guilford Press.

Segal, Z. V., Williams, J. M. G., & Teasdale, J. D. (2002). *Mindfulness-based cognitive therapy for depression.* New York: Guilford Press.

Seligman, M. E. P. (1995). The effectiveness of psychotherapy. *American Psychologist, 50,* 965–974.

Shafran, R., Cooper, Z., & Fairburn, C. G. (2002). Clinical perfectionism: A cognitive-behavioural analysis. *Behaviour Research and Therapy, 40,* 773–791.

Shafran, R., Fairburn, C. G., Nelson, L., & Robinson, P. H. (2003). The interpretation of symptoms of severe dietary restraint. *Behaviour Research and Therapy, 41,* 887–894.

Shafran, R., Fairburn, C. G., Robinson, P., & Lask, B. (2004). Body checking and its avoidance in eating disorders. *International Journal of Eating Disorders, 35,* 93–101.

Shapiro, J. R., Berkman, N. D., Brownley, K. A., Sedway, J. A., Lohr, K. N., & Bulik, C. M. (2007). Bulimia nervosa treatment: A systematic review of randomized controlled trials. *International Journal of Eating Disorders, 40,* 321–336.

Steele, A. L., Bergin, J., & Wade, T. D. (2011). Self-efficacy as a robust predictor of outcome in guided self-help treatment for broadly defined bulimia nervosa. *The International Journal of Eating Disorders, 44,* 389–396.

Steinhausen, H. C. (2002). The outcome of anorexia nervosa in the 20th century. *American Journal of Psychiatry, 159,* 1284–1293.

Steinhausen, H. C., & Weber, S. (2009). The outcome of bulimia nervosa: Findings from one-quarter century of research. *American Journal of Psychiatry, 166,* 1331–1341.

Stice, E., Presnell, K., Groesz, L., & Shaw, H. (2005). Effects of a weight maintenance diet on bulimic symptoms in adolescent girls: An experimental test of the dietary restraint theory. *Health Psychology, 24,* 402–412.

Striegel-Moore, R. H., Silberstein, L. R., & Rodin, J. (1993). The social self in bulimia nervosa: Public self-consciousness, social anxiety, and perceived fraudulence. *Journal of Abnormal Psychology, 102,* 297–303.

Strober, M., Freeman, R., & Morrell, W. (1997). The long-term course of severe anorexia nervosa in adolescents: Survival analysis of recovery, relapse, and outcome predictors over 10–15 years in a prospective study. *International Journal of Eating Disorders, 22,* 339–360.

Sullivan, P. F., Bulik, C. M., Carter, F. A., Gendall, K. A., & Joyce, P. R. (1996). The significance of a prior history of anorexia in bulimia nervosa. *International Journal of Eating Disorders, 20*, 253–261.

Teasdale, J. D., Moore, R. G., Hayhurst, H., Pope, M., Williams, S., & Segal, Z. V. (2002). Metacognitive awareness and prevention of relapse in depression: Empirical evidence. *Journal of Consulting and Clinical Psychology, 70*, 275–287.

Thompson, R. A., & Trattner Sherman, R. (2012). *Eating disorders in sports*. New York: Routledge.

Treasure, J., Claudino, A. M., & Zucker, N. (2010). Eating disorders. *Lancet, 375*, 583–593.

van Furth, E. F., van Strien, D. C., Martina, L. M., van Son, M. J., Hendrickx, J. J., & van Engeland, H. (1996). Expressed emotion and the prediction of outcome in adolescent eating disorders. *International Journal of Eating Disorders, 20*, 19–31.

Vandereycken, W. (2003). The place of inpatient care in the treatment of anorexia nervosa: Questions to be answered. *International Journal of Eating Disorders, 34*, 409–422.

Vitousek, K., Watson, S., & Wilson, G. T. (1998). Enhancing motivation for change in treatment-resistant eating disorders. *Clinical Psychology Review, 18*, 391–420.

Walsh, B. T., Kaplan, A. S., Attia, E., Olmsted, M., Parides, M., Carter, J. C., et al. (2006). Fluoxetine after weight restoration in anorexia nervosa: A randomized controlled trial. *JAMA, 295*, 2605–2612.

WHO. (1995). *Physical status: The use and interpretation of anthropometry. Report of a WHO Expert Committee. Who Technical Report Series 854*. Geneva: World Health Organization.

WHO. (2000). *Obesity: Preventing and managing the global epidemic. Report of a WHO Consultation. WHO Technical Report Series 894*. Geneva: World Health Organization.

Wilson, G., Vitousek, L., & Loeb, K. (2000). Stepped-care treatment for eating disorders. *Journal of Consulting and Clinical Psychology, 68*, 564–572.

Wilson, G. T. (1996). Acceptance and change in the treatment of eating disorders and obesity. *Behaviour Therapy, 27*, 417–439.

Wilson, G. T. (1998). The clinical utility of randomized controlled trials. *International Journal of Eating Disorders, 24*, 13–29.

Wilson, G. T., & Fairburn, C. G. (2002). Treatments for eating disorders. In P. E. Nathan & J. M. Gorman (Eds.), *A guide to treatments that work* (2nd ed., pp. 559–592). New York: Oxford University Press.

Wilson, G. T., Grilo, C. M., & Vitousek, K. M. (2007). Psychological treatment of eating disorders. *American Psychologist, 62*, 199–216.

Wilson, G. T., Wilfley, D. E., Agras, W. S., & Bryson, S. W. (2010). Psychological treatments of binge eating disorder. *Archives of General Psychiatry, 67*, 94–101.

Wing, R. R., & Phelan, S. (2005). Long-term weight loss maintenance. *The American Journal of Clinical Nutrition, 82*, 222S–225S.

Wonderlich, S. A., Gordon, K. H., Mitchell, J. E., Crosby, R. D., & Engel, S. G. (2009). The validity and clinical utility of binge eating disorder. *International Journal of Eating Disorders, 42*, 687–705.

Index

abdomen. *See* stomach

adolescents. *See* younger patients

adverse effects, 70, 72

anorexia nervosa: diagnosis, 5, 11, 15, 19; diagnostic criteria, 5, 15; treatment, 9, 113. *See also* underweight; weight regain; weight maintenance

antidepressant medication, 12, 14, 79, 121

anxiety disorders, 5, 19

appearance. *See* mirror use; shape; stomach

asceticism, 5, 22

assessment: clinical impairment assessment (CIA), 57; eating disorder questionnaire (EDE-Q), 57; initial, 53, 54

barriers to change, 101, 162–163, 203, 205, 207, 293–294, 310

binge eating: binge analysis, 80

binge eating disorder, 3, 11–12, 14, 16, 33, 78–79, 110; course, 14; diagnosis, 19, 78

BMI. *See* body mass index

body checking. *See* shape checking; weight checking

body image. *See* feeling fat; mirror use; weighing; weight

body mass index (BMI), 70

bones, 32, 202

broad CBT-E. *See* enhanced cognitive behavior therapy (CBT-E)

bulimia nervosa: diagnosis, 5, 15, 19; DSM-V criteria, 9; treatment, 36

case conceptualization. *See* formulation

CBT. *See* cognitive behavior therapy (CBT)

CBT-E. *See* enhanced cognitive behavior therapy (CBT-E)

checking. *See* dietary restraint; shape checking; weight checking

CIA. *See* clinical impairment assessment (CIA 3.0)

clinical depression. *See* depression

clinical impairment assessment (CIA 3.0), 57; questionnaire, 287

clinical perfectionism. *See* perfectionism

cognitive behavioral theory, 20–22, 28, 30, 33–34, 37, 40, 118

cognitive behavioral therapy (CBT), 8

cognitive restructuring, 41

comorbidity: psychiatric, 8, 56

core low self-esteem. *See* low self-esteem

core psychopathology, 18, 21–22, 24, 35

delayed eating, 155

depression, 5, 10, 19, 62–63, 79, 87, 120–121, 252–253

diabetes, type-2, 14, 79–80

diagnostic migration, 17

337

About the Author

Riccardo Dalle Grave is head of the Department of Eating and Weight Disorders at Villa Garda Hospital, Italy. This highly specialized department houses eighteen inpatient beds, fourteen day-care beds for eating disorder patients, twenty beds for severely obese patients, and an outpatient service for eating disorder and obesity patients. It was thanks to his experience in this department that he conceived the original stepped-care approach for treating eating disorders, based entirely on enhanced cognitive behavioral therapy.

In addition to his clinical and research activities, he is on the editorial board of the *European Eating Disorder Review*, *Eating and Weight Disorder*, and the *Journal of Eating Disorders*. He is also editor of the Italian journal *Emozioni e Cibo*, past president of the Italian Association of Eating and Weight Disorders (AIDAP), member of the executive board of the Italian Society for Obesity (SIO), and a member of both the Eating Disorder Research Society and the Academy of Eating Disorders. Among other works, he has published numerous peer-reviewed scientific articles, and is author of several books and book chapters on the treatment of eating disorders and obesity.